Subject to Biography

SUBJECT TO BIOGRAPHY

Psychoanalysis, Feminism, and Writing Women's Lives

Elisabeth Young-Bruehl

Harvard University Press

Cambridge, Massachusetts
London, England
1998

Library of Congress Cataloging-in-Publication Data

Young-Bruehl, Elisabeth.
Subject to biography : psychoanalysis, feminism, and writing
women's lives / Elisabeth Young-Bruehl.
p.   cm.
Includes bibliographical references and index.
ISBN 0-674-85371-7 (hardcover : alk. paper)
1. Women—Biography—History and criticism.   2. Biography as a
literary form.   3. Psychoanalysis and feminism.   4. Women and
psychoanalysis.   I. Title.
CT3203.Y68 1998   98-22417

Contents

Introduction

At a recent American Psychoanalytic Association colloquium on biographers' relationships with their subjects, I found myself sketching a theory about biographical motivation, one I have entertained during the last ten years, while I was writing the essays in this book. The theory had occurred to me originally as I wrote along on *Anna Freud: A Biography,* and had grown more elaborate when I began to practice as a psychoanalyst, which I at first did as though psychoanalyzing were a kind of biography-writing in which two people work together to recover and reconstruct a life story. I have never written about my theory, so I felt no scholarly compulsion to offer it in a finished form; I could just toss it into the ring and hope that it would further the conversation.

The presenter for the colloquium was Diane Middlebrook, author of a forthcoming biography of the jazz musician Billy Tipton, who, when he died in 1989 at the age of seventy-five, was discovered to be a woman. Middlebrook had deftly entertained the room full of psychoanalysts with the story of how she slowly investigated, through painstaking and awkward interviews with Billy's wives and lovers, the details of his disguise and of his behavior in bed. How was it that none of his women knew that he was a woman? For which abilities and practices did his women sing his praises as a lover? It seemed to me that Middlebrook, taking up the delicate and titillating task of finding out how another human being goes about being gendered and goes about being sexual, had provided a remarkably clear illustration of my theory about a central motivation for people to write biographies. So, I ventured to say my piece.

I said, first, that my years of practicing as a biographer and as a psychoanalyst had allowed me to marvel again and again at how much

▼ ▼ ▼ ▼ ▼

human sexual satisfaction and general happiness depend upon two people, of whichever sex, each with a central fantasy of contentment, finding each other and finding that their fantasies seem to fit together as though by design—like the two sides of an arch. As I said this, there came into my mind an image of the great Lion's Gate arch at the ancient city of Mycenae in Greece, where two sculpted stone lionesses, who have long since lost their enameled heads, face each other in serene, still power. Such a fantasy fit is itself a fantasy, an ideal, for happiness really depends more on the partners having a capacity to tolerate the fit's deficiencies, all the wobbling and uneven settling and adjustments over time. There is a very fine line between thinking of our human condition as poignantly fragile and changeable and thinking of it as tragically insusceptible to constancy.

A second thread of my idea was that fantasies of contentment involve many complex interweavings of sexual currents and affectional needs, but, I think, they all reflect a desire that humans have—a universal desire, perhaps—to be both sexes and, even more fundamentally, to be two people in relatedness, having intrapsychically a love affair or a loving relationship. Psychoanalysts have written about the desire to be both sexes as common in the latency period, but they have pathologized it, insisting that it is one of those desires for omnipotence that should be gotten over for the sake of mental health. Cultures in which androgynes play an important part are more forgiving, although it is unusual for a culture to have a Tiresias and not require him/her to pronounce who gets more pleasure out of sex, men or women—that old competitive game. While my colleagues smiled at this, I thought to myself that I should consider how a desire to be both sexes in some proportion (not usually 50-50, more often tipped, say 75-25, which allows for more peace) relates to a desire to be both genders, feminine and masculine. Maybe many people mix these desires, to be both sexes and to be both genders; or one desire preponderates in some people and the other in others? "Small wonder I have never written about this—the possibilities are fissioning," I said to myself.

Aloud, I pulled the second thread further. The desire to be both sexes, and to have the pleasures of the female and the male, masculinity and femininity, is related to the desire to be two people. If you are in your mind and heart two people, you in a couple or you contemplating a couple, you can experience in yourself—rehearse in the theater of yourself—what you have known of human relatedness and what you may be able to envision. Your two-people self is part of your ego ideal,

▼ ▼ ▼ ▼ ▼

which draws you on in your quest for relatedness. Some cultures provide a clear corresponding cultural ideal or a religious image: here are Yin and Yang, which you are and which you can emulate in their balance. When you do find another person to be in relationship with, the desire recedes into the reality—which is, of course, still suffused with fantasy, especially the fantasy that you have found your fit. I didn't say so at the colloquium, but I have recently come to think that this fantasy of being two people in relatedness stems from an earlier developmental level than the one that generates the desire to be both sexes. It seems to me rooted in the caretaker-infant relationship, as a matter of desired affection and care, which then seeps over into more sexual desires.

Coming to a third point, I suggested that a biographer can enact with her or his subject a version of this fantasy complex. Researching and writing the biography, you have in your mind "the subject" who lived an independent life—and left all the traces of it that you are collecting and fashioning into a portrait—but who is you and yours for the duration of the work. Biographers sometimes have a crucial dream in which the subject appears and announces that she or he has been waiting a lifetime for just such a perfectly fitted biographer. I remembered to myself how Anna Freud had helped me in one dream to rearrange the last two chapters of my biography of her and in another dream to set, like a cameo, an image of her in her essential relationship with her father, the master dreamer. She, a very old woman, being pushed along in her wheelchair by her loving nurse, like a baby in a stroller, was wearing her father's woolen winter coat. The perfect couple—all of us.

The biographer's version of the fantasy-fitting complex has not much to do with whether the biographer and the subject are of the same or opposite sexes, similar or different genders. The biographer relates in the medium of fantasy to the subject's fantasy, insofar as it can be found. And it may be that the biographer relates less to the specific content of the subject's fantasy than to the feeling that the subject *had* a fantasy of contentment, the feeling of kindredness. A woman who dresses for the better part of her adult life as a man and makes love to a woman who has the fantasy that she has found in this man a man who can really understand a woman and is tremendously excited by her, making her feel that she can really excite a man, is a woman-man who clearly has a great deal to teach a biographer about the power of fantasy, and a great deal of power to mobilize biographical fantasy: Ah, here is someone who has been . . . everything, to whom I will be . . . everything. I believe that human beings are distinguished from the animals by, among other char-

▼ ▼ ▼ ▼ ▼

acteristics, the ambitiousness of their images of themselves, by their narcissistically organized creativity.

But men and women who do not so explicitly or elaborately dedicate themselves to the dressing for and the living out of their fantasies make, each in his or her own way, fine teachers, too. Everyone has something about fantasizing to teach the somebody who imagines himself or herself as the perfect listener to that person. Take a woman who managed to create a family life with another woman, mother of children, in which the first woman was not the father or the husband, or the mother or the wife, but . . . everything, or nothing conventionally classifiable. A psychoanalyst! That was the Anna Freud whose story I imagined myself the right biographer to write.

But that was not the story of Anna Freud which I wrote. I did not want to write a biography on the basis of my fantasy or even my idea that all people in one way or another share this complex fantasy of being both sexes and having two selves inside themselves who are related as they would like to be related. My theory, in fact, as I noted, occurred to me while I was writing Anna Freud's biography, and at that time I did not trust it at all, or even understand it. I was afraid that this was one of those ideas that just registered my own idiosyncrasies or my own narcissism. Dangerously subjective. And, besides, I believed that a biography is not the proper place to present a theory. A theorizing biography would reveal my failure to recognize my subject, respect her, pay her regard.

Because I held this general belief about biography-writing, I put various aspects of what I had to say in a theoretical vein about Anna Freud into a series of essays composed between 1988 and 1997. And those are collected here in *Subject to Biography*. They descend from several earlier pieces, which I wrote in the six years after I published my first biography, of Hannah Arendt, in 1982, and then collected in another book of my essays called *Mind and the Body Politic*. Biography-writing often, I have observed, induces in those who do it such after-the-biography efforts to theorize—or to gather up loose ends, express second thoughts, complain about the task and ask for sympathy, settle scores or argue with other writers, reflect in tranquillity, recuperate from living with the subject or from the necessity of moving along after finishing with the subject's biography. In 1991, I published a book called *Creative Characters*, which was of the cathartic after-the-biography theorizing sort, but which was also a treatise on characterology.

Trying to acknowledge rather than become anxious about the intri-

▼ ▼ ▼ ▼

cacies of biography-writing, I decided to title this essay collection *Subject to Biography*. The phrase seemed to me to gesture toward both sides of a complex relationship, and toward the many sides of a complex problem—the biographer's subjectivity. The biographer subjects the subject to study and writing. But the biography and its subject also subject the biographer to the claims of the biographer-subject relationship and the biographer-biography relation. This web of bonds constitutes in its specific form the problem I have been circling: How does the biographer's subjectivity fit the subject's life and story?

After I left the New York colloquium, I settled myself on the train home to Philadelphia and scribbled a very rough draft of the paragraphs you have just read. If I sent this theory of a biographical motivation into the world cross-genre-dressed as an introduction to my essay collection, I had imagined, I could suspend my doubts about whether it is wild psychoanalysis or a generalization which shows nothing more than the inside of my head. Put forward informally, as an introduction to my psychoanalytic way of thinking, the theory could have the same status it had just had at the colloquium: something to ponder and talk over—something to play with—work in progress—reminiscence or reconstruction—not a "scientific" psychoanalytic thesis.

I was deciding to bend one of my rules of writerly self-governance: never send out in print an idea you have not had the opportunity to consider thoroughly in conversation. I have this rule because I believe that the best ideas are generated in conversation—they are the sparks that fly when mind strikes mind or when you have another's mind in and on your mind for an interior conversation. Conversations, further, are better vetting venues than the solitary confinements of composition for combing ideas of their foreign bodies, straightening out their tangles and exaggerations, shaping them into careful form.

This rule of mine, which reflects, of course, an ideal of thinking, also guarantees me a certain confidence that ideas I publish, because they have already been talked over often, will not be idiosyncratic in the negative sense of the word—the idiot sense. They may be characteristic of me, but they will not be, because of that subjectivity, disconnected from other people. Grounds are there for hope, then, that they will strike a responsive chord in readers.

This ideal of conversational thinking, in turn, reflects my preoccupations. All my writing life, I have been compelled to explore a single range of questions and themes, which I can summarize fairly simply:

▼ ▼ ▼ ▼ ▼

What is it, psychodynamically, that makes people think as they do and understand or not understand each other accordingly? What makes their conversation possible, or not possible? I take an interest in people's ideas, and do intellectual history, but my main focus is on where their ideas come from. When I was younger and using the philosophical language I learned as Hannah Arendt's student, I approached these questions philosophically, although always with more interest in people's unconscious minds than Hannah Arendt had. Eventually, in a psychoanalytic essay called "What Theories Women Want," I named the approach I have evolved for myself "psychotheoretical criticism."

My working draft about the desire to be both sexes or genders and to entertain a fantasy couple is a psychotheoretical search for a general statement, about people—and that is what makes me so unsure and tentative about it. During the decade in which the essays in this volume were composed, I worked on a lower rung of generalization to outline a characterology. Writing about hysterical, obsessional, and narcissistic types (and mixtures), I tried to say only that all people can be described as of a character type, more or less pure or mixed. Further, I argued, people's ideas grow from and are shaped by (among other factors) their characters—different kinds of ideas come from different kinds of characters. From within this schema, a fantasy about being both sexes would look different depending on whether it was entertained by a narcissist, a hysteric, or an obsessional character type.

While I was arranging *Subject to Biography*, consulting my files to reconstruct the dates when the essays were written, I remembered how unsure I had been about this characterology as it was evolving. The most striking evidence of my hesitancy was filed away in a cabinet that has the unpsychoanalytic title INACTIVE FILES. There, in a folder labeled "1991 Lectures," was a faded dot-matrix printout of a lecture on the origins of creativity, which I recognized, flipping through it, as an overview of *Creative Characters*'s characterology. I had completely forgotten its existence.

When I read the manuscript through, I remembered writing it in a mixture of excitement and apprehension. It was a romp through various books I love, an exuberant romp because I had decided not to try to argue for this character typology but just to play with it, go for it, and try to share with my audience my enthusiasm for it. I was trying to sustain a mood: Well, even if this fascination with characterology is just some reflection of *my* character, perhaps it will stimulate some good conversation. That is the same mood I was in without effort at the American Psychoanalytic Association while I was chatting on about the desire to be both sexes, two people, and biographically coupled.

Delineating the three character types in my manuscript, I dashed from Freud, representing the narcissistic type, to a British literary sampler of the hysterical type—Yeats, Wilde, Hopkins—and on to Anna Freud, Simone Weil, Gertrude Stein, and Marguerite Yourcenar, four examples of the obsessional type. It was fun, and lots of good reading went into it. I also remember spending happy hours wandering around my study reciting the Hopkins poem I was going to quote in the lecture, recalling the poetry class I took as an undergraduate at Sarah Lawrence College. It was Muriel Rukeyser who had taught me in that class how to read Hopkins's "sprung rhythm": putting many lines of his on a blackboard, she had marked with colored chalk the syllables that should be stressed and sung them out. Performing the poem to my audience at the Princeton University Public Lecture Series for 1991 turned out to be the best part of my stint. I could feel my hearers enjoying the verbal music— being drawn into the circle of Hopkins's conversation with God by his music. But no good conversation with me or for me was stimulated. It was one of those occasions where the guest lecturer comes in, speaks a prepared piece, and then says good night. Nothing interactive.

My deflation after the lecture was connected to the apprehension that had punctuated my mood of enjoyment while I was writing it. A kind of crisis of confidence was precipitated. This characterological theory of which I was—and still am—so enamored had made its public debut the year before in *Creative Characters,* which then promptly sank out of sight without a review in the popular or academic media. My confidence had been shaken then, but no crack appeared in it until this lecture, when I looked beyond my conversational circle and realized that my preoccupations in the area of character study ran counter to the current of the various "postmodernist" discourses then cascading through the academy, where biography was considered a kind of retrograde genre for people who had not properly problematized the notion of "the self," or "identity." Lapsing into a time of self-doubt, I filed away— buried—the manuscript of the lecture because it symbolized for me my questions about the characterological work I had done while I was no longer subject to biography.

In my lapse of confidence, I began to understand that being a biographer is not something that I was or did between the covers of two books, during two periods of my life. That is, I have never not been thinking from within a relationship and a relationship in which I was, and remained after the biography, the biographer. And this simply means that in the relationship I always said: "In thinking things through with you, I tell your story, I know your life—that is part of what thinking is, caring for you and your story." But I had, as I finished the biography-writing time, gotten caught up in the idea that "the biographer" was a role I had to outgrow: How could I write what I had to say until I could stop writing about what these two women had to say? I was thinking of being subject to biography as a kind of service or servitude or apprenticeship. This notion, however, flowed against the much more important, deeper, and—in me—older one that thinking is conversational, that ideas spring up in conversation and are shaped and formed in conversation. And it also felt counter to my newer idea that biography-writing can be a field for the playing out of fantasies, which is not a negative possibility—it is not *mere* subjectivity.

What I had been through was a kind of adolescence: I broke away from my original, originary, understanding of thinking and conversation, looking for freedom to speak in my own voice, only to come to the conclusion that I had not been unfree in the first place—my voice was not subservient in the conversations; it was originated by them and sustained by them. Similarly, my fantasies about the biographical relationship were not confining or traps of subjectivity unless I construed them that way.

While I was getting over my mis-construction of myself, I often found myself reverting to *Anna Freud* and finding many occasions to tell friends, students, and lecture audiences how I came to write that book. I was reconstructing or correcting myself with the story of how Lottie Newman, Anna Freud's Vienna-born literary executor, invited me to lunch at her home near New Haven and, as she served the thick Viennese coffee, proposed that I write Anna Freud's biography. We went down into her basement, where she had six big steamer trunks full of Anna Freud's papers, which had been shipped from England en route to the Library of Congress. Like a fairy queen with a fabulous treasury, she proclaimed these papers mine for as long as I needed them. "You can come here every day and read them all! I will help you with the German handwritings!" I felt a surge of fatigue so strong that it overcame the effects of her coffee.

From Lottie Newman's luncheon, I went directly to the office of my psychoanalyst in New Haven, Hans Loewald. I rambled on to Loewald for most of my session about how weak and exhausted I had felt looking at those papers, imagining the work they represented, the years and years of commitment. I illustrated the challenges that interviewing Anna Freud's contemporaries would bring by recounting how Richard Newman, Lottie's psychoanalyst husband, had answered my questions about Anna Freud, whom he had known intimately. Was she, I had asked him, a lesbian—or was her partnership with Dorothy Burlingham a professional partnership? a Boston marriage? Would it be the biographer's task to brave the homophobia of psychoanalysis with a lesbian life story? Mischievously smiling at me, getting ready for one of those psychoanalytic maneuvers in which the ball gets effortlessly hit back in your court, he replied in his refined Texas drawl: "Sweetheart, those two ladies lived together *harmoniously,* really *harmoniusly,* for *fifty years*—now, I ask *you,* could that be a sexual relationship?" Hans Loewald laughed—quite a departure from his usual silence. I resumed my ramble about how impossible it would be for me to undertake the biography, although I did admit that writing the biography of Anna Freud, and thus a kind of biography of Sigmund Freud, and a kind of history of psychoanalysis, would be a splendid project for *someone.* As I got up to go, Loewald, a tiny, wizened man with exquisite manners, made his characteristic little bow of farewell, but then cleared his throat to speak. This was another surprise, for he had never uttered a word at the leave-takings. "Perhaps I should not, but somehow I feel compelled to observe to you that you have changed your mind," he said.

On my way home, an instruction formed in my mind: "Biography is your destiny. Do not kick against your destiny." And then a little later: "Your character is your destiny." *Ethos anthropoi daimon*—thus spake Heraclitus. The trick is to know what your character is. So, I did write Anna Freud's biography, and then I wrote the characterology.

During the years between 1992 and 1996, while my crisis of confidence over my character and my characterology was resolving, I spent most of my writing time extending the characterology into the territory of "applied psychoanalysis," and onto the topic of where prejudiced thinking comes from. A book called *The Anatomy of Prejudices* resulted, a work in which the philosophical, feminist, and psychoanalytical trainings I have had all speak, as they do in this collection. I thought often about my midlife adolescent crisis of confidence, considering how it had influenced my decision to train as a psychoanalyst, but I didn't write anything that directly reflected it, other than in my personal journal. I did, however, write an essay about Hannah Arendt for a 1995 conference on her work. It is focused on Arendt's "exemplary independence" both because

▼▼▼▼▼

I thought a message about exemplary independence would be a good one to send out into a world in which political positions have become very homogenized, and because I myself obviously needed a reminder about staying independent of trends and fashions in the intellectual world. Then, when I was invited to a conference on biography and philosophy at New York University in 1996, I decided to make a kind of credo about thinking and relatedness, using not my psychoanalytic language but Hannah Arendt's philosophical one—my intellectual native tongue.

The short lecture that I gave is not included in this collection because its opening pages are too technical and scholarly, too much of a lexicon of Greek philosophical concepts. In those pages, I was touring Greek and Roman models of philosophical *Lives,* or presentations of philosophy in the medium of biographies. My purpose was to frame an image—an ideal—of what biographers could and should contribute in the present historical moment to renewing what is best in the Greco-Roman heritage, which is, I argued, not any kind of achieved truth but a way of looking, a way of thinking, a way of living the examined life. In the second part of the lecture, I went on to give the image:

I believe that in our cultural moment, I said, we need *Lives of the Philosophers,* whether of noncontemporaries or contemporaries, written by those who are trying to rediscover the historical and individual developmental sources of philosophy; to rediscover a way of living-and-thinking. Or, to put this sense of what philosophy is even more strongly: a way of thinking for sustaining living—something more fundamental than pursuit of an independently existing truth, more fundamental than concern for doctrine and succession. What I am invoking is thinking—presented in life-story–telling—as a way of relatedness to others in friendship and hospitality, and as a way of finding or refinding the world as a home; philosophy as a therapy for displacement and world-loss.

In the twentieth century, Karl Jaspers was the philosopher more than any other who gave his attention intently and profoundly to the writing of biography. Biography-writing was crucial to his search—he called it a "loving struggle"—for a philosophy "that does not cognize objects" but "elucidates and makes actual the being of the thinker." This is a philosophy that essentially is communication—but its method is biographical and autobiographical: it elucidates and makes actual the being of the thinker.

Jaspers wrote many short biographical studies—of his friend Max Weber, of Leonardo, Descartes, Goethe, Schelling—a long study of Nietzsche, and, most important, four massive volumes of *The Great Philoso-phers*. These volumes, which Jaspers thought of as a "world history of philosophy," are the incarnation of his conviction that we live in a cul-tural moment of "humankind," a moment when technological means have brought about a global age, when peoples of all specific cultures can and do communicate and a unity of humankind is concretely imag-inable. In this situation, the great philosophers can be studied—encoun-tered—as revealers of humankind; they represent the self-interpretation of human beings in their commonality. As Jaspers put it,

> We hope to enter into the world of the great philosophers, to make ourselves at home in it, because it is only in their company, the best there is, that we can attain to what we ourselves are capable of being . . . Admittance is open to all. The dwellers in that land are glad to answer provided that we know how to inquire. They show us what they are. They encourage us and make us humble. A great philosopher wants no disciples, but [people] who are themselves. With all our veneration, we come close to them only if we ourselves philosophize.

I think of a philosopher's biography as a form of philosophical com-munication that reveals who the philosopher was and who the biogra-pher is—but not simply in their subjectivities; rather, as communicants in the circle and situation of philosophizing that Jaspers has invoked. The biographer is in the biography telling the story of the philosopher's life and thought so that the philosopher would be able to recognize herself and feel the caring recognition of herself. But the biographer is also there representing the people who have heard and will hear this story, pass it down, connect it with other stories to make a collective representation. The biographer should certainly strive for literary excel-lence and truthfulness in the sense of historical accuracy; but her own sense of the contribution that her work can make to communication with and among readers is more an answer to the question "Did you grow in the work; did you find your capability with your subject?" The biographer's growth is then the sign of what is possible for the reader.

Jaspers's purpose was to make what his student Hannah Arendt once called "a common room." In the common room of her own *Men in Dark Times*, she had gathered a very diverse group of biographical por-traits, about whom she spoke in Jasperian terms:

> [Even] in the darkest of times we have a right to expect some illumination, and that . . . illumination may well come less from

▼▼▼▼▼

theories and concepts than from the uncertain, flickering, and often weak light that some men and women, in their lives and in their works, will kindle under almost all circumstances and shed over the time span that was given them on earth . . . Eyes so used to darkness as ours will hardly be able to tell whether their light was that of a candle or that of a blazing sun. But such objective evaluation seems to me a matter of secondary importance which can safely be left to posterity.

We expect some illumination in our times, and we expect it from people, and from ideas as they come from people in relation to other people, from conversations. There are many reasons why biography as a genre expanded its share of the global publishing scene exponentially in the 1970s and 1980s, and why memoirs and autobiographies followed suit in the 1990s, but this expectation of illumination is, it seems to me, the chief reason. People want to read about people—real people even more than fictional characters—because so many current fictional characters seem so intellectualized and heartless. Biographies, although usually, unfortunately, without much literary excellence, are about people in the full-bodied, full-emotioned, socially intricate way Euro-American novels were during the time now known by academics as "modernist."

The "back to the people themselves" movement among readers is related to the way in which reflections on transference came to the forefront of psychoanalytic theory of technique in the 1970s and 1980s, to be followed in the 1990s by reflections on countertransference and on psychoanalysis as a "two-person model." This development answered a sense among a generation of younger analysts—now in their fifties—that many of their elders had become caricatures of The Freudian Analyst, austere, self-enclosed, and mostly silent creatures, too given to imposing theories on patients; not given enough to paying attention to their patient's feelings about them or to their own listening. The critics were interested in how an analyst can be real—get real—with patients without losing what is important about analytic neutrality and without turning into a counselor or a confidante or a kind of professional friend. In terms of influence, this development was and is the feminization of psychoanalysis or the transformation of psychoanalysis by feminism (about which I wrote in the essays collected in Part II of this volume).

The readers wanting to read about people and the analysts wanting to be people were and are, like the thinkers thinking in conversation, and perhaps like the biographers being and having a couple in mind, all part of a world-historical trend that I was trying to invoke in my lecture

▼▼▼▼▼

on biography and philosophy. Since then, I have made the exciting discovery that there is a historian who has written about this trend in its multifarious manifestations: Theodore Zeldin, in *An Intimate History of Humanity*, a title in which the word "humanity" refers not just to the human population of the planet but to an ideal of encounter between people and among peoples that is emerging in a new form. "Today humanity is above all an ideal of caring and kindness extending to every age and to every living being."

Not surprisingly, Zeldin works like a biographer and like a therapist as he explores this ideal and contrasts it with ideals—for example, of conquest and power—that have preceded it. Like a biographer, he interviews individuals, collecting life stories. Asking his subjects about their hopes and their regrets, he finds that each is "restrained by attitudes inherited from origins long forgotten." Like a therapist, then, he points out those long-forgotten origins to his readers, showing as he does that restraint can be overcome by knowledge and the attentive kindness of an informed listener. The approach is biographical and therapeutic, but Zeldin's frame is wider: "Instead of explaining the peculiarity of individuals by pointing to their family or childhood, I take a longer view: I show how they pay attention to—or ignore—the experience of previous, more distant generations, and how they are continuing the struggles of many other communities all over the world, whether active or extinct, from the Aztecs to the Babylonians, to the Yoruba and the Zoroastrians, among whom they have more soul-mates than they may realize."

What Zeldin found with his biographical-therapeutic method was that the people he interviewed had in common an aspiration to travel and meet other people, to be listened to and to listen. "The age of discovery has barely begun." The harbingers of the age of discovery are clear, however, especially in the rise of feminism as an international movement and a climate of opinion, which, in its most general sense means the education of women as people capable of making a world in which they can meet people and be met as people, recognized not ruled. "Only when people learn to converse will they begin to be equal."

By making a narrative—a reflexive self-biography, psychoanalytic and philosophical, full of different angles of vision and levels of generalization—I wanted to consider in this introduction why contemporary scholars write biographies. I wanted to think out from my own case and to do so by proceeding biographically: by gathering up unpublished ideas, drafts, texts and invoking offstage conversations; by presenting

▼ ▼ ▼ ▼

the influences of private admonitions and confusions on public presentations; by reproducing the mental stuff and motion of a writer while writing and wondering what human commonality the writing will reflect and establish—a writer widening into her world. So this piece of writing is not like the essays collected here, but it is what their author, their thinker, is like in her being. Subject to biography.

▼ ▼ ▼ ▼ ▼

PART I

THE PRACTICE OF PSYCHOBIOGRAPHY

1

The Biographer's Empathy
with Her Subject

When I was asked to take up the topic "the biographer's empathy with her subject," I immediately, because the two biographies I have written are of German-speakers, translated my task: "Was ist Einfühlungsvermögen fur ein Biograph?" This response shows you in a quick stroke the most obvious dimension of biographical empathy. It is a kind of homing instinct for the territory of the biographical subject's emotional and intellectual formation and, in general, of her formative experiences. It is a mimetic movement, unpremeditated, but based upon the biographer's reflective habits of a lifetime, which tracks into the subject's ways of thinking and talking about herself.

Einfühlung, I thought as I continued considering my assignment, is a word and an activity which my first biographical subject, Hannah Arendt, would as a young woman have referenced automatically to her own biographical work during the late 1920s on Rahel Varnhagen, the most famous German Jewish salon hostess at the turn of the eighteenth century. *Einfühlung* only came into the technical vocabulary of German aesthetics in the 1870s, but its conceptual ancestry was in the distinction between imagination and reason that had been articulated so often during the French Enlightenment. Imagination had emerged in German Romanticism as the supreme cultural capacity, the mark of aesthetic sophistication, and all the people in the German salons would have lined themselves up with it and against coldly universalizing reason. They would have celebrated all particular, unique manifestations of human personality, all individual talent and genius, and thrown themselves into the "unbounded communication and unrestricted intimacy" that Arendt cited as the ideals of the day. They would have felt toward their peers as

▼ ▼ ▼ ▼ ▼

the young Hannah Arendt felt toward Rahel Varnhagen—that she should be able to tell Rahel's story *as Rahel herself would have told it.*

Later in her life, however, Hannah Arendt would have contrasted empathy, *Einfühlung,* as a passive according-with-another's-thought, to that active *Selbstdenken* recommended by the greatest representative of the German Enlightenment, Immanuel Kant. Thinking for yourself meant achieving an "enlarged mentality," a mentality not confined to a single subjective view, another's or your own, but able to range freely, to become a general view by virtue of encompassing and transcending all views. Romanticism's adored empathy had to be left behind, Arendt had come to think, to achieve good judgment. Her revised view was, I think, based upon historical experience with how the ingredients of Romanticism in general could be and were adopted and distorted by the intellectuals who served fascism. The lesson Arendt had learned about the arrogance of empathy—the notion that it is, ultimately, possible to achieve a kind of magical unity of subjectivities with kindred spirits, an illusory intimacy that can, then, be turned exultantly into a public life—is a lesson of very great importance. And it teaches anyone who wants to think about empathy—as I do here—to construct the concept modestly, limitedly. As Hannah Arendt liked to say, "No Schwarmerei!"

For my second biographical subject, Anna Freud, on the other hand, a woman whose entire "higher education" had taken place in the school of the Vienna Psychoanalytic Society, *Einfühling* would have had different associations. As a young woman, she would have tracked the word right to its first locus in her father's writings, his 1905 book *Jokes and Their Relation to the Unconscious.* Later, when she was her father's collaborator, she would have remembered his return to the topic in 1921, and before her mental eyes would have floated the German version of these words from *Group Psychology and the Analysis of the Ego:* "A path leads from identification by way of imitation to empathy, that is, to the comprehension of the mechanism by means of which we are enabled to take up any attitude at all towards another mental life."

It was her father's life and oeuvre by which Anna Freud oriented herself conceptually and emotionally, and she would have worked within this secure frame to evaluate later uses of "empathy." Both as Heinz Kohut employed the term in his "self psychology" and as Melanie Klein's followers developed it, "empathy" was a candidate for Anna Freud's lengthy blacklist of psychoanalytic notions that have been ruined, first with overuse and then with fetishization. Empathy, one could frequently hear it argued in the late 1970s, was *the* analytic requirement, the key

▼▼▼▼▼

to unlock all the mysteries of transference, the royal route capable of completely connecting one unconscious to another, and such arguments put Anna Freud on high defensive alert. She had her own version of the fear of Romanticism that had moved Hannah Arendt.

Not surprisingly, given their common cultural milieu, both of my biographical subjects were very historically minded. Asked to think about a concept like "empathy," they would both have set out on the kind of orienting mental tour that every German-speaker of their vintage knew as "origin and development" (*Ursprung und Entwicklung*). Both of my subjects were intellectual historians, with or without the title, by commitment and by imitation and by cultural formation (*Bildung*). Anna Freud always began her written contributions to psychoanalysis with a paragraph of historical situating, and she also wrote many predominantly historical papers, particularly in her later years, when she feared that the history of psychoanalysis was being forgotten or misused. Hannah Arendt learned historicity—to use the philosophical term, *Geschichtlichkeit*—in the seminars of her teacher Martin Heidegger, later briefly her lover, who as a matter of course began every reflection of his own with a mental trip to the pre-Socratic Greek philosophers and into the poetic treasuries of early Greek philosophical language. Heidegger was, and Arendt learned to be, a philosophical etymologist.

If I myself, as the biographer for these two women, had not learned—in fact, learned directly from Hannah Arendt, in her seminars—to imitate this fundamental mode of intellectual orientation, it would, simply, have been impossible for me to write about them and their work. On the other hand, neither of my subjects was an intellectual conservative, shackled by the inheritances and traditions in which they so carefully situated themselves. Their originalities, however, bloomed slowly, even though both had been remarkably precocious as children and as adolescents. They were both, interestingly, able to march forth as independents only after they had long passed the periods of their apprenticeships—indeed, only after they had passed their fortieth birthdays. Anna Freud had to work her way through a long mourning for her father, a journey that she certainly never completed—as if such journeys could be completed!—but on which she did come into her own as a contributor to psychoanalysis. Hannah Arendt had to be alienated from Heidegger and politically exiled, cast out of her German heritage in the most concrete of ways, exiled into the New World, before she committed herself to what she called "a new science of politics," an intellectual revolution, a vision for the future.

▼ ▼ ▼ ▼ ▼

For myself, the intellectual milieus of first German philosophy and then psychoanalysis are my place of exile—they are what I left home into, left home for, in the late 1960s, when I was in my early twenties. And these biographical subjects of mine, Arendt especially, who was my teacher, were for me like figures in a "family romance," a new and better, more elevated and self-flattering heritage. They were the means for my adolescent break with my past. And twenty years or so have been necessary—that is, I have had to be in my forties—for me to finish creating this place of exile for myself, and then to be done with it; to construct it and, in the process of writing through it, to deconstruct it, to use the work to find my way back over that break and into a domain of reconciliation. My empathy with my two biographical subjects is grounded in identification and imitation.

But these terms "identification" and "imitation" are vague, and the way in which I have been showing you what they mean for a biographer has also been, so far, quite intellectualized. I have set them in terms of reaching toward the subjects' culture. Let me now change registers, and stop presenting my two biographical subjects in their similarities. For considering my empathy with them more concretely, it is their differences that matter most.

I never felt any difficulty in empathizing with Hannah Arendt, because I felt that in some very fundamental ways we were alike (and I feel that likeness even more strongly now, more than ten years after I finished the biography, than I did while writing it—because I have grown into it). Let me illustrate this with an anecdote. I once remarked to Hannah Arendt that she must have found the strident attacks mounted against her and her controversial book *Eichmann and Jerusalem* (1961) very painful to endure. She gave me one of her intent, lesson-delivering looks and said, "Does it matter?" She was not denying her pain, she was just doing what she always did—putting her experience into a political perspective, subsuming her personal story in a larger history. And this is just what I had wanted and expected her to do when I made my remark. Later, I designed my biography to present her lesson to my readers—acting as an intermediary, so to speak—and this meant that I constructed an image of my readers as people who would want and expect such a lesson just as I had.

The likeness I felt with Hannah Arendt was in type of mental life, and, more fundamentally, type of character—we are both what I would describe as productively narcissistic. In terms of abilities, we lived and

▼ ▼ ▼ ▼ ▼

always will live on different planes completely, but I could—without apology or embarrassment—understand myself as a lesser version of her. With Anna Freud, however, I never felt this similarity of kind (if not scale). I experienced her as "other." And I understand this difference, now, as a matter of character as well. Hers was, in psychoanalytic terms, an obsessional character, and I, though I have obsessional traits, am not an obsessional character.

The majority of biographies are written like-to-like in characterological terms, although I am sure that many are written in the mode of constructing a character to be a like, forcing the subject into the biographer's type rather than discovering the similarities in the writing. Only the discovering mode, not the forcing mode, seems to me to involve empathy—indeed, forcing a person into your likeness is an excellent definition of lack of empathy. But, at any rate, biographers are drawn to subjects who are like themselves, usually in ways that the biographer is initially not consciously aware of. However, it is also possible to write across characterological types, and what happens in this instance—when the biographer is capable of it—is a process of part identifications, comparable to the incorporation of part objects. With Anna Freud, for example, I could feel myself identifying with her lucid mind, but not with her very restricted sexuality; with her physical energy and her energy of mind, her wit, but not at all with her physical presence, her embodiedness; with her sense for tradition, but not with the severest parts of her superego.

For the dimensions of Anna Freud that I could not, would not, take in, I had to cultivate, not just exercise, what might be called empathy-to-difference. Not simple empathy, but overcoming-antipathy, a kind of second-order or reinforced empathy for what is forever foreign in another. For example, I remember very vividly that one day, near the beginning of my archival research, I came to a screeching halt before a sentence in an otherwise uninteresting business letter. Anna Freud's sentence, referring to a homosexual applicant for training, said categorically, "I know from past experience that it is no good for any kind of course, or any kind of institution, to permit people with sexual abnormalities." I hated this sentence—for myself, and for all homosexuals who have had to endure psychoanalytic intolerance and pathologization—and continued to hate it until, many months later, I found Anna Freud's unpublished clinical reflections on male homosexuality and began to understand what the sentence meant to her, how it protected her, how it represented her. She was, I discovered, willing to question herself,

▾ ▾ ▾ ▾ ▾

analyze herself, on this topic, and, slowly, to alter her view. My hatred, encapsulated so that it did not flow out into my work, dissolved, and was replaced with a kind of cautious regard.

When you find yourself cultivating empathy, you also surely know that no empathy with a person you have incorporated and identified with ever rises up automatically on the basis of the incorporation or identification, as a natural by-product. Any empathy depends, its seems to me, on a certain form and degree of self-consciousness. You have to know—and this is a matter of insight—the role that the subject plays in your wish structure and your ego ideal; you have to make this role conscious to the degree that you can. The reason that this insight is the necessary precondition for empathy is that empathy is feeling the other person's desires in the mode of comparison, and for a comparison you must be able to tell the difference between the subject and yourself.

The usual—indeed, the clichéd—way of describing empathy as "putting yourself in another's place" seems to me quite wrong. Empathizing involves, rather, putting another *in yourself*, becoming another person's habitat, as it were, but without dissolving the person, without digesting the person. You are mentally pregnant, not with a potential life but with a person, indeed, a whole life—a person with her history. So the subject lives on in you, and you can, as it were, hear her in this intimacy. But this, as I said, depends upon your ability to tell the difference between the subject and yourself, which means to appreciate the role that she plays in your psychic life. Such insight is the ground on which you can distinguish between what you want for yourself, which you may be seeking partly from her, and what she wanted for herself, which she obviously did not seek from you (though you may supply part of what she wanted in the biography).

Let me return again to my subjects to show you what I mean by linking insight and comparison of desires in this definition of the biographer's empathy. I came to feel very strongly as I lived with Anna Freud lodged in my mind that she had most deeply wanted—all her life, and so strongly that her obsessionality had grown up around this pearl of desire as a denial of it—something to which I gave the nontechnical name "tenderness." I came to feel that she had felt perfectly secure in her father's love for her, but not in his tenderness, a deeper and more frighteningly incestuous level of his love; and I came to feel that she had, as a small child, basked in the tenderness of her nurse but had received relatively little tenderness from her overworked mother and her frustrated aunt, the other two of the troika of women who cared for her.

▼ ▼ ▼ ▼ ▼

I felt in her a quest for the nurse. And I felt this as the chord underlying her intimate friendships with women and supplying the enormous tenderness—filtered of sentimentality at his request—that she lavished upon her father. Coming to this picture of Anna Freud's desire, her *Ur-Wunsch* if I may call it that, I did not consult my own desires and say, "I can empathize with this." Rather, I said, this is not the desire that determines my relationships with women or with men, but this is a desire that I find frightening even to think about—*so it must be mine in a way that I do not yet understand.* Her need sent me on a self-quest. And on that quest, I empathized with her out of both gratitude and anticipation for what she would teach me. And I gave her, in turn, my biographical tenderness.

Similarly, as I lived with Hannah Arendt lodged in my mind for the years of writing her story (and still), I felt that there was a basic desire in her for understanding, a passion for finding the meaning of history, *Weltgeschichte.* I felt, but could not assert in the biography directly for lack of evidence, that this desire was a vastly ramified, extended quest for the meaning of her father's illness—for his syphilis, his paresis, and his death when she was seven years old. Leaving aside her very justifiable philosophical skepticism about the arrogant knowledge claims so often made by psychoanalysts, her aversion to psychoanalysis seemed to me a sign that what she really wanted to know about was, precisely, madness and death-by-madness. But what she directed her formidable intellect toward was the madness of history, and particularly the completely paradoxical fact that a small and unpowerful people like the Jews had been drawn into the storm center of twentieth-century European politics and set upon with a viciousness unknown in previous human history. She was an unlocker of secrets. And with this character-organizing desire, one that is, I would argue, central to the character type that I would call narcissistic, I felt completely in accord. And I was, at the time of that biography, quite content to have this need displaced onto, worked out in the medium of, history and a historical-biographical narrative. Hannah Arendt played in my mind the role of the legitimator of a quest for understanding. I was aware of this, and it helped me to give her, in turn, my biographical understanding.

The way in which I have chosen to reflect on the biographer's empathy with her subject is influenced by a study I wrote called *Creative Characters.* In this book I considered three broad types of creativity, which, I argued, rest on and represent three broad character types. Both the char-

▼ ▼ ▼ ▼ ▼

acters and the creativities were, in many different modes, biographically illustrated in this book. But *Creative Characters* is a work of theory, not a biography, and it was very obvious to me as I wrote it that I had nothing like the identificatory engagement with the people whose biographies I was sketching that I had had with Hannah Arendt and Anna Freud. The difference was, I think, something like the difference between using case material for illustration in a theoretical paper and writing a case study.

When you write an illustrative biographical vignette (perhaps also a brief biography), I would like to suggest, you exercise with particular intensity a biographical empathy that is rather different than the two sorts that I have already sketched—empathy for cultural formation and empathy for core, formative desires. Let me just say one thing quickly and in closing about this third kind of empathy. This is, I think, empathy directed at the subject's life over time. It follows a life line, it moves along the shape of a life and is particularly sensitive to turning points, junctures, moments of high density—particularly as the subject herself constructs these, sometimes in the form of those complex condensations of experience that Freud called screen memories. People have, I think, a feeling for the form their lives have taken or are taking, and people usually have an image or images by which they present this form to themselves. The biographer must discover that image or images.

When you write a full-length biography, turning-point images slowly emerge to you and you use them to frame the book, to organize the book so that the book reflects them. For example, you divide a book at the moment that your subject goes into exile, as both of my subjects did, for this moment has an iconic quality in the minds of exiles. But, then, behind such a life-capturing image you will, inevitably in my opinion, find another sort of image, one capturing how the life story was made internally. Some people will indicate that their life story consists, for example, of their efforts—more or less successful—to learn how to control their energies, their drives, their desires; others will indicate that their lives consisted of efforts to shape their youthful chaos into something contoured, of self-fabricating; yet others show you that over the course of their lives they tried to purify themselves of hated ingredients, pollutions, bad habits, taints. Such images are icons of peoples' feelings about themselves. They are their feelings about themselves distilled, condensed, as unconscious dream-thoughts are condensed into the manifest content of a dream.

Empathizing with such icons of feeling is empathizing in a visual mode, not the hearing mode, the listening mode that I described earlier

▼ ▼ ▼ ▼

when considering empathy toward the incorporated desiring subject. It is the most highly synthetic kind of empathizing, and seems to me to involve the ego's synthesizing functions more than the "hearing the incorporated other" mode does. This is, so to speak, portrait painter's empathy, the kind that puts a story—something that exists over time—into an immediately graspable space.

Now, there are surely more modes of biographical empathy than the three I have tried to describe here briefly, but these are the three most familiar to me, the three that I can recognize in my own practice of biography writing and biographical sketching, and I offer them as such.

▾   This was the plenary address at the April 1992 meeting of the American Academy of Psychoanalysis in Washington, D.C., and then it was published in *Academy Forum,* 36 (1992): 9–11.

▾ ▾ ▾ ▾ ▾

2

Psychoanalytic Reflections
on Creativity

In his essay on Edgar Allan Poe, the poet Charles Baudelaire offered a general reflection on the importance of adolescence in the development of character, genius, and style:

> All those who have reflected upon their lives, who have often turned back their gaze in order to compare their pasts with their present life, all those who have learned the habit of ready self-analysis, know what an immense share in man's definitive genius is due to his adolescence. It is then that things stamp themselves deeply upon the tender and responsive mind: it is then that colors are vivid, and the senses vocal with a mysterious tongue. The character, the genius, the style of a man are formed by the apparently vulgar circumstances of his first youth. If all the men who have come upon the world's stage had set down their impressions of their boyhood, what an excellent psychological dictionary we would have!

Baudelaire, it seems to me, underestimated the psychological dictionary that exists in the works of men and women who have come upon the world's stage as creators, as originators of works of art. This dictionary is little read, however, because a guide for its use, a guide to how character, genius, and style—to use Baudelaire's terms—define each other, has not been developed.

I think that such a guide could be built up with the help of a notion I call the character-ideal. My idea is that in their late adolescences creative people form for themselves—sometimes consciously, but usually unconsciously—a guiding image of the character they wish for, the sort of genius that will be able to subtend, to be the origin for, their style,

▼ ▼ ▼ ▼

their creativity. This guiding image or character-ideal is formed on the basis of the character an adolescent has: it is an idealization of an existing state of psychic affairs; it is a projection on the basis of a developmental history.

Sigmund Freud offered the very rich idea that people form images of ideal societies—utopias—and of natural processes and orders on the basis of their internal perceptions of themselves. He called these images "endopsychic perceptions." His idea was that people project outward their crucial developmental icon, the story of their Oedipus complex; and he assumed that they idealized this story in the projecting, that is, that they projected not how things had truly been Oedipally with them, but how they wished things had been—and still were. They projected what he called "the family romance." So, we find our traditions full of societal stories about magnificent Founding Fathers and natural-historical stories about the cosmos having been commanded into being by a Creator Father or a divine Demiurge, and so forth. Religions and philosophies are, in sum, psychic stories, family romance fantasies, turned outward and writ very large.

I find this idea of Freud's provocative, if rather too focused on Oedi-pal desires and too patriarchal to compass, say, Mother Earth images; but I want to add something to the idea. It seems to me that adolescents, at one remove of libidinal development from the "sexual efflorescence" (as Freud called it) of the Oedipal period, tend to have "endopsychic perceptions" of another kind than children have. They perceive them-selves, their psychic apparatuses, in terms of how the apparatuses are, or are not, ordered. In the upheaval of adolescence, they long for order, for an independent New World of psychic order, to which psychoanalysis has, since Erik Erikson's work of the 1960s, given the name "identity."

This adolescent image of mind-body order, this character-ideal, is, I think, apparent in creative works of all sorts—literary, philosophical, visual, musical, and so forth. It is the origin, as Freud noted, for projec-tions of the ideal society and images of the cosmos. But I think it is also the origin for creative people's images of creativity: it determines the way they imagine creative processes, their own and others'. Theories of creativity are expressions of "endopsychic perception" of creativity in action. This is, by the way, the reason why—I think—the search peren-nially conducted by psychoanalysts for *the* key to creativity, *the* creative process, is a perfectly futile and misconceived search, as is the recent feminist search for *the* creativity specific to females. There are creative processes, in the plural, and these stem from different creative charac-

▼ ▼ ▼ ▼ ▼

terological types, which are not specific to the two sexes, though they may have particular differences that are sex or gender specific.

I am not a clinician, but a biographer. Someone who has written and read the kinds of stories of adolescence about which Baudelaire spoke. It is on the basis of biographical study that I have come to the conclusion, a hypothetical one, that there are basically three different kinds of character-ideals or images of ideal psychic order developed by adolescents in the course of their identity quests. What I would like to do here is to sketch in very summary terms these three types and then offer three biographical illustrations of them.

The first type is an image of wild forces brought under control by a commanding figure, a figure of such charisma that it can over time, evolutionarily, bring about order without violence, by sheer force of will or personality or authority.

In the history of psychological inquiries into the nature and processes of creativity, it is Sigmund Freud who has most persuasively made this type of character-ideal the centerpiece of his theory. Freud, of course, argued that creative work depends on a person's ability to sublimate, to channel and dedicate libidinal forces, the wild resevoir of the id, to cultural purposes. Freud portrayed the creator as a person of strong, charismatic ego, a person who, as he said in his biographical essay on Leonardo da Vinci and reiterated in the late small essay called "Libidinal Types," works from a narcissistic characterological base.

The second type of image of ideal psychic order or character-ideal features a figure who works upon matter that needs shaping, molding, forming. This image is artisanal: a well-ordered self is a self in which one part has been able to make the other part beautiful. In some creative people of this character-ideal sort, the fabricating image is, however, one of reproduction rather than production. These people imagine the psyche as having two parts, one male and one female, which together make a "child of the soul" (as Plato called the poet's work).

Theories of creativity generated by people of this second creative characterological type take two general forms according to whether the emphasis is on production or reproduction. If the emphasis is on production, these theories of creativity present images of the self splitting and then reuniting through a molding or sculpting process. The split-off molder or sculptor is very often presented as an impostor, or a poseur, a figure who can assume many guises and then bring the material or to-be-formed part into accord with those guises. If the emphasis is on repro-

▼ ▼ ▼ ▼ ▼

duction, the bisexuality or androgyny or hermaphroditism of the psyche is emphasized and celebrated—as bisexuality or homosexuality in object choice is often practiced. Males often speak of themselves, as Friedrich Nietzsche did, as "male mothers," and they sing the praises of the female's capacity for giving birth. Females analogize their creativity to their procreativity, but imagine that they have in themselves a paternal, inseminating figure (who is very often modeled on their father). In theories of this sort, inspiration plays a large role—and it is conceived of as an ability either to inseminate or to be inseminated. Not sublimation, but splitting is the key creative mechanism for people of this sort.

The third type of image of ideal psychic order or character-ideal is one in which a true self, a pure or uncorrupted self, throws off or strips itself of all impurities, all mere matter, all corruptible flesh, all shackles that keep it from creative flight or prevent its salvation. This is the image fundamental to all who conceive of order as arising from spiritual discipline, achievement of undistracted attention or concentration, and, usually, sexual abstinence or at least some very regulated form of asceticism or so-called Platonic love.

Creativity, according to people of this third sort, has more to do with a state of mind than an actual product or achievement in the world. Worldly products are, at most, a record of a process of transcending the world, escaping its corruptions, finding peace, serenity, purity—though worldly products may be very highly valued for their pedagogical or their exemplary force, their status as manuals of salvation or prevention of illness. Spiritual exercises, meditation, periods of self-humbling and self-denial are typical of this Stoic, or one might even say, Buddhistic modality. The libidinal organization or character type that is the basis for this type of creativity and theorizing about creativity is, usually, the character Freud called "anal", which is known diagnostically as "the obsessional character."

What I have noted is very condensed and abbreviated, and I think it will make more sense with illustration. I am going to present first a sketch of Sigmund Freud in his adolescence, to illustrate the type of character-ideal in which psychic order is imaged as charismatic "political" control over wild energies. Then I am going to present a composite portrait of a group of turn-of-the-century British lyric poets. This portrait, which will focus on William Butler Yeats but range to Oscar Wilde and Gerard Manley Hopkins, will illustrate the second type of character ideal, the one in which a part of the self shapes and molds another part or in which

▼ ▼ ▼ ▼ ▼

a part is father and a part mother to a child of the soul. Finally, I am going to present a group of four women who shared neither genre, nor historical period, nor native culture: two French-speaking women of different generations, Simone Weil and the Belgian Marguerite Yourcenar, an Austrian, Anna Freud, and an American expatriate, Gertrude Stein. This group will illustrate the spiritual self-stripping or self-transcending ascetic character-ideal type. I hope these three different biographical methods will give some idea of how biography can contribute to the "psychological dictionary" of adolescent experiences that Baudelaire envisioned and that I am trying to locate.

In his youth, the controlling figure in Sigmund Freud's character-ideal had a number of sources—it was a composite of Hannibal, Napoleon, Napoleon's Jewish general Messena, Garibaldi, the leaders of the French Revolution. Freud indicated autobiographically that when he was an adolescent a slightly older contemporary, Heinrich Braun, later a prominent socialist leader, lent him a library of political histories and inspired his admiration personally. When he was a grown man, contemporary figures were assimilated to the ideal, as Kolomon Szell was during the Hungarian crisis of 1898. But, given the role that Rome played in Freud's imagination, it seems that Hannibal had a kind of pride of place among the exemplars. For Freud to visit Rome meant direct emulation of the conquistador's greatness—and Freud had to avoid for years making what felt like such a naked display of ambition. In his later adult life, Freud's character-ideal was more and more frequently associated with Moses.

About the controlling figure in Freud's character-ideal, we can say—generally—that he is a thoroughgoing independent, a rebel who does not stop short of his goals or his establishment of himself as the authority second to no other man, even if—like Moses—he must overcome great personal weaknesses to succeed. In him there are no unresolved questions about obedience to other authorities, including the parental (specifically paternal) one. Furthermore, he leads without having to subdue his followers: they follow in deference to his charisma, and when they do have a period of rebelliousness against him, his charisma deters them—and he is able to be restrained and in authoritarian control over his emotions until it does. He is Moses as Freud described him in his essay on Michelangelo's statue of Moses in Rome: "the giant frame with its tremendous physical power . . .[is]. . . a concrete expression of the highest mental achievement that is possible in a man, that of struggling

▼▼▼▼▼

successfully against an inward passion for the sake of a cause to which he has devoted himself" (13:223).[1]

It is in relation to self-control that the politically constructed character-ideal seems to have been most important for Freud. The leader behaves toward the people as reason or a strong ego should behave toward the id. The human figures in the ideal character rule (as Freud noted of the French revolutionaries) by their sheer force of intellect and their fiery eloquence. Or, as Freud said in his *Group Psychology and the Analysis of the Ego* of the ideal leader: "his intellectual acts were strong even in isolation, and his will needed no reinforcement from others." The leader is a man of "masterly nature, narcissistic, but self-confident and independent." In his later years, it seems to have become important to Freud that his ideal character figure—who was then Moses—be an outsider, not a product of his group but someone who brought the group a redemptive vision from elsewhere. The ability to live as an outsider, a pariah, and to bear scorn and hatred had become crucial in the character-ideal. Again and again, Freud noted that his Jewish heritage was not a theology but a character—a phylogenetic heritage for enduring pariah-dom.

The development of the character-ideal figure from earlier "family romance" figures is signaled the fact that Freud imagined that his father—a man not heroic, without a masterly nature—looked, as he lay flushed and red-faced on his deathbed, like Garibaldi (4:228, 247). He related to his father through the medium of the idealized father figure, who was the human figure of his character-ideal. The character-ideal was also tied to an earlier sexual ideal. The character-ideal's figure is a ruler of people, but he must also have a history of sexual preparation for such greatness. As Freud said in general, not just of political figures: "A man who has shown determination in possessing himself of his love object has our confidence in his success in regard to other aims as well. On the other hand, a man who abstains for whatever reasons, from satisfying his strong sexual instinct, will also assume a conciliatory and resigned attitude in other paths of life, rather than a powerfully active one." This passage presents the typical form of character-ideal measuring: the ideal is set out—it is possession, success—and then ("on the other hand") the failure is envisioned—lack of possession, unsuccess.

Freud as an adolescent had every reason to find himself headed for unsuccess when he failed to approach, much less possess, his first love, a girl named Gisela Fluss. To his friend Eduard Silberstein, the sixteen-year-old Freud gave a literary account of his interior obstacle, a pre-

▼ ▼ ▼ ▼ ▼

monition of the account he would later give of Shakespeare's Hamlet as a character caught in an unresolved Oedipal dilemma: "This sentiment for Gisela appeared like a nice sentiment in spring, but my nonsensical 'Hamlethood,' my shyness, prevented me from indulging in conversation with the partly naive, partly educated young lady." Ten years apparently passed between this episode and his next sexual adventure. Then he had every reason to find his arduous, prolonged, but ultimately successful courtship of Martha Bernays a much more satisfactory augury for the future, and he told his fiancée repeatedly that she was his salvation from a life with no meaning.

It is hard to think that this story of salvation is not reflected in Freud's description of the kind of narcissism characteristic of males. The sexual instincts are at first attached to the satisfaction of the self-preservative, nutritionally focused ego instincts, Freud argued, and they carry this attachment into later loves or object choices. So, men attach themselves continually to versions of the woman who nourished them (and, to a lesser extent, of the father who protected them): "Complete object-love of the attachment type is, properly speaking, characteristic of the male. It displays the marked sexual over-valuation which is doubtless derived form the child's original narcissism and thus corresponds to a transference of that narcissism to the sexual object. This sexual over-valuation is the origin of a peculiar state of being in love, a state suggestive of a neurotic compulsion, which is thus traceable to an impoverishment of the ego as regards libido in favour of the love object" (14:88).

A second kind of narcissism, moving a person to seek continually a version (an idealized version) of himself or herself in lovers, often combines with narcissism of the attachment type, but it can also predominate over the attachment type—particularly in women and male homosexuals, Freud argues. In Freud himself, both kinds of narcissism seem apparent, with the attachment type taking the upper hand in the period when he courted Martha Bernays.

The narcissism mixture in Freud is also revealed in his career plans. After his adolescent "Hamlethood" episode with Gisela Fluss, who was so much a creature of Freud's narcissistic fantasy and so little a real girl, Freud made two decisions: he gave up his goal of preparing himself with a law degree for a political career, and he gave up the possibility of an artistic avocation. The restraint he decided to put on his artistic and speculative imagination soon meant turning away from speculative philosophy as he encountered it in the classroom of Franz Brentano. But

▼▼▼▼▼

the refusal of an artistic self-ordering seems also to have been crucially tied to his sexual experience. When Gisela Fluss married, Freud joked elaborately with Silberstein about this girl they called "Ichthyosaura" as though she were prehistoric, a dinosaur: "Herewith this period ends, here I submerge the magic wand that has contributed to its organization: a new time may commence without secretly active forces, a time that does not need poesy and fantasy. Nobody may search for a principle [a girl] in the alluvium or diluvium or elsewhere but in the present, nowhere but among the children of human beings but not in the grisly primordial past." Poesy and fantasy, associated with this ill-fated affair, were ruled out—as was what I have called the artisanal character-ideal.

Ruled in as careers were natural science (as presided over by Goethe) or medicine. The difference between artists and scientific people was, then, built in autobiographical terms into Freud's theory of sublimation. As he noted in an essay entitled " 'Civilized' Sexual Morality and Modern Nervous Illness": "in the vast majority of cases, the struggle against sexuality eats up the energy available in a character, and at the very time when a young man is in need of all his forces in order to win his share and place in society . . . An abstinent artist is hardly conceivable; but an abstinent young savant is certainly no rarity."

What the abstinent young savant Sigmund Freud could not do without for the development of his scientific career was authority figures. Freud attached himself to a succession of male protective authority figures, chief among them the physiologist Ernst Brucke, who, as Freud much later dramatically proclaimed, "carried more weight with me than anyone else in my whole life" (20:253). Consciously, Freud turned political leadership over to these figures, but unconsciously he converted his own self-leadership ambitions into another field—science. Brucke was an emmulatable leader in the manner of Freud's ideal, a real-life Garibaldi; he dreamt of Brucke's "terrible blue eyes by which I was reduced to nothing" (5:422).

It is possible to see Brucke as an ideal or what the analyst K. R. Eissler calls an "ideal superego figure," a corrective image to Freud's weak father, but it is also important to see him as a leader, the head of an institute bearing his name—that is, as fit to influence the figure in Freud's character-ideal. Freud's ego, his reason—to speak nontechnically—was to have dominion in his psyche, not as an artistic or magical Prospero with a wand, but as a political figure, an authority, commanding obedience without resorting to violence. In the more abstract terms of the character-ideal: Reason (the ego) was to rule over unreason (the id)

▼ ▼ ▼ ▼

without ever rebelling against destiny or against what cannot be influenced because it is—like death—beyond our control. Reason's ally in exerting control was to be psychology, as Freud later (in a May 25, 1895, letter) told his friend Wilhelm Fliess: "A man like me cannot live without a hobby horse, without a dominating passion, without—to speak with Schiller—a tyrant, and he has come my way. And in his service I know no moderation. It is psychology."

The social vision in which this character-ideal was projected outward also featured instinctual life undergoing a slow devolution in the process of civilizational evolution. Explicitly, Freud viewed the microcosm of the individual and the macrocosm of society as sharing a story—but in the manner common among his contemporaries, he claimed that the microcosm recapitulates the societal story, ontogeny recapitulates phylogeny. Freud's ideal became to avoid despising the erotic instinct by sublimating it—controlling it without repression. He thought of the result as a special type of civilized character, while, in general, he viewed the emergence of character types as a phenomenon of civilization. "The differentiation of the individual character, which is so marked in our day, has only become possible with the existence of sexual restriction" (9:196).

The particular way in which Freud conceived of the voice of the controlling ego or Reason is obvious in his texts—for, as Baudelaire indicated, character, genius, and style are linked. People of genius who create literary texts, and over time an oeuvre, project their character-ideals into their style or their form or their choice of genre or their working method as well as into a social vision or a natural philosophy. In Freud's case, what this means is that his texts, singly and in relation to each other, are dialogic in a particular sense: they present a leader, the main voice in the texts, and other voices—specific dissenting theorists, propounders of anticipated objections, or choruses of unnamed critics. As the text unfolds the opposition is given its say and then stilled while what is valuable in the oppositional views is peacefully assimilated to the dominating view, Freud's psychoanalysis. Like the Roman emperors, Freud gave citizenship in his empire to willing former opponents and banished the unwilling to outer darkness. The dialogue is quite foregrounded and theatrical in the late work called *The Question of Lay Analysis,* but it operates everywhere in Freud's oeuvre, frustrating readers who find their criticism has already been anticipated and defeated.

Let me turn now to a group portrait to illustrate the character-ideal that features two parts, one crafting the other or both coupling to produce a

▼ ▼ ▼ ▼ ▼

child of the soul. I will take up a group who, collectively, followed Oscar Wilde's well-known advice: "Create yourself! Be yourself your poem." Richard Ellmann, Oscar Wilde's most sophisticated biographer, noted in general that "the measure of the greatness of the Wildean hero is the extent to which he has altered the raw material of his life into something quite different. So far as his passions emerge they are ignoble and uninteresting, part of an unpleasant, irrelevant reality, a subject for the naturalist and not for the true artist." Wilde did not imagine character as a channeling of forces of libidinal disposition or natural temperament; he imagined character as replacing nature, and he exalted the completely artificial self.

Among turn-of-the-century British aesthetes, it was the word "personality" that came to denote the crafted self. As Ellmann noted in his biography of Yeats, aptly subtitled *The Man and the Masks*:

> The implication of the esthetes' conception of the artistic personality is that a man is really two men. There is the insignificant man who is *given*, whether by God, by society, or simply by birth; there is the significant man who is *made* by the first . . . In literature the splitting up of the mind is accomplished near the end of the century by two books, *Dr. Jekyll and Mr. Hyde* (1885) and *The Picture of Dorian Gray* (1890) . . . The last decade of the century is thronged by extravagant *poseurs* like Lionel Johnson and Aubrey Beardsley; even James Joyce, growing up in this atmosphere, says he felt compelled to construct "the enigma of a manner." The attempt to achieve a rarefied, synthetic self is implicit in Pater's extreme preoccupation with style, his method of rewriting innumerable times so that his finished phrase would resemble as little as possible the one that had come initially into his head.

William Butler Yeats, as Ellmann shows, was well suited for internal division and quite able to exploit his state by virtue of his childhood revolt, "which could only be a half-revolt, against his father and his father's world." As a late adolescent, he adopted the notion of himself as two beings and began to write from it, with it. Then, when Yeats associated himself with the magical adepts in the Order of the Golden Dawn, his vision was projected outward, as Ellmann shows: "From the attempt to achieve personal transmutation it was only a brief step to the attempt to achieve a more general transmutation. The Order taught that its doctrines should affect daily life. Many members of the Golden Dawn felt that they had the additional obligation of becoming 'a perfect instrument for the regeneration of the world.' " Yeats, thirty years old, but still

▼ ▼ ▼ ▼ ▼

shy and sexually quite inexperienced, expected sociopolitical Armageddon and envisioned a "civilization about to be born." Crafting a self and conjuring a civilization into being were two ranges of the same character-ideal in action.

For men at the turn of the century, both the political character-ideal evident in Freud, analyst of the Oedipus Complex, and this artisanal ideal went under the aegis of father-son struggle: they are ideals of conflict stilled by political authority or artistic skill triumphant over the "given," the self tied to the past and to paternal authority or precedent. But the father-son conflict is most obvious in the artisanal ideal, because it involves not just an image of authoritative control assumed, but one of construction—and construction entails destruction, violence wrought. The divided self can be at once father-identified and parricidal—even if, as in the Daedalus and Icarus story, the parricide has to be disguised, so that the artificer father survives rather than dying himself. "Who doesn't desire his father's death?" Ivan Karamozov asked—and he clearly meant no question at all. Yeats's concurrence was expressed first in an unpublished play he wrote when he was turning twenty, again at the age of thirty-eight in "The Death of Cuchulain," and on through two different translations of Sophocles' *Oeidpus Rex* and a play involving parricide written shortly before his death in 1939.

But the specific forms that the artisanal character-ideal takes in males, although clued to the specific forms of Oedipal conflict, call for a more complex reading along what Anna Freud called "developmental lines." The Wildean poseur, for example, artistically defends himself as an obsessional does—his character is like a fully lived out obsessional ceremonial, a ceremonial turned into a way of life, a childhood lack of control and a fear of passivity turned into active self-shaping.

With others, the self-shaping imagery may relate more to self-gestating than to fabricating. Character-ideals presenting one part of the self or psyche raising and educating another, or one part giving birth to a work of art that represents a facet of the self, or one part tied to a "civilization about to be born," are rooted in very early childhood experiences but reactivated with adolescent envy for pregnant women. Goethe's envy of his younger sister's pregnancy is an example that has been biographically studied. As much as Wilde abhorred Byron and Byron's heroes, Goethe had admired the English poet's "true poetical power" and his capacity to bear and rear his work naturally. The Platonic tradition of relating divine inspiration or madness and impregnation is echoed in the apostrophe to Byron recorded in Goethe's conversations with Johann

Eckermann: "with [Byron] inspiration supplies the place of reflection. He was obliged to go on poetizing; and then everything that came from the man, especially from his heart, was excellent. He produced his best things as women do pretty children, without thinking about it or knowing how it is done."

Among the late-nineteenth-century British aesthetes, one of the most explicit and sustained presentations of psychic procreation and male mothering (to use Nietzsche's phrase) was crafted by Gerard Manley Hopkins. His poem, dedicated to his friend the poet Robert Bridges, can stand as a representative of the sexual corollary of the artisanal character-ideal projected into a work:

> The fine delight that fathers thought; the strong
> Spur, live and lancing, like the blowpipe flame,
> Breathes once and, quenched faster than it came,
> Leaves yet the mind a mother of immortal song.
> Nine months she then, nay years, nine years she long
> Within her wears, bears, cares and combs the same:
> The widow of an insight lost she lives, with aim
> Now known and hand at work never wrong.
>   Sweet fire the sire of muse, my soul needs this;
> I want the one rapture of an inspiration.
> O then if in my lagging lines you miss
> The roll, the rise, the carol, the creation,
> My winter world, that scarcely breathes that bliss
> Now, yields you, with some sighs, our explanation.

Inspiration can be thought of as the divine spur to self-crafting, as it can be thought of as spiritual impregnation. But it can also be experienced and conceptualized quite differently, as a process of unburdening. People with character-ideals of the third type I sketched above, the ascetic or spiritual type, speak as T. S. Eliot did in "The Use of Poetry and the Use of Criticism" about what inspiration feels like:

> A disturbance of our quotidian character which results in an incantation, an outburst of words which we hardly recognize as our own because of the effortlessness ... [To] me, it seems that at these moments, which are characterized by the sudden lifting of the burden of anxiety and fear which press upon our daily life so steadily that we are unaware of it, what happens is something negative: that is to say, not "inspiration" as we commonly think of it, but the breaking down of strong habitual barriers—which tend to reform very quickly. Some obstruction is momentarily whisked

▼▼▼▼▼

away. The accompanying feeling is less like what we know as a positive pleasure, than a sudden relief from an intolerable burden.

Disburdening or what I have called self-stripping is the action of the ascetic or spiritual character-ideal. Stoical or sexually overstrict religious traditionalists of Eliot's sort often project such an ideal. But stripping the self of all its accidentality or materiality, revealing the essential self in its purity, can serve many purposes, and not the least among them is escape from psychic and social conditions in which being female seems a limitation, an inadequacy.

In her biography of the French philosopher Simone Weil, Simone Petrement described her subject as a *lycée* student: "As for the plans she had already formed, her whole conception of what she wanted to do with her life, it was—as she herself later said—a great misfortune to have been born female. So she decided to reduce this obstacle as much as possible by disregarding it, that is, by giving up any desire to think of herself as a woman or to be regarded as such by others . . . Her parents called her 'Simon,' 'our son number two,' and 'our *cagne* boy.' When Simone wrote to her mother while at Henri IV [her *lycée*], she even went so far as to speak of herself in the masculine gender and to sign her letters 'your respectful son.' " Simone Weil gave up her femininity for the gender she regarded as generic: she joined, as it were, mankind.

But her project also had quite specific purpose within her family context, in the shadow of her astoundingly precocious mathematician brother André and in the atmosphere of her mother's contempt for feminine frailties and silliness. In her "Spiritual Autobiography," Weil recalled that:

At fourteen I fell into one of those fits of bottomless despair that come with adolescence, and I seriously thought of dying because of the mediocrity of my natural faculties. The exceptional gifts of my brother, who had a childhood and youth comparable to those of Pascal, brought my own inferiority home to me. I did not mind having no visible successes, but what did grieve me was the idea of being excluded from that transcendent kingdom to which only the truly great have access and wherein truth abides. I prepared to die rather than to live without that truth. After months of inward darkness, I suddenly had the everlasting conviction that any human being, even though practically devoid of natural faculties, can penetrate to the kingdom of truth reserved for genius, if only he longs for truth and perpetually concentrates all his attention upon its attainment. He thus becomes a genius, too, even though

▼ ▼ ▼ ▼ ▼

for lack of talent his genius cannot be visible from the outside. Later on, when the strain of headaches caused the feeble faculties I possess to be invaded by a paralysis, which I was quick to imagine as probably incurable, the same conviction led me to persevere for ten years in an effort of concentrated attention that was practically unsupported by any hope of results.

The sibling rivalry, the competition for prowess as a penetrator into a romanticized kingdom of truth, the stress on her own "invisible" equipment, give this passage all the marks of the Freudianly defined "masculinity complex," but what is important in the context I am developing is Simone Weil's solution: paring herself down to an ascetic, rarefied attentiveness. The purity does not come, as with Oscar Wilde, from self-shaping—rarefaction or transformation by constant reworking—but by elimination, purgation. It is no psychic accident that Simone Weil later ended her life in a martyrdom that took the form of self-starvation, anorexia.

A person of this character-ideal type might also describe her life and her writing style with words like these: "I try to eliminate what isn't essential, and I try not to give in, as I did in my youth, to the temptation to add ornament. Back then I thought it was necessary to round off each sentence. Now I look instead for the sharpest possible sentence, the simplest images, and I don't try to be original at all costs. In fact, I don't try anything at all; my writing is the way it is." This woman, cited from a collection of her interviews appropriately titled *With Open Eyes,* is the Belgian-born novelist Marguerite Yourcenar, the first woman ever to be initiated into the Académie française. She was speaking of the style she had first worked for in *Alexis,* a *récit* or monologue penned by a young man explaining to his wife that he is a homosexual and cannot continue in their marriage. Yourcenar published the book when she was twenty-six, in 1929. Later she declared that she hoped to be like the central character in her novel *The Abyss,* Zeno, who is a mystic pursing a goal typical of the self-purifier: to "die a little less besotted than he was born."

Near the end of her life, at the age of eighty-three, Yourcenar told an interviewer about the character-ideal she had had since her youth—even before she produced a collection of male literary characters to present the ideal, and before she had achieved a lean, graceful prose style to announce it.

YOURCENAR: "I don't mean to say that I will be fundamentally different—whatever I am I have probably been all my life—but

▾ ▾ ▾ ▾ ▾

I shall at least have gotten rid of a lot of excess baggage, or so I hope."

INTERVIEWER:: "For you, then, life is primarily a matter of divestiture."

YOURCENAR: "Yes, certainly, but it is also a matter of enrichment. One sheds one's clothing in order to be bronzed by the sun's rays."

For Yourcenar, the spiritual discipline that lets an individual being (un être) understand that he or she is an essence (l'être) was a matter of course in much of the ancient world, in the Stoic quarters of Greece and Rome that she knew well as an amateur classicist, and also in the East. "Generally speaking, one must try against considerable difficulty to achieve what Hindu sages describe as a state of 'attentiveness,' in which you get rid of three-quarters or nine-tenths of what you seem to think but really don't. Ordinarily, a person merely assembles bits and pieces of pre-existing ideas. All these must be eliminated and one's thought focused on nothing; the effect is quite salutary."

In Marguerite Yourcenar's social vision, all human particularities and differences were eventually to be overcome. Men and women would know themselves as humans; homosexuality and heterosexuality would become, simply, expressions of sexuality; people would come to respect animals and plants as fellow creatures, citizens of one world. The corollary to Marguerite Yourcenar's cosmopolitanism is a spiritual feeling for the cosmos that is almost pantheistic. Her assault upon egoism, which she equated with lack of perspective on the oneness of creatures and nature, is most intense in her two-volume autobiography, one volume of which provides a history of her mother's family and one a history of her father's family, and neither of which takes her own story past her first month of life. She is embedded in, undifferentiated from, her people, their land.

In comparison to Simone Weil and Marguerite Yourcenar, Gertrude Stein, who was born in 1874, some twenty-five years before the French-speaking contemporaries, conceived of the process of stripping the self down to its essentials in temporal rather than spatial terms. She eliminated past and future and focused her attention only on the present. Having encountered William James's characterology when she was a student at Radcliffe, she concluded that every individual has a character— she called it "the bottom nature"—that never varies, which means that the present is the past being repeated and the future is what the present will be when it repeats itself. In her dualistic characterology, people are

▼ ▼ ▼ ▼ ▼

either of the "independent dependent kind" or of the "dependent independent kind," and the words and deeds of people within these two types
are endlessly, infinitely repeated. Or, as she said of the book called *Three
Lives*, in which she first embodied her vision of psychic order: "In that
there was a constant recurring and beginning there was a marked direction in the direction of being in the present although naturally I had
been accustomed to past present future, and why, because the composition formation around me was a prolonged present." The literary language for expressing this temporal a-linearity or amorphousness was to
be a language, she concluded, stripped of sentence structure and burdensome rules: "The question is, if you have a vocabulary have you any
need of grammar?"

In Gertrude Stein's image of psychic order there was also—not surprisingly—no structure, no division; she completely rejected Freud's theory of the unconscious. As she firmly said of herself (in the third person
singular, writing the *Autobiography of Alice B. Toklas*): "Gertrude Stein
never had subconscious reactions." Similarly, she claimed that there are
no differences between people who want no differences between them:
she insisted as she wrote Alice B. Toklas's autobiography that she and
her friend were one, and then she went right on to insist that she could
write the autobiography of America—a book called *The Making of the
Americans*—or even *Everybody's Autobiography*. Her social vision was an
expanded version of her character-ideal, which was an ideal of a singular
psyche, without fixed order, stratification, structuration, or differentiation.

Stripping the self down to essentials, purifying it, can be ac-
complished in spirits as different as Simone Weil's—self-castigation or
rebuke; and Marguerite Yourcenar's—ecstatic nature worship; and
Gertrude Stein's—self-congratulation. It can also be undertaken for quite
different purposes, by quite different psychic means. Anna Freud offered
a classic description of one such means in an autobiographical passage
on "altruistic surrender" in her 1936 book *The Ego and the Mechanisms
of Defense*. "Altruistic surrender," which is a means of stripping the self
of forbidden wishes by making over the wishes to others, can also translate easily enough into a social vision, as Anna Freud herself noted during an informal discussion of her idea that was recorded in *Analysis of
Defense:*

> If you can't get what you want yourself and enjoy it yourself
> because it's prohibited by internal conflict, well at least somebody

▼ ▼ ▼ ▼ ▼

else can get it, and you can enjoy it there through what you call vicarious enjoyment—which is certainly worthwhile. But that isn't all. At the same time the process liberates, or creates an outlet for aggression. What I meant was that originally the individual wants to pursue his or her instinctual aims aggressively. "I want it, I'll have it, I'll fight anybody who won't give it to me." This aggression becomes impossible and forbidden when the fulfillment of the wish becomes impossible and forbidden, but now with the altruism you can fight for somebody else's fulfillment of the wish with the same aggression, the same energy. So you have both your libidinal vicarious pleasure, and you have an outlet for your aggression. It's surprising that not more people are altruists!

Many democratic and anarchistic social visionaries, of course, have conjured up a harmonious world in which there would be no divisions among masterful leaders and followers, people-shapers and peoples-shaped, in which all people would do unto others as they wish others would do unto them, or in which each would get according to his or her needs. But Anna Freud was able to imagine what nonhierarchical social harmony would actually require psychologically—that is, that all people find appropriate others whom they can help to do what they once wished to do for themselves but could not. In such a world, there would not be philanthropists and recipients of philanthropy, do-gooders and possibly quite resentful gooders-done-to—another form of hierarchy—but rather altruism that would be as universal as the universality of forbidden wishes. Each person would give according to his or her psychological need, and each would get an outlet for forbidden wishes and aggression.

It really is surprising that not more people are altruists! But, then, if it is the case, as I've been arguing, that people can only be creative in the modes that their characters permit and promote, we would all do better, for ourselves and for others, to celebrate our diversity than to try—unless we are characterologically suited for it—to redistribute our aggression. In the multicultural spirit of the moment—so welcome—this essay is meant to celebrate multi-characterism.

▼   This essay, which reviews and extends some of the themes of my book *Creative Characters,* was prepared as a lecture in the Princeton University Public Lectures series for 1991. It has not been published before.

▼ ▼ ▼ ▼

3

Reflections on
Anna Freud: A Biography

The touchstone text for the contemporary burgeoning of American feminist biography is Nancy Milford's *Zelda*, first published in 1970. This burgeoning that *Zelda* heralded has now been large and long enough—some twenty years—for a period of assessment to have begun. And the touchstone retrospective text is Carolyn Heilbrun's *Writing a Woman's Life,* which appeared in 1988 and has since occasioned a great deal of commentary.

As Heilbrun and others have noted, *Zelda* offered many of the ingredients that can now be said to be typical of feminist biographies: a woman is rescued from both historical neglect and the shadows cast over her by the men in her life; she is allowed her own voice in the form of much quotation from her unpublished letters and manuscripts; she is not measured by male standards for female success or failure, diagnosed by male psychiatric categories, or fitted into male notions of female types; her private and domestic life is not cordoned off as a "separate sphere," but viewed in relation to her public life and achievement. What *Zelda* does not offer, however, is concentration on either the adult Zelda Fitzgerald's bonds with other women or the child Zelda's pre-Oedipal bond—or lack thereof—with her mother. These two ingredients have come to the fore in feminist biography writing during the 1980s, and their debts are to feminist theorizing about female friendships and to psychoanalytic object relations theory.

Also much more obvious in recent feminist biographies than in *Zelda* is a claim, explicit or implicit, about the value of the relations between biographer and subject, and a celebration of the subjectivity of biographers who have given up worshipping before the patriarchal

▼ ▼ ▼ ▼ ▼

shrine of "objectivity." A collection of essays called *Between Women,* published in 1984, offers many variations on the theme of how important to women biographers are their subjects and their subjects' lives. The biographer-subject relationship is presented as one of reciprocity, and its terms are the terms of confidence between friends or female family members. Carolyn Heilbrun, with a slightly different emphasis, claims that women writing—and then reading—biographies find in them alternatives to the one plot traditionally deemed acceptable to women, "the marriage plot," and that these alternatives include especially living and working with other women.

The history of feminist biography writing in the last twenty years, toward which I have been gesturing broadly, is part of a larger transformation in American middle-class feminism: its evolution from a liberation struggle, a business of rebellion and rescue, to a more analytical after-the-upheaval-phase in which alternative ways of knowing and living are being struggled for. Among the most interesting measures of this evolution is the conversion of psychoanalysis, one of the chief enemies of feminism in the late 1960s and early 1970s, into one of the chief sources of feminism's critical work on ways of knowing and living. When Kate Millett published *Sexual Politics* in 1970, psychoanalysis seemed the very quintessence of misogyny; more recently it seems like the most powerful tool for understanding misogyny and for illuminating how deeply and pervasively gender identities are constructed.

On the biographical front, this shift is apparent in the use of psychoanalytic theory in biography, which I have already mentioned, and it has been celebrated with a shelf of biographies of women psychoanalysts. We have had full-scale lives of Lou Andreas-Salomé, Marie Bonaparte, Helene Deutsch, Karen Horney, Melanie Klein, and shorter studies of other analysts of the first and second Freudian generations. My own work on Anna Freud belongs here. And the story I had to tell offered an especially intense version of the questions that lie behind all of these biographies. Very summarily: What did psychoanalysis mean to these women? How did they understand themselves in its terms and live their lives under its influence? How did they, as women, interpret Freud's views on female psychology? Psychoanalysis was, as is well known, one of the few areas of medicine or psychology in which women were accepted, at least in the early decades, on an equal footing with men and in which they have made pioneering contributions—including the enormously important adaptation of psychoanalysis to child analysis. What

▼ ▼ ▼ ▼ ▼

relation had this historical fact to psychoanalytic theory of female sexuality and psychology?

When I wrote my biography of Anna Freud, I, of course, had these questions in mind, along with a great many others that did not come from a specifically feminist frame of reference. But biographies are not, in my opinion, the textual place for posing theoretical and interpretive issues as such; they are life stories, and their literary virtues, it seems to me, stem from the biographer's commitment not to stray too far from the subject's own way of knowing and living, not to leave her side for the role of the judge, the assessor, the theoretician. The life story should not be directly used for purposes external to it, or forced to answer questions over which the subject herself did not ponder.

But now I am writing an essay, not a biography, and my intention is to return to *Anna Freud: A Biography* without my biographer's scruples. Specifically, I want to take up on the basis of my own experience with my subject three topics that are—as I have tried to indicate—woven into the history of contemporary feminist biography. First, I want to say a bit about what it was like to write Anna Freud's biography, in order to test out on my memories the current notion that the relation between feminist biographer and subject is one of reciprocity and friendship or familyarity. Second, I want to comment about the dimensions of Anna Freud's life that most recommend her as an exemplary figure to those interested in women living and working together. Then I want to turn to the relationship between Anna Freud and her father, *the* father of psychoanalysis and *her* psychoanalyst. As much as any period in the history of psychoanalysis, the period of Anna Freud's analysis was crucial for the development of Freud's views on female psychology, and I want to consider what he learned from his daughter, and she from him, and me from both of them, specifically about the conditions of feminine creativity.

In the still very limited literature on the experience of women writing biography, the theme that figures most prominently might be called idealization-disillusion. Female biographers have written of themselves as turning to their subjects, consciously or unconsciously, in search of an ideal—an ideal mother, an ideal friend or sister, a sexual ideal, an ideal of productivity, and of creativity, an ideal liver of life—and in some way, often more than one way, being disappointed. The disappointment can take many forms: the subject turns out to be not what she seemed; she keeps secrets or destroys the evidence that would have let her biographer know her; she does something the biographer finds repellent; she is not the example she was expected to be; she is antifeminist.

On the basis of my own memories and those noted by other biographers, this disillusioning process is the experience (or, usually, series of experiences) on which the success or failure of a biography hangs. If it occasions only anger, rage, and a reenactment of childhood disappointment with family or friends, the biography will be blocked by a wall of hostility—frequently, a wall papered over with too much admiration, too obvious an effort to restore the initial idealization in whatever terms are still feasible. The biography will be distorted by the biographer's need to express her loss or to cover it up.

If, on the other hand, the disillusionment is worked through to realism, which means for the biographer both acceptance of the subject for who she was and analysis of the biographer's own idealization of the subject, then it is invaluable to the book. Judging from the literature on biography writing, realism can be achieved when the specific ideal has become known to the biographer, when the biographer's "family romance" stands somehow revealed. But in my own experience, the realism required another step, or perhaps it was a step in a slightly different direction. What I found was that I idealized in the mode I would like to be idealized myself. The mechanism is narcissistic: the subject is constructed as how you wish to be in the eyes of some one or ones; you are looking, in the medium of the subject, for the you who would be most lovable to someone else or to you yourself (which may come to the same thing). I noticed that when I became disappointed in Anna Freud during my work, as I did, for example, while I considered her rigid views on homosexuality (which I'll come back to later), I would also intensify my reaction by charging her with failing me, which meant she was not being the idealized being I identified with for myself, for my own needs.

I don't think my experience would sound familiar to a biographer who tended to operate more by, say, identifying with the subject as with a missing (perhaps maternal) loved one, or a twin, or to a biographer whose main mechanism was to rid herself of a burdensome self by writing the self out into a biography—two other modes I have noted in the literature on biography-writing. Employing the schema of "Libidinal Types" Freud offered in a 1931 essay, I could make the same claim on a theoretical level by noting that narcissistic types, erotic types, and obsessional types do not have the same experiences—including as writers of biographies. But, for people of my sort, whose work has a clear narcissistic function, and for whom in earlier life "family romance" figures had primarily a self-aggrandizing or self-idealizing function, achieving realism about the biographical subject requires both self-acceptance—overcoming the need for being idealized—and a keen appreciation of how the subject and the biographer differ psychically and in behavior and works. The accent has to be on difference, on disrupting the complex mirroring role the subject comes to play in the biographer's psyche.

More generally, leaving aside the specificities of characterological types among biographers, I feel that it is reasonable to view biography as, initially, autobiography in the mode of the biographer's basic needs; and to say that any biography that finishes in that mode is bound to be a failure as a biography—although it may be an interesting autobiography. For any biographer, it is crucial to identify the mode of basic need and work both with it and against it. Or, more accurately, to work with it in order to work against it.

Let me say what this cryptic advice means by returning to my own case. Potentially distorting idealization of the subject (and of one's own self in the process) is quite different from admiration of her achievements, which I think makes a *fine* emotional foundation for biographers of my sort. The reason that admiration is so fine a foundation is that it keeps the difference (which always exists) between the biographer's and the subject's work clear, lively, charged; and the biographer must try to work to the subject's mode and level, earn admission to her circle. The focus on work also takes the emotional heat off the subject herself and promotes the realistic idea that there is no simple relation between the strengths and weaknesses of her personality and the strengths and weaknesses of her work. Your critical faculty is neither overactivated nor paralyzed when admiration guides it, although I should say candidly that being critical in this mode is more difficult than it is when the hostility of disillusionment sharpens one's mind.

This kind of admiration, I want to claim further, is affectively very close to envy. Envy is usually thought of as something to be conquered, something ignoble and even vicious. In some traditions, like the Christian one, envy is one of the top seven vices, rightfully in the company of sloth, avarice, gluttony, lust, and the rest. Similarly, within the psychoanalytic context, envy—perhaps interpreted as penis envy in women—is usually presented as something to be gotten over, worked thorough. But it seems to me that envy has achieved this generally bad reputation by being confused with the commonly appearing range of destructive and self-destructive reactions to envy, that is, by being confused with reactions in the form of efforts to tear down, castrate, or reduce to the envier's level the subject of the envy, which efforts are always destructive of any independent abilities the envier has. Envy need not, however, express itself negatively; it can be renewing and releasing for the envier if it is recognized and converted into its similar, admiration. In psychoanalytic terms, this is a creative-conscious use of the defense known as reaction formation (and it is quite different from the unconscious disguising of hostility or disillusionment with admiration that I noted before). In nonpsychoanalytic terms, I think Goethe meant the same process when he remarked: "Confronted by outstanding merit in another, there is no way of saving one's ego except by love."

Rather than some fantasized reciprocity or friendship or confidence between biographer and subject, some biographer-flattering equality, I think that analyzed disillusionment together with envy-turned-to-love focused on the work can make an emotional modality strongly conducive to judicious biography. This combination may serve well only biographers of one psychic or libidinal type, but I think that there are probably similar mechanisms at work among other types.

What I have tried to sketch about the psychology of biography-writing is, I think, quite relevant to the specific difficulties of writing biographically about Sigmund and Anna Freud. The biographical literature on Sigmund Freud, almost entirely written by men, is shot through with the most complex kinds of self-elevating identification with him and his genius, and also with many examples of envy of his achievement turned to malice (and only very few of envy turned to loving admiration). He is certainly the most complex subject for psychoanalytic biography, for he is the originator not only of psychoanalysis but of that genre, too, and his finest achievement in it—the study of Leonardo da Vinci—is still, despite all its faults, the touchstone of the genre. Freud so towers over his followers and his biographers that he is vastly intimidating to almost all except those whose self-elevating narcissistic bond with him is very strong (as was the case with Ernest Jones) and those whose envy-and-malice toward his work is palpable.

Freud is also the key figure in all biographies of his followers, whether they be lifelong adherents or schismatics. The followers are spoken of as sons and daughters, of course, and the psychodynamics of the Oedipal or even pre-Oedipal periods are invoked to track the familial interaction of "the Freudians." In the case of Anna Freud, all of this historical habit was aggravated by the fact that she, unlike any of the other followers, really was his child, his daughter. This fact meant, I

▼ ▼ ▼ ▼ ▼

think, that she has been treated to what might be called doubly-the-daughter evaluations.

Not surprisingly, I found when I began my biography of Anna Freud that there existed a kind of taken-for-granted assessment of her among historians of psychoanalysis. It was that she had contributed nothing original to psychoanalysis but was merely a superbly talented applier of her father's theories and techniques to children. As the titles of the two existing biographies said summarily, Anna Freud was *Her Father's Daughter* and lived *A Life Dedicated to Children*. Daughters, as a simplistic version of psychoanalytic theory has it, have no reason to overcome their fathers, and no reason to grow up.

The usually unspoken corollary to this view of Anna Freud was the assumption that in the Freudian circle, or the Freudian church, originality was not tolerated, which meant that the truly original became dissenters and schismatics. Freud, so this assumption went, was rigidly and authoritarianly against innovations unless they were his own. In the early days, male disciples departed—Alfred Adler, Wilhelm Stekel, Carl Jung, Otto Rank, Wilhelm Reich, and so forth—and later female followers dissented, chief among them Karen Horney and Melanie Klein. Originality became linked to rebellion. So, the proof of Anna Freud's epigonic status was that she stayed, and, indeed, stayed in an almost wife or nurse role.

Behind these layers of assumption were two others. One was that originality in psychoanalysis was the prerogative of lonely and misunderstood rebels, not of adherent groups or collective enterprises. And the other was that originality came from work with adults, not children, and on the epic level of metapsychology, not out of slow accumulation of comparable cases and comparable data. If these assumptions are not determining your views, Anna Freud looks like the great innovator of her generation, not on the rarefied plane of speculative metapsychology or models of the mind, which is so often privileged, particularly by non-practitioner historians, but in other ways. For example, she was a methodological innovator: she did research. That is, she set up experimental situations—nurseries, clinics—and she devised methods for data collection and analysis, for comparative work and for longitudinal studies. This was totally new, since psychoanalytic theory had been developed by Freud and his first followers only on the basis of their therapeutic practices with whatever individual adults turned up looking for help. Anna Freud worked with colleagues, predominantly female, to share what their individual practices taught them and to devise observational, nonanalytic learning methods. For another example: Over decades of work she slowly gave up an idea that had been key to her father's views of early childhood development. He had assumed that the psychiatric classifications appropriate to adult neuroses are appropriate, also, to childhood neuroses; that there is continuity between childhood and adult neuroses, the latter being repetitions and complications of the former. Anna Freud insisted on two things: children's pathologies are not the same as adults' pathologies, and there are childhood pathologies— she called them developmental pathologies—which fall outside psychiatric classifications altogether. Innovations like these do not summarize easily, and their results are not simple; otherwise they would have spread into the whole of psychoanalysis and child psychiatry and child development, which they unfortunately have not.

The research and training units organized by and dominated by women with which Anna Freud was associated, usually but not always as the prime mover, were, I think, unique in the history of science. They were, first of all, made up largely of women with no scientific background who were trained on the job to observe, to take notes, to let concepts come forth as they synthesized their material. Their work never lost touch with the anecdotal, with the texture of children's lives; their generalizations never lost the "let me tell you a story" richness more common among artists than experimentalists of any sort. They were, second, very obviously familial groups, groups in which the work functioned familially—either because the workers were émigrés who had been deprived of their native homes and families, or because they were single women and widows for whom the children were like foster children. Third, they were groups that took in and worked with subjects marginal to science and medicine—blind children, physically handicapped children, culturally complicated and multilingual children, welfare children, children with borderline pathologies, and so forth. It seems to me that, without a doubt, such groups would never have grown up under male leadership or with predominantly male members; in patriarchal contexts, these groups did "women's work." And it seems to me not coincidental that the predominantly male historians of psychiatry and psychoanalysis have paid them no more mind than the predominantly male leadership of medical-psychoanalytic organizations, which have always refused full membership status to child analysts without full training in adult analysis.

These quick sketches of Anna Freud's achievements are highlighted to convey my opinion that all of the reasons for which she has been

▼ ▼ ▼ ▼

underacknowledged have a strain of sexism to them. She was merely a daughter, only a woman, she worked in groups—largely consisting of women—and she did women's work, with children. So my biography fitted well into the feminist rescue-and-reparations tradition that aims to eliminate these strains and give credit where credit is due. But the feminist project was, in this case, quite interwoven with a critique of psychoanalysis itself in the ways that it was—so to speak—part of the problem and not part of the solution.

Insofar as it can be reconstructed biographically, Anna Freud's analysis with her father seems to have been quite fateful for his views on female psychology. It confirmed for him his basic insight that all people are bisexual psychologically and perhaps also anatomically or in some as yet unexplored way also biologically. Most people are either preponderantly masculine or preponderantly feminine in terms of their physical attributes, their mental sexual characteristics, and their preferences in sexual objects and aims or practices; but in no person is the interplay of all these attributes, characteristics, and preferences simple or predictable from one variable to the next.

This basic insight makes perfect sense to me. But, more specifically, in the early 1920s his daughter's analysis helped confirm Freud in his corollary view that a particular female type, Anna Freud's type, in whom the tendency toward anal eroticism, clitoral masturbation, penis envy, father (more than mother) identification, and masochistic beating fantasies are compounded, is something like the epitome of female bisexuality—what might be called characterological female bisexuality. All that remained for him to add to this female type in the late 1920s was the insight that a strong, indeed undissolved, pre-Oedipal mother-bond lay hidden behind all of the female bisexual type's more manifest masculinization and enmeshment with the father.

Freud's ideas about the pre-Oedipal period seem to have come to him when he renewed his analysis of his daughter after a hiatus caused by his first cancer surgery, and when she had arranged a family for herself in the form of a partnership with Dorothy Burlingham and a kind of adoption of Dorothy Burlingham's four children, who were also her analysands. In this new family, Anna Freud played both maternal and paternal roles, and retained her bisexuality in terms of aim preference by being ascetic. She also retained her role in her own family, as her father's collaborator and companion and nurse, as her mother's rival—manifestly, a rather stereotypically feminine, unending Oedipal triangle. The cross-

▼ ▼ ▼ ▼ ▼

currents in this period of Anna Freud's life were intense and swift: there was instant parenthood, without biological motherhood, and continuing opportunities for infantilization; there was reconciliation of sexual conflicts and avoidance of them in asceticism; there was a movement out of the original family and stasis in it, both as a daughter and as an analysand. It seems that Anna Freud's analysis itself had the mixed result of freeing her from her intellectual inhibitions (particularly about writing) and from her compulsive masturbatory activity, while leaving her dominating love for her father—and his needy love for her—quite untouched, however intricately it may have been explored.

To a biographer, as, I imagine, to the Freuds themselves, Anna Freud's young adulthood defies any simple assessment. The Freuds, given the tenets of psychoanalysis, had every reason to rejoice in her obvious professional success and in her pleasure in her new family, and every reason to wonder whether this success and this happiness had come at some psychic cost not yet paid in full. The challenge to a biographer of the situation, I think—and thought as I wrote—was precisely not to judge it, not to try to package it neatly, but to set it out in all its ambiguity for the reader's contemplation. As far as readers are concerned, this also meant to set the situation out as a challenge to what preconceptions readers might bring to it. For examples: readers might assume that asceticism is equivalent to developmental failure, that spinsterhood (to use an old-fashioned term) is necessarily emotionally threadbare; that homosexuality, whether involving sexual acts or only fantasies, is by definition pathological or, on the other hand, that homosexuality without sexual activity could only be a figment of a biographer's homophobic imagination because it is not to be found in real life; that a father-daughter analysis is some kind of incest, or, as one analyst argued to me, some kind of world-historical courage of experimentation. Many kinds of preconceptions . . .

What could not be met (at least not by me) in meeting the challenge of these and other preconceptions, however, was the theoretical challenge of the female bisexual type Anna Freud represented to her father. I would like to say now, in this nonbiographical context, that I think Freud's fascination with this type and his lengthy analytic relationship with his daughter led him to a major distortion.

Since his early *Three Essays on the Theory of Sexuality*, Freud had imagined female (and male) development mono-linearly, in terms of stages on a single path. Variations came from arrests or fixations or regressions (or combinations of these). In the essays he wrote during and after Anna Freud's analysis, he further hypothesized "normal" femininity, or a "normal" predominance of femininity over masculinity, as a working through or overcoming of this type, as though this type were a necessary stage. But he also put this hypothesis in a larger context. Freud seems to have gotten into the habit of thinking of the epitome of female bisexuality as the key intersection at which paths diverge toward (1) normal (heterosexual) femininity, (2) the "masculinity complex" continued perhaps in combination with homosexuality, and (3) asceticism. That is, he imagined the complete female Oedipus complex as something like a station where a trunk line ends and three local lines begin. And Anna Freud seems to have adopted this habit and even to have rigidified it in the sense that she, unlike her father, thought of the local line to homosexuality as pathological. (It is not clear how the asceticism line was judged.) Her assessment seems to me to represent her own fear, but it is important to note that the entire medical-psychiatric psychoanalytic establishment of her generation (female as well as male) reinforced her view for her.

To my mind, the idea that there is one line of female (or male) development that branches off in different directions during the heightened bisexuality of the Oedipal period is too simple. It seems to me to be much richer, and much less teleological, to think that there are many stories of female development, starting from many sorts of genetic (physical and psychological) inheritances and environmental influences and going in many directions, some of which are pathological and some of which are not. That is, there are many ways to be "normal"—in the sense of relatively unconflicted, or, as Freud once put it, only ordinarily unhappy—and many ways to be ill.

Ironically enough, it is Anna Freud's own concept of "developmental lines" that, of all the contributions in psychoanalysis, most lends itself to a reconceptualization of the sort I am invoking. And it is this richness in her thought that allowed me, *as* her biographer, to be disappointed with her and admiring of her in the same quick psychic dance-step. For her and for all women, her developmental lines concept implies that the criteriological or classificatory question to put should not be "Has she reached the biological destiny of motherhood or not?"—that is, it should be a psychological and not a biological (and teleological) question.

By my view of things, Anna Freud's adulthood was quite a psychically harmonious one, while by the trunk line and three local stations Freudian model, she failed to be "normal." My biography of her represents, although it does not theoretically discuss, my viewpoint, both in

▼ ▼ ▼ ▼ ▼

the sense that it fends off judgmental preconceptions, Freudian and otherwise, and in the sense that it lets Anna Freud speak for herself in her nonprofessional, private correspondence and private conversation voice on the question of whether she looked upon her life with regret or with satisfaction. This way of doing things is, I think, a feminist way of doing things. But it is not one that puts pre-Oedipal bonds or relations with women at the center of a story. Rather, it gives these their complex place in a complicated story, without judging them in advance to be crucial or determinative.

And by my view—to say one last thing on this topic—there is something to be learned here about the creativity of women with powerfully influential and creative fathers. The commonly accepted male model of originality in face of such a father (or his symbolic equivalent in a predecessor) is "anxiety of influence" and rebellion. Originality is overcoming. But what I think can be observed in Anna Freud's case is creativity in the mode I described above as envy-turned-to-love. I think that Anna Freud envied her father's creative work—and that this envy was part of her envy of masculinity in general—but that she saved herself from the common destructive and self-destructive reactions to such envy through her love of him and through creating for herself what he never had except in her—a group of coworkers loyal personally and professionally to her and to the cause she represented, a female world in which she was the object of loving envy. Psychoanalysis was her father's; the research that was to revise it slowly and carefully (not overthrow it) and make it soundly scientific was hers. That this form of creativity is limited (particularly in the mode of criticism) seems obvious—but it also seems obvious that it is no more limited than creativity that is restricted by the modalities of rivalry and dependent on a patriarchal object of rebellion. The challenge of the one kind of creativity is achieving a critical stance; the challenge of the other is achieving anything other than a critical stance. Both of these challenges, the one faced by adherents and the one faced by schismatics, it seems to me, can and do grow from reactions to sweepingly systematic creative efforts of Sigmund Freud's sort. But they can never produce such efforts.

When I think of Anna Freud in retrospect, after the end of our years of in-my-mind working association, I think that I am glad I never felt the need to try to imaginatively befriend her or to build a relationship of confidence with her—I am fortunate to have real people in my life for that. But I still glance at the eight volumes of *The Writings of Anna Freud*

▼ ▼ ▼ ▼ ▼

that sit in their blue jackets on the shelf near my desk and feel the same admiration of them that I have felt ever since I set up my camp next to them some six years ago. Good differences make good neighbors, I think to myself, as the good plurality of female stories makes good story-telling in biographies.

▼   This essay was originally prepared for the American Pychoanalytic Association's 1991 meeting in New Orleans. I was invited to an annual event called "Meet the Author," for which I was asked to reflect on my biography of Anna Freud. The essay was subsequently published in the inaugural volume of *Biography and Source Studies,* 1 (1994): 149–160.

▼ ▼ ▼ ▼ ▼

4

Looking for Anna Freud's Mother

The evolution of Sigmund Freud's views on female psychology is directly and dramatically linked to his youngest daughter's psychology. In an essay he wrote in 1919 and then in another, written in 1925, he registered two crucial revisions of the general picture of female development presented in his *Three Essays on the Theory of Sexuality;* these steps prepared the way for his last and most influential statements, "Female Sexuality" (1931) and "Femininity" (1933).[1] The 1919 and 1925 essays both depend heavily on the insights Freud gained as he analyzed his daughter. The confidentiality of the analytic situation is protected in the essays, but they nonetheless report Anna Freud's analysis as he conducted it in two phases, between 1918 and 1922, and then between 1924 and 1925.

In my biography of Anna Freud, I was able to track in considerable detail the course of her analysis by weaving Freud's reports in "A Child Is Being Beaten" (1919; 17:175–204) and "Some Psychical Consequences of the Anatomical Distinction between the Sexes" (1925; 19:243–258) together with three types of material written by Anna Freud herself. She left in her literary estate both a series of poems and prose pieces dating from the period of the first analysis, and her early correspondence, chiefly with Lou Andreas-Salomé and Max Eitingon, the two of her father's colleagues and friends with whom Anna Freud was closest. In the public domain, she left her first clinical paper, "Beating Fantasies and Daydreams," published in 1922, which is both a commentary on "A Child Is Being Beaten" and a thinly disguised report on her own case.[2]

The richness of this documentation, the detail it yielded, presented me with a big temptation: to go on and find Anna Freud's story continued in "Female Sexuality" and "Femininity," the essays in which Freud

▼ ▼ ▼ ▼ ▼

stressed the role of the mother in a girl's early development. The further possibility that was offered by constructing Freud's late essays on female psychology as episodes in his daughter's story was alluring: that I would also find Anna Freud's mother, who had eluded many another type of biographical detective work and remained as a shadowy figure in my family album. Such historical and biographical neatness! The story of Freud's views on female psychology and the story of Anna Freud's analysis are the same story! I imagined myself showing in Freud's theory and in Anna Freud's analysis the importance of the mother as not just a nurturer but a love object and also the importance of the pre-Oedipal period as far more than just a stage of oral erotism. As these demonstrations proceeded in my fantasy, the very specific mother I had been unable to create in Anna Freud's biography—Martha Freud—came into view, like a painting under a palimpsest.

I am going to re-create this crossroads in my work, and show a biographer's dream interrupted by lack of information just as it was about to come true. Sympathy over my frustration would be appreciated, but I also have a larger purpose in reconstructing this path to a piece of "applied psychoanalysis." Walking to the end of it, I think I learned something, and I would like to share it.

Both Sigmund Freud's "A Child Is Being Beaten" and Anna Freud's "Beating Fantasies and Daydreams" are illustrations of Freud's dictum that the Oedipus Complex is the nucleus of the neuroses. Freud studied male patients whose beating fantasies reflected both the mother love–father rivalry familiar to him since the 1890s and the mother identification and "passive" or "homosexual" father love that had assumed more and more significance in Freud's work after *Three Essays on the Theory of Sexuality*. His four female patients had beating fantasies that clearly reflected the Oedipal situation Freud had always emphasized for females: father love–mother rivalry—the converse of the male's configuration. But he also saw that the females he studied, who fended off incestuous wishes by assuming male disguises in their own fantasies, often ended up with powerful father identifications. The father identifications seemed to him defensive: they further protected the girls from incestuous wishes, and eventually protected them from any kind of sexual involvement—made them safely ascetic. There is no mention in the essay, however, of what should logically have been the corollary of the father identification: daughterly mother love.

▼ ▼ ▼ ▼

The case study Anna Freud wrote, on the other hand, is not comparative. She concentrates on one subject—a girl who is very like herself—and takes as her particular subject the role of sublimation in the girl's mental life. Her patient eventually gives up her beating fantasies and their climax, an act of masturbation, for what she calls "nice stories," a superstructure which has been relieved of the sexual content of the beating fantasy. Eventually, the nice stories are also transformed, into short stories. The desired gratification is no longer masturbation but praise from a reading audience. What becomes of the girl's desire for her father or of her sexual life in general is not clear; and the girl's mother is not even so much as mentioned.

Freud's essay, by contrast, does imply that the male fantasizers were more or less overtly homosexual (or mother-identified) and that the females were more or less asexual and able to overcome their father love only through father identification. Freud was impressed enough by the differences between the male and the female beating fantasies, despite the fact that all the fantasizers were in love with their fathers and in conflict over their intense masturbation activity, to be shaken in his conviction that males and females undergo analogous developments until they diverge at the Oedipal crossroads. But the differences between the male and female fantasies were not pursued in the essay, which ends, rather, with a general reflection on repression that rejects two unsatisfactory theories: Alfred Adler's notion that both sexes repress "the feminine" and Wilhelm Fliess's idea that both sexes repress the mental sexual content opposite to their anatomical sexuality. Freud argued against the "sexualization of repression" because he was impressed by the variety of repression.

This same theme runs into the case study of a female homosexual published in 1920, where Freud concludes with a tabulation of three sets of characteristics that must be accounted for in any adequate understanding of homosexuality—or of heterosexuality: physical sexual characteristics, mental sexual characteristics (masculine or feminine attitude), and kind of object choice. (Earlier, in *Three Essays,* he had also added a fourth: kind of aim, preference for type of sexual activity.) These characteristics, he notes in the 1920 case, "up to a certain point, vary independently of one another, and are met with in different individuals in manifold permutations" (18:170). Researchers who concentrate their attention on object choice will miss the fact that male homosexuals, although they chose male lovers, "have experienced a specially strong fixation on their mother" (18:171). He does not make a similar general

▼ ▼ ▼ ▼

claim about female homosexuals, although the subject of the case study was a female homosexual. This young woman's attachment to her mother, Freud had noted, was important: but he viewed it as secondary, that is, as an attachment that assumed great importance for her when her love for her father was bitterly disappointed. (The same can be said of the 1915 case of a female's paranoia "running counter to psychoanalytic theory.") Once again, daughterly mother love is invoked but not explored.

Freud made two important statements about infantile sexuality after the 1920 case, "The Infantile Genital Organization" (1923; 19:141–145) and "The Dissolution of the Oedipus Complex" (1924; 19:173–179), but both of these repeat the basic premise about female development that Freud had laid down in *The Interpretation of Dreams* (1990) and *Three Essays on the Theory of Sexuality:* the first love of the little girl is for her father, as the first love of the little boy is for his mother, and their developments are therefore analogous, mirror images. So, it was momentous when this premise, held for thirty years, was abandoned in "Some Psychical Consequences of the Anatomical Distinction between the Sexes" (1925).

Freud did not himself herald the shift in his views. He simply says of males and females that "in both cases the mother is the original object" (19:251). Later he speaks vaguely of the girl's "affectionate relation to her mother." The purpose of the paper is not, really, to explore this relation; it is, rather, to ask how the relation comes to an end, how the girl comes to turn toward her father. Penis envy, which had always been a key ingredient of Freud's theory of female development, takes on a function in this paper that it had not had before: the girl turns away from her mother because she holds her mother responsible for the fact that she has come into the world so ill-equipped. The route of this turn can be complex and involve a displacement: the girl displaces her hostility toward her mother onto a sibling, claiming that the mother is fonder of the sibling. In general, penis envy converts easily into jealousy.

One would expect Freud's biographers to wonder what brought about the realization that girls, like boys, first love their mothers— though it is very interesting to note that not one of Freud's male biographers, from Ernest Jones to Peter Gay, has found the matter worth puzzling over. What impresses Freud's male biographers is how little, despite the Oedipus Complex, mothers figure in Freud's case studies of males, and how Freud's attention to the Oedipus Complex seems to have kept him from exploring the pre-Oedipal period *in males*. It is assumed

▼▼▼▼▼

that Freud's pre-Oedipal relationship to his own mother somehow troubled his view of mothers in the case studies and obscured from his view the pre-Oedipal period in males. This veil, of course, then extended to the pre-Oedipal period in females as well. "Freud, it seems, had good reason to find the subject of woman somewhat mysterious, even a little threatening," says Peter Gay in *Freud* after making an argument of this sort.

Actually, the matter seems a bit more complex. But I want to pause here to note that the Freud biographers are participating in a trend that now dominates psychobiography. Psychobiography, as Freud and his immediate followers practiced it, focused on the Oedipal period. But since the late 1940s, psychobiography, which always seems to follow trends within psychoanalysis—because it is, after all, "applied psychoanalysis"—has been more and more frequently conducted as a search for mother love in the first two to three years of life. There have been very few psychobiographies of women until quite recently, but the search for the pre-Oedipal period is also a trend in them, and one augmented by feminist writings on female development such as Nancy Chodorow's *The Reproduction of Mothering.*[3]

Freud's pre-Oedipal relationship to his mother—whatever that may have been—was not responsible for three facts that need to be taken into account. First, Freud's views on the importance of penis envy for women were articulated in the context of debates among his followers. They had been resoundingly seconded by Karl Abraham in 1920 in a very influential article, "Manifestations of the Female Castration Complex." In this essay, Abraham, even though he had a special interest in oral erotism, did not, however, speak of daughterly mother love. Only shortly later, in 1923, Karen Horney had come forth with a dissenting view: penis envy, she argued, is a secondary formation, something which develops after a little girl is disappointed in her love of her father; it does not turn her toward her father. This debate converged with another.[4]

Melanie Klein arrived in Vienna six months before Freud wrote "Some Psychical Consequences of the Anatomical Distinction between the Sexes" (1925) to give a startling paper, one that sounded to Freud's circle like a replay in slightly different terms of Otto Rank's "birth trauma" theory, which had recently provoked such a split in the little psychoanalytic movement. The central trauma of infancy, Klein argued, is weaning. Babies of both sexes form their first object relation to their mother's breast—it is a "part object" for them—and this relation is the foundation of all others. Sexual differentiation does not take place along

▼ ▼ ▼ ▼ ▼

Freudian lines: the girl does not really turn to her father—for any reason, certainly not penis envy. Mother love was certainly the centerpiece of this paper, but the girl's love was not a specific topic.[5]

Freud, in other words, had two oppositional views, very different from each other, to take into account in 1925. Both questioned his views on penis envy. At the same time a second factor came into play: Freud had in his own practice in Vienna a number of women who were, as patients, of a different sort than were the women he had treated earlier in his career. These were professional women, psychoanalytic trainees. The "masculinity complex," as Freud understood it, was pronounced in them; they seemed living arguments for his claim that he had underestimated the effects on a woman's character of penis envy.

Anna Freud was one of these trainees. And I think that it is reasonable to argue—I did so in my biography—that a third fact that needs to be taken into account in considering Freud's change of viewpoint is that "Some Psychical Consequences of the Anatomical Distinction between the Sexes" contains another case study of Anna Freud. Freud himself links the essay to his earlier "A Child Is Being Beaten" with the following remark:

> Even after penis-envy has abandoned its true object, it continues to exist: by an easy displacement it persists in the character-trait of jealousy . . . While I was still unaware of this source of jealousy and was considering the phantasy "a child is being beaten," which occurs so commonly in girls, I constructed a first phase for it in which its meaning was that another child, a rival of whom the subject was jealous, was to be beaten. This phantasy seems to be a relic of the phallic period in girls. The peculiar rigidity which struck me so much in the monotonous formula "a child is being beaten" can probably be interpreted in a special way. The child which is being beaten (or caressed) may ultimately be nothing more nor less than the clitoris itself, so that at its very lowest level the statement will contain a confession of masturbation, which has remained attached to the content of the formula from its beginning in the phallic phase till later life.   (19:254)

The connection between intense masturbation, the beating fantasy, and jealousy of a sibling is palpable in Anna Freud's life, and it is important to note that the sibling who was her chief rival, her next older sister, Sophie, had, in fact, always been her mother's favorite girl child and had secured her special place even more firmly when she became the first

▼ ▼ ▼ ▼ ▼

producer of grandchildren. After Sophie's death in the 1921 influenza epidemic, Anna Freud became a kind of surrogate mother to her sister's two little boys—in a sense, she took her sister's place.

Sophie Freud Halberstadt's boys were three and eight years old in 1922, when Anna Freud, having finished the first of her analyses, took care of them for two months in their home in Hamburg. The youngest, Heinz, was her first toddler observational subject, while Ernst was the age of the elementary school children she had taught for five years in Vienna. Her letters home to her father from Hamburg are full of reports about the boys. And Anna Freud, twenty-seven years old, in the role of the surrogate mother, seems to have identified with her own mother, whom she had almost always tended to present as a rival in all the documents preceding this Hamburg stay.

To note this mother identification without qualification, however, is inadequate. For Anna Freud had, as an infant, been cared for by a *Kinderfrau,* a woman named Josefine and called Jo by her charge. She had also had as another mother figure her aunt, Minna Bernays, her mother's maiden sister. When she was caring for her nephews, she had the assistance of a Hamburg relative of her brother-in-law's, and she called this woman a "good Minna," but that does not make clear whether she spoke from identification with her mother or with the *Kinderfrau.* What the day-to-day relationship of Martha Freud, Minna Bernays, and the *Kinderfrau* Josefine was is not determinable; how they existed in relation to each other in Anna Freud's memory is not evident in the surviving letters. There are only clues.

In 1922, Anna Freud visited several times in Göttingen with Lou Andreas-Salomé, who had spent a month with the Freuds in Vienna the previous December. Sigmund Freud had clearly brought his colleague into his household to befriend his daughter and to offer her a quasi-analytic relationship with a woman—a model woman of great intelligence and sensitivity, respected as an analyst and as a writer. Lou Andreas-Salomé referred to Anna Freud in letters to Sigmund Freud as "Daughter Anna," but this mother was like none of Anna Freud's other mothers.

It was to Lou Andreas-Salomé that Anna Freud confided her reaction to the surgery performed on her father's jaw in the spring of 1923 and then the major surgery the following fall designed to stem what had been diagnosed as cancer. She announced that she would never leave her father, and that she was quite satisfied to stay at home with him as his nurse, secretary, helper, companion. She displaced her mother and

▼ ▼ ▼ ▼ ▼

her aunt from these roles, and the new configuration in the household was apparently not pleasing to either of the Bernays sisters.

Anna Freud's analysis was renewed in the spring of 1924, when her father had recovered sufficiently to work with patients again, and it went on for at least a year, up to the time when Freud began to write "Some Psychical Consequences of the Anatomical Distinction between the Sexes." When Freud had drafted his paper, he presented it to an audience of two on his summer vacation: Anna Freud and Lou Andreas-Salomé. Anna Freud had just joined her family on vacation after attending in Vienna the funeral of her *Kinderfrau,* Josefine, who had died in a hospital on the outskirts of the city where the Freuds had provided for her financially. Anna Freud told several of her correspondents about the funeral, and affirmed that Josefine was (as she said to Max Eitingon), "the oldest and most real relationship of my childhood." Whether memories of her infancy were stirred by this funeral, she does not say.

Both Anna Freud and Lou Andreas-Salomé reacted to Freud's paper with enthusiasm—Anna Freud suggested that she read the paper to the September meeting of the International Psychoanalytic Association—and also responded with their own work. Lou Andreas-Salomé wrote a short story (unpublished and unavailable), and Anna Freud prepared a brief report for a December 1925 meeting of the Vienna Psychoanalytic Society called "Jealousy and the Desire for Masculinity." The report was based on her first analytic cases—two females, one child and one adult, whom she had often discussed with her father while he was formulating his ideas.

That Freud's paper depended upon the second phase of his analytic work with his daughter and also on her first cases, which she reported to him, seems clear. In Anna Freud's early life, the hostility she felt toward her mother, and her own jealousy of her sister and of others, were related to her penis envy, her "masculinity complex." But what does not emerge from Freud's paper or any of Anna Freud's correspondence is the still elusive topic of daughterly mother love or anything about the complexities of having more than one mother figure.

It is at this point that certain passages in Freud's next essay on female psychology loom up. In early 1931, he drafted the paper called "Female Sexuality," which responded to the continuing debates led by Horney and Klein over his views—although he wrote without mentioning his 1925 paper, and treated the debates as though they had arisen spontaneously, not in relation to his own work. By this time, Anna Freud had

▼ ▼ ▼ ▼

entered into a kind of partnership or "Boston marriage" with Dorothy Burlingham, an American woman, separated from her husband, with four children, all of whom had been treated analytically by Anna Freud. The two friends shared the upbringing of the children, traveled together, and had just bought a country house together, a place where they and the children and friends could retreat from Vienna on the weekends. Also a recent development in their lives was Dorothy Burlingham's termination of an analysis she had undertaken with Theodor Reik and her transfer to a new analyst, Sigmund Freud.

Freud reminded his readers at the beginning of "Female Sexuality" that it had long been a psychoanalytic tenet that females must negotiate a change in genital zone, from clitoris to vagina. That they also had to negotiate a change from their original love object, the mother, to the father was something that had become apparent more slowly. "The way in which the two tasks are connected with each other is not yet clear to us" (21:225), Freud notes, and then turns to his clinical context with this passage:

> It is well known that there are many women who have a strong attachment to their father; nor need they be in any way neurotic. It is upon such women that I have made the observations which I propose to report here and which have led me to adopt a particular view of female sexuality. I was struck, above all, by two facts. The first was that where the woman's attachment to her father was particularly intense, analysis showed that it had been preceded by a phase of exclusive attachment to her mother which had been equally intense and passionate. Except for a change in her love-object, the new phase had scarcely added any new feature to her erotic life. Her primary relation to her mother had been built up in a very rich and many-sided manner. The second fact taught me that the *duration* of this attachment had also been greatly underestimated. In several cases it lasted until well into the fourth year— in one case into the fifth year—so that it covered by far the longer part of the period of early sexual efflorescence. Indeed, we had to reckon with the possibility that a number of women remain arrested in their original attachment to their mother and never achieve a true change-over towards men. This being so, the pre-Oedipus phase in women gains an importance which we have not attributed to it hitherto.   (21:225–226)

To square this claim with his earlier notion that the Oedipus Complex is the nucleus of the neuroses, Freud proposed to call the girl's mother attachment the "negative oedipus complex," and he stressed that in this stage she is active toward her mother as a little boy is. Then he went on to wonder why this pre-Oedipal or negative Oedipal stage had not appeared to him, and speculated that it might have undergone an especially inexorable repression, or else that he had "gained this impression because the women who were in analysis with me were able to cling to the very attachment to the father in which they had taken refuge from the early phase" (21:226).

These passages might fit Anna Freud, whose attachment to her father was certainly strong—to say the least—and whose tie certainly had not been dissolved by her analysis, conducted as it was *by her father.* And, if Freud was making statements about his daughter, the implications are tremendous: he would, then, be seeing her attachment to him as a secondary formation, something she clung to strongly as an escape from the earlier attachment, not for its own sake; and he would be seeing her attachment to women, her reluctance to take up with any man other than himself, as also a function of her mother love, not of her father love. And Anna Freud herself would, as an analysand, have come to the same conclusions—insofar as the therapeutic situation allowed.

These seemed to me fascinating possibilities. But how would one go about testing whether the description really does fit Anna Freud? Or to specify in exactly what way it might fit Anna Freud? This is the point where information fails, where the documents run out. Anna Freud wrote poems, prose pieces, and letters about her two periods of analysis, and thus made it possible to link her case to her father's work intricately; but in the early 1930s she had no intimate correspondents. Lou Andreas-Salomé was aging, ill, unable to visit; Max Eitingon had disappointed Anna Freud and removed himself from her confidence. In her later correspondence and in a series of dreams she wrote out and interpreted after her father's death, there is not one indication that she understood herself as crucially determined by her early mother love. On the contrary, she continued to interpret herself in terms of the classic Oedipal configuration, and she continued to express a great deal of ancient grievance against her mother and her aunt Minna Bernays, both of whom she portrayed as too strict, too controlling, too rigid—that is, as interferers with pleasures, forbidders, and, I think it is safe to infer, toilet trainers and masturbation punishers. Quite specifically, Anna Freud held her mother responsible for not telling her, when she was about thirteen, that a doctor had prescribed an appendectomy for her: Anna Freud went to the hospital under false pretenses and was taken by surprise to find that

▼ ▼ ▼ ▼ ▼

surgery was planned. Both in and of itself and insofar as it may have echoed earlier prohibitions and punishments—specifically "castration" threats—this incident helped seal Anna Freud's hostility toward her mother.

The most common form that Anna Freud's ancient grievance took was the complaint that Martha Freud, who gave a good deal of concern to make-up and wardrobe, criticized her plain face, bottom-heavy figure, and doughty, sexless clothing. (Anna Freud's one concession to elegance was to wear with pride the necklaces her father gave her on her birthdays.) The seriousness of her complaint, in which appearance certainly stood for reality, presentation for essence, is obvious in the letters to Lou Andreas-Salomé, in which Anna Freud often thanks her older friend for accepting her and loving her just as she is, without demanding any changes or hoping for any improvement. The second most common form the grievance took was the complaint that the Bernays sisters were too military about meal times, stipulating the exact moment at which meals were to begin and the exact menu, which was to be consumed down to the last morsel. Anna Freud's revenge on this regime was to conduct a series of experiments in her first nursery, the Jackson Nursery, that showed toddlers to be quite capable of feeding themselves a nutritionally balanced diet if they were presented with a smorgasbord of possibilities and left to eat at their own pace.

These are very suggestive details, but because, as I noted, there is also little direct documentation to illuminate Anna Freud's early childhood or to bring into focus the three maternal figures, separately or in relation to each other, there was no choice for me but to test Freud's theory on Anna Freud's later childhood and adulthood—using Freud's own terms, which would have been the terms familiar to Anna Freud. For example, in "Female Sexuality," Freud offers one such way of testing in relation to later childhood. He notes that in their play children convert passive experiences into active ones: "When a doctor has opened a child's mouth, in spite of his resistance, to look down his throat, the same child, after the doctor has gone, will play at being the doctor himself, and will repeat the assault upon some small brother or sister who is as helpless in his hands as he was in the doctor's" (21:236). This triumph of activity is something that obviously caught Anna Freud's attention, for she studied it in detail in *The Ego and the Mechanisms of Defense* (1936), under the title "identification with the aggressor" or the aggressor's aggression.[6] (Interestingly, she cites the example from a similar passage in her father's *Beyond the Pleasure Principle* [1920: 18:3–64], not from "Female Sexuality," and there is no evidence that this essay was particularly significant for her.)

But there is also, of course, the libidinal identification Freud had first studied as part of the process of superego formation; we might call "identification with the caretaker's care" the mechanism that is apparent when a girl feeds and cleans her doll or takes care of her animals. As Freud put it: "the little girl's preference for dolls is probably evidence of the exclusiveness of her attachment to her mother, with complete neglect of her father-object" (21:237). In Anna Freud's case, though, it does seem that it was the *Kinderfrau*'s ministrations, not the mother's, which were reproduced. Martha Freud did not, for example, nurse her youngest; the baby was bottle-fed by the *Kinderfrau* while her mother took a long time to recuperate from a strenuous pregnancy—her sixth pregnancy in eight years, and not a very desired pregnancy at that. Later, it was the *Kinderfrau*, Josefine, who taught Anna Freud to knit and launched her lifelong habit of knitting little clothes for dolls and for other people's babies. And this habit was a facet of Anna Freud's life work: she was herself always a *Kinderfrau*, a person who took care of other people's children—as an elementary school teacher, as a child analyst, as surrogate mother to her nephews and the Burlingham children, as a director of nurseries and a clinic. It should be noted, however, that it is identification which is apparent here, not active taking of the mother figure as a love object, the "negative Oedipus Complex."

There may be some confirmation for this conjecture about identification with the *Kinderfrau* in the fact that Freud carefully noted in 1931 that "someone such as a nurse" can take the mother's place as chief feeder and washer. Similarly, in his 1933 essay "Femininity," he speaks of the mother "and the figures of wet-nurses and foster-mothers that merge into her" (22:118). But Freud does not comment on how multiple mothering can affect a little girl. On this count, it seems to me feasible to conjecture that Anna Freud's identification with the *Kinderfrau*'s child care sustained a split: the *Kinderfrau* was the good mother, while Martha Freud, who was the mother of six children, not the caretaker for one, who was the disciplinarian, and who was later the rival for the father's attention, was the troublesome mother, the object of hostility. Of course, such a split could not have been total, and the love Anna Freud felt for her mother was obvious at the time of Martha Freud's death, when the intensely private Anna Freud mourned her openly—to the surprise of people familiar with their tensions. But even such mourning may have been tinged with regret that her mother was not the one with whom she

▼ ▼ ▼ ▼ ▼

could comfortably be a crying, needy child, be passive and taken care of. At least I suspect this to be the case from the fact that it was in the year of her mother's death that Anna Freud prepared for delivery (but never prepared for publication) a justly famous lecture called "Fear of Passivity."

My conjecture about this splitting or dividing of ambivalence seems to me to be supported very graphically by a similar split that was evident in the last year of Anna Freud's life, when she, the last living member of her immediate family, was reduced to a state of childlike dependency after a stroke. Then she had a stubborn, controlling, rigid caretaker to be angry with, to hate—her maid, Paula Fichtl—and a good one, a *Kinderfrau,* the former nursery school teacher Manna Friedmann, who kept her company, shared her knitting projects with her, enjoyed German songs and stories with her. Anna Freud, citing her loyalty to the maid, who had been with the family for half a century, refused to place her in a home; she kept Paula in the house and made herself and her good *Kinderfrau* miserable by doing so.

When Freud turned in "Female Sexuality" and the later essay "Femininity" to manifestations of intense and long mother love in adult female life, he offered an example that had been part of psychoanalytic observation for many years and that he had earlier written about in "The Taboo of Virginity" (1918; 11:191–208). Women often behave in their first marriages in a complex or layered way. They take a husband who is modeled on their fathers, but they replay with the husband the drama of their mother love, with all its passion and hostility, all its ambivalence. This is a particular instance of a general claim that the girl's mother love will be, in some form, carried into her adult object choices: she may vacillate between currents running from her mother love and currents running from her father love; she may return to her mother love after the disappointment of her father love (as Freud had suggested was the case with the female homosexual), and so forth.

In Anna Freud's case, there was no heterosexual later love. There was also no diminution of her father attachment—thus no return to a mother love current in a homosexual mode. It seems to me that what appeared was an equipoise reflected in the choice of a female companion, Dorothy Burlingham, a mother with four children, and the maintenance of the father attachment. Since neither relationship was sexual, they did not conflict on that plane; this was, as it were, psychological bisexuality without physical sexuality. Such an arrangement, of course, would presuppose a great capacity for sublimation—but no one who knew Anna

▼ ▼ ▼ ▼ ▼

Freud had any question about her accomplishments as far as this psychic function was concerned, and her life work stands as a monument to her capacities.

This conjecture, however, leaves many unanswered questions. Was there a period of active mother-figure love, a "negative Oedipus Complex," prior to the *Kinderfrau* identification? What became of the hostility directed toward her mother? Were there female objects of hostility other than Martha Freud (and perhaps Minna Bernays, as her mother's ally) and Paula Fichtl? Did the split between good and bad mother figures I have proposed have other manifestations, for example, in Anna Freud's work and in her work settings, her nurseries and clinics, where so many women joined her enterprises? How did the intellectual mother figures like Lou Andreas-Salomé fit into this scheme? Did Anna Freud mother her surrogate children in the *Kinderfrau* way or the mother way or some mixture of the two split-off ways or some reaction to the splitting off of ways?

These questions are hard enough, and they are not illuminated by any mention in Freud's texts on female psychology of friendships or animosities among adult females or of adult females' choices of profession or types of work—his texts are exclusively concerned with how heterosexual love and marriage are related to early childhood events. It is tempting, nonetheless, to read general passages of his essays with these questions in mind. For example: "A woman's identification with her mother allows us to distinguish two strata: the pre-Oedipus one which rests on her affectionate attachment to her mother and takes her as a model, and the later one from the Oedipus Complex which seeks to get rid of her mother and take her place with her father" (22:134). In Anna Freud's case, as I am developing it, the difference is that the two strata seem to have been predominantly tied to two different mother figures.

But there are also other, quite specific passages in these late essays that are suggestive about Freud's—and Anna Freud's—view of her early development. For example, considering Anna Freud's long struggle with masturbation and beating fantasies, about which both father and daughter wrote, one can easily imagine her as the subject of his remarks in "Femininity" on a girl trying to free herself from masturbation:

> She does not always succeed in this. If envy for the penis has provoked a powerful impulse against clitoridal masturbation but this nevertheless refuses to give way, a violent struggle for liberation ensues in which the girl, as it were, herself takes over the role of her deposed mother and gives expression to her entire dissat-

▼ ▼ ▼ ▼ ▼

isfaction with her inferior clitoris in her efforts against obtaining satisfaction from it. Many years later, when her masturbatory activity has long since been suppressed, an interest still persists which we must interpret as a defence against a temptation that is still dreaded. It manifests itself in the emergence of sympathy for those to whom similar difficulties are attributed.   (22:127–128)

One can hardly imagine anyone in a better position to give sympathy to people struggling with masturbation conflicts than a child psychoanalyst, and one can hardly find a child psychoanalyst in whose work masturbation conflicts receive more attention than they do in Anna Freud's work.

I have now advanced a series of conjectures about the first years of Anna Freud's life and about her relations with her mothers. My technique has been to comb through Freud's essays looking for traces of Anna Freud's story and then to test the results against relationships, configurations, in her later life. As I have said repeatedly, the conclusions are only conjectures, and I did not include them in my biography because I really cannot prove—which in biography means document—them. Further, they have not produced what my vision of a neat merger of stories— Anna Freud's, her father's, psychoanalysis's—promised: that the vague figure of Martha Freud would emerge. On the contrary, my conclusions reduce her to a function: the bad mother, the object of hostility. Similarly, the question I raised and left hanging about what Freud's changing views on female psychology have to say about Freud's own psychology has simply clouded over.

The impasse I have created could also easily be made more complicated by another standard psychobiographical strategy: a turn to the current literature. For example, with Anna Freud's case in mind, it is very instructive to look at the work of contemporary child analysts— heirs to Anna Freud's theory and practice of child analysis—on children with beating fantasies. Kerry and Jack Novick, in an article called "The Essence of Masochism" (1987), reported on their observations and analyses of a number of girls and boys with beating fantasies and compared their materials, arranged along a developmental line, with adult cases. Being contemporaries, they, of course, give a good deal of attention to pre-Oedipal mother-child relations, and they conclude, not surprisingly, that "descriptions of a mutual lack of pleasure on the part of mother and baby were universal in the fixed beating fantasy sample and have recurred in all our subsequent cases of masochistic pathology where

▼ ▼ ▼ ▼ ▼

social history data have been available." (But there is no mention of a case of multiple mothering.)[7]

The Novicks note as common a great deal of aggressive behavior in their beating fantasy patients' toddler years—and this, too, is in line with Anna Freud's reputation in her family as a naughty child (her father's affectionate nickname for her was "Black Devil"), although she seems to have been really more saucy and impish than truly violent. The mothers of the Novicks' patients were generally unable to contain their children's aggression or to tolerate their messiness and anal play. This, too, accords with the impression one gets of Martha Freud and Minna Bernays, if not of Josefine. The episode of Anna Freud's appendectomy could very well be described with this observation from the Novicks' paper: "parents of patients with masochistic pathology seem unable to protect them from repeated exposure to overwhelming experiences." But the "repeated exposure" is a bit strong for the case, and the following claim about puberty and adolescence does not fit the case well at all, even though the result is similar: "The fathers of the girls continued and intensified their denigration of the mothers and actively involved themselves in overstimulating relationships with their daughters from the oedipal phase on, with the result that a component in the masochistic pathology of the females was intense bisexual conflict and severe penis envy."[8]

Anna Freud, a child with a troika of mothers, fits some but certainly not all of the Novicks' mother-child generalizations. But she was not the child of either a remote, disinvolved father or an overstimulating one; she was the child of a loving, observant, concerned, but passionately preoccupied one. And, so, this route, too, of comparing child-analytic clinical results with what little can be seen of Anna Freud's childhood leaves the biographer with more opportunities for "wild analysis" than sure narrative units.

I have sketched three types of biographical badlands: (1) the subject's writings run out and cease to give confirmation for hypotheses; (2) the contemporary documentation—in this case, Freud's essays—becomes teasing, suggestive, rather than sure; and (3) independent clinical generalizations, not concerned with the particular case, give a bit of confirmation mingled with a great number of mirages. In effect, I have just shown the essential difference between psychobiography and psychoanalysis. To put the matter very simply: in psychobiography there is no next session; one cannot wait for further associations, transference manifestations, or acting-out episodes to lead beyond an interpretative

▼ ▼ ▼ ▼ ▼

impasse—to show that at this point in the work I am right, wrong, or some mixture of right and wrong.

But the matter can be put less despairingly: psychobiography is designed neither for therapy nor for theory (or metapsychology); these are not its purposes. A psychobiographical narrative unit is different from an analytic reconstruction. In addition to the general outlines of a life, what we learn, I think, from psychobiography is something about the features of a life that are never clearly documented, which do not leave clear traces, which are not simply evidentiary. For female biographical subjects born before or near the turn of the century, these features have to do primarily, it seems to me, with the complexity of mothering—even though so many famous women have been very obviously deeply father-directed, in the mode of love, or of identification, or both.

In Anna Freud's case, the complexity is mysterious, but not, on the other hand, unusual in what might be called an extended-mothering bourgeois family. We might call to mind contemporaries of hers with similarly strong male identifications in relation to a single father figure who were similarly mothered by many women: Willa Cather, for example, or Gertrude Stein for another. Sorting out what contributions to the subject's psychology are made by each or any of the mothering figures is nearly impossible. Mothers and grandmothers and nurses merge; sisters and aunts slip generations; "role models" and ego ideals are indistinguishable. In sociological terms, one of the main reasons why Martha Freud is so vague a character in Freud biographies is that both before and after her marriage she was a woman embedded in an extended female domestic world, and such a world is very difficult to reconstruct beyond the level of social roles. At the level of who meant what to whom, there is mostly silence. Sigmund Freud's family was also, of course, a predominantly female, multigenerational one (with nurses) organized around a single father figure—and compounded by a complex mixture of Jewish traditions and free-thinking elements. It was a family—like the one Martha and Sigmund Freud raised—in which it would not be difficult to name the boys' rival or the little girls' male love, but in which it would be much more difficult to sort out the mothers.

Methodologically, psychobiography has a great deal to learn from intrapsychically focused studies of families. And this learning needs to be added to what two decades of fine feminist scholarship has already revealed about how historical an institution motherhood is and how intricately patriarchal cultures shape both that institution and children's identities developing within it. But even feminist scholars have a ten-

▼ ▼ ▼ ▼

dency, when they turn to biography, to focus in on the mother-child dyad, and to isolate it from anything but the nearby Oedipal triangle. Sibling groups, extended and multigenerational families fade away. The rest of childhood, the latency and preadolescent and adolescent years, with all their added complexity of new venues and new relationships, also tend to fade away in explanatory terms if not in narrative terms. Psychoanalytic family study is a book of reminders, a technique of question-posing. But from within the ranks of child psychoanalysts there are also, of course, people who pay particular attention to larger family contexts and full developmental lines—and Anna Freud was certainly foremost among these, and the one who had the most influence on several generations of others.

What I learned from my interpretative impasse, the collapse of my dream of perfect biographical and historical order, was to pay more attention to my subject's range of vision: her ability to survey a full family network and to range over the whole of an individual's developmental course. My project became to place the mystery of Anna Freud's mothering consistently in that range. What I came to was a less spectacular but nonetheless satisfying sense of biographical and theoretical orderliness: the notion that the range in Anna Freud's thought had its debt precisely to her plural mothering.

▼ This essay was originally the 1989 Edith Neissen Memorial Lecture for the Chicago Institute for Psychoanalysis. Later it was published in *The Psychoanalytic Study of the Child*, 44 (1989): 391–408.

▼ ▼ ▼ ▼ ▼

5

Anna Freud as a
Historian of Psychoanalysis

If we count roughly from 1908, when Freud's first disciples began to meet together in Vienna, and allow about fifteen years for a generation, there have been six generations of psychoanalysts, and the history of psychoanalysis has been written on their persons. For it is, of course, a characteristic of this science that it is transmitted from one generation to the next by a unique means, the training analysis: the science is practiced on its future practitioners, altering them in its terms, structuring into them a relationship with an analyst and, by this peculiar descent, with the first analyst. Until recently, psychoanalysis has hardly had a history or a historiography of the conventional textual sort, although it has since the 1950s had a huge outpouring of biographical—predictably, psychobiographical—studies devoted to the first analyst, Freud.[1] What textual writing there has been of psychoanalysis's history has largely followed the biographical path, too: Freud's first small circle and the outstanding first trainees have been the subjects of biographies, most of them focused on the subjects' relationships with Freud and on psychoanalysis's schisms.

Freud's early followers were not historians of their science, but when Hitler's rise to power in Germany forced many European analysts to emigrate, they—the first generation of trainees, Anna Freud's generation—took it upon themselves to survey the state of their science and prepare it for export, even, perhaps, for survival, and they became, thus, its first textbook writers, engaging in a historical mode common to other sciences—though certainly very seldom so urgently pursued. They tried to show what in psychoanalysis's territory could be considered secure knowledge, what was still tentative, and what was unexplored. Otto Fen-

▼ ▼ ▼ ▼ ▼

ichel's *Psychoanalytic Theory of the Neuroses* is perhaps the best work in this genre and time. Soon afterward, with Ernest Jones's research on his biography of Freud and with the completion of James Strachey's monumental *Standard Edition,* including its invaluable apparatus, the materials and means for the next generation to write the history of the psychoanalytic theory of the neuroses that Fenichel and others had presented began to become available. But just then came a turn in psychoanalysis's fortunes that had two dimensions, each of which was detrimental to psychoanalysis as a science and as a science with a history. The first dimension was the cultural hostility toward psychoanalysis (interpreted as a conservative or counter-reformist enterprise) in the late 1960s, and the second was a rash of internal splittings of psychoanalytic organizations into rivalrous camps battling for dominance. The cultural hostility was reflected in the many biographies of Freud, each of which linked him to some kind of repressiveness. The internal fissuring heavily reinforced a tendency already existing in training programs: that they were aimed at teaching a given school's technique, and gave very little attention to training in the history of psychoanalytic concepts, theory construction, or the collective enterprise of building up the science qua science, for which historical consciousness is key.[2]

I think that one of the most interesting ways to take stock of these developments is to look at Anna Freud's reaction to psychoanalysis's externally and internally embattled state. In 1965, she had, of course, completed her enormously important and synthetic book *Normality and Pathology in Childhood,* and this book, significantly, contains in its first two chapters the most complete history of child analysis that exists—a history in the Fenichelian manner, one that maps what can be considered secure knowledge about child development and then indicates which areas are in need of investigation, and which are unexplored. But over the next ten years, while she continued to initiate one important research project after another at her Hampstead Clinic, Anna Freud obviously grew uneasy. And the result was a series of papers in the mid-1970s in which she wrote more and more frequently as a historian.[3] She clearly felt the need to prepare and present a general historical assessment, and the papers she wrote again and again opened with variations on this sentence (from one written in 1976): "It is the privilege of age to view present happenings in the light of past experience . . ." (7:193). But she also had a political purpose. Thinking that institutional psychoanalysis might finally be ready to reconsider the second-class status conferred from the beginning on child analysis, and more generally intending to

▼ ▼ ▼ ▼ ▼

remedy the bifurcation of analytic training into adult training and child training, she presented the history of psychoanalysis and child analysis as what she thought it was—an institutional travesty.[4]

I want to offer here an interpretation of these historical papers of Anna Freud's, because they are, I think, a neglected resource for understanding what psychoanalysis has become in the last several decades. But before I do that I want to make a few remarks about Anna Freud as a historian of psychoanalysis, to consider how it came about that Anna Freud, of the figures in her generation, should have emerged as the one most historically minded. (I should note, however, that these remarks are not going to be psychobiographical, because the psychobiographical issues involved are too complex to explore here.)

Anna Freud was, of course, not just the daughter of the founder, but the daughter analyzed by the founder, bound uniquely in this recapitulatory process that I noted as unique to psychoanalysis among the sciences. She was grounded in her father's life and work more completely, more emblematically as it were, than any other psychoanalyst, and she had to play—particularly after his death—the role of his representative, his intellectual executor, his living shrine, his museum-keeper, his vestal. But she was very skeptical about biographies of her father; indeed, she considered all biographies, even Jones's, which she aided in many ways, to be intrusions into his—and her—privacy. Her daughterly loyalty protected her from becoming fixated on the biography genre while it also kept her attention fixed on the future. She wrote history only for the sake of the future, with the conviction that the only kind of memorialization her father would have approved was the continued health and growth of psychoanalysis. Her attitude sometimes led her to use her own work as a historian of psychoanalysis defensively, to keep up her father's tradition of pointing out the true path and naming the schismatics, a practice that might have made her not so much a historian as an apologist, or even a catechist. But defensiveness was not her usual mode in print—even though she was a conservator, in the deepest meaning of the word—and it is interesting to consider why not.

In the first place, Anna Freud had the great advantage of viewing herself as working in a field other than her father's, something which no analyst of adults has done or can do.[5] And she had the sanction for this view right from her father, who wrote a sentence in 1925 (as part of the preface to August Aichhorn's *Wayward Youth*) that divided the history of psychoanalysis into two parts—his part and her part: "children have

▼ ▼ ▼ ▼ ▼

become the main subject of psychoanalytic research and have thus replaced in importance the neurotics on whom its studies began." As far as she was concerned, her father had basically laid down what there was to know about adults and particularly about adult neurotic (although not psychotic) psychopathology; all innovations in his domain she viewed as merely adjustments, refinements. But child and adolescent analysis was another matter. From her analytic field she anticipated and helped bring about two achievements that could really be described as novel, as true innovations in psychoanalysis. One was the delineation of childhood pathologies in their own terms, not as infantile neuroses that might be rewritten or reedited in adulthood. And the second was the creation of a full descriptive framework for normal development. As she noted:

> Reconstruction from adult analysis inevitably is weighted toward pathology to the neglect of normal developmental happenings; [for] it is always the conflictual and unsolved which does not come to rest in an individual's mind, which welcomes the opportunity to re-establish itself in the transference situation and thus captures and monopolizes the analyst's attention. In contrast, the satisfied impulses, the successful adaptive conflict solutions disappear by entering the fabric of the personality. They are outgrown with little incentive left for revival at a later date.
>
> Thus, while the analysts of adults become expert in tracing psychopathology back to its earliest roots, only the child analysts appear to hold the key to the description of the course taken by normal adult development.   (8:85)

It is interesting to note how frequently Anna Freud conceded to analysts of adults (and over topics in the domain of the psychoses, to medical practitioners) the territories of debates about adult psychopathology and histories of those debates. For example, when she was called upon to comment on a discussion between Leo Rangell and André Green that took place in 1975, the topic of which was how and to what extent classical psychoanalytic technique should be altered to deal with psychotic patients, she contented herself with framing the issue in a particular way: She framed it so that her hearers could, as she said, "construct their own personal picture of the future of psychoanalysis, following either one or the other of the two protagonists." She wanted to convey, subtly but firmly, that any discussion of whether or not to adjust psychoanalytic technique should be thought about with the whole future of psychoanalysis in mind. She was trying to train her hearers to think "in

▼ ▼ ▼ ▼ ▼

the best interests of psychoanalysis"—if I may adapt her well-known maxim "in the best interests of the child."

Her position here was, again, I think, a function of her conviction about the centrality of child and adolescent analysis to the present and future of psychoanalysis. This conviction also allowed her to maintain the excitement and curiosity—the sense of pioneering—that she had had since her youth and that she attributed to her generation in general. In 1975, when she was beginning to write her historical papers, Anna Freud offered a description of the satisfied and excited attitude toward psychoanalysis that she thought had become so difficult for younger analysts to find in their own terms, their own times:[6]

> We [of the initial generation] felt that we were the first who had been given a key to the understanding of human behavior and its aberrations as being determined not by overt factors but by the pressure of instinctual forces emanating from the unconscious mind; that we were the first, therefore, to see mental illness as a battle between rationality and irrationality; that we also were the first to possess a method, namely, free association, for breaking down the barrier between consciousness and the unconscious; that this method was applicable to ourselves as well as to our patients, thus reducing the difference between the mentally ill and the mentally healthy and altering the relationship between therapist and patient from one of the dominating authority to one of shared endeavor; that our new technique of inquiry and exploration of resistance and transference was identical with our technique of cure; and, finally, that, apart from suggestion and hypnosis, we had no rivals in the field of mental treatment.[7]   (8:177)

As a pioneer—a perpetual pioneer, always going forward—Anna Freud stood for history as a map of territory traversed. This is the attitude her historical papers clearly show, and which I would like to convey by mapping her map. It is not complicated. In fact, it has only three regions or, as I shall call them, themes.

The first of her themes always went under the title "the widening scope of psychoanalysis." Here she tracked how her father had widened his scope over the course of a lifetime of work, including work with his first collaborators: "from the neuroses to the psychoses; from sexual inhibitions to the perversions; from character disorders to the delinquencies; from adult psychopathology to adolescence; from adolescence to childhood," as she once put the catalog (8:83). Then she tracked how the

▼ ▼ ▼ ▼ ▼

scope of psychoanalysis had continued to widen later. On the unambiguously positive side of this continued widening, she laid—as I noted—developments in child and adolescent analysis. But she also noted difficulties and frustrations. For example, the widening of scope had, eventually, produced a condition in which analytic understanding was greater in scope than analytic therapy—many of the mental conditions that could be explored could not be cured. In this category, for example, she placed many childhood developmental pathologies as well as many adult psychoses and borderline cases (8:183).

Anna Freud's second theme—to which I have already referred above—bore the title "from psychopathology to theory of normal development." And this was the historical theme that most emphasized the pioneering role of child and adolescent analysis. In connection with this theme, she argued frequently and forcefully for giving child and adolescent analysis institutional parity with adult analysis—which would at least eliminate the anomalous condition of the avant-garde area of research being staffed by the second-class citizens. Similarly, she argued very strongly that psychoanalysis had done itself a great damage by contradicting Freud in its policy toward nonmedical practitioners; and she was quite aware that the hostility toward lay analysis cast a deep shadow over child analysis, a field where many nonmedical people worked. In many papers on questions of training, Anna Freud always tried to bind together what others had historically tried to put asunder—psychopathology and normality, adult and child analysis, medical and nonmedical practitioners.

It was in connection with this theme "from psychopathology to theory of normal development" that Anna Freud constructed a history of methods within child analysis. She came forward in 1957 to acknowledge Ernst Kris as the first historian of child analysis, and to accept his claim that child analysis up to 1950 had had two periods, one before and one after the 1920s, when Freud broached the structural theory, the second anxiety theory, and the dual instinct theory, and when observation emerged as a source of knowledge along with analytic research based on reconstruction in the analysis of adults and children.[8] Anna Freud herself had been skeptical about direct observation as a research method and about the contribution that direct observation could make to knowledge of normal development, but she took the occasion of the 1957 memorial lecture for Ernst Kris to correct herself and, further, to set herself in opposition to a then emergent trend of considering as analytic data only indirect and direct manifestations of transference. Her sense

▼ ▼ ▼ ▼ ▼

in 1957, confirmed in her retrospections of the 1970s, was that a third methodological period in child analysis's history was beginning, one marked by innovative combinations of analytic reconstruction and observation in research focused on normal development.

At about the same time in the late 1950s, Anna Freud articulated a second idea about normal development that became crucial to her later work and central in her later historical reflections. Viewing development as a process extending from birth through late adolescence, to the phase of character consolidation that is the transition from late adolescence to adulthood, will show, she argued in her 1958 classic "Adolescence," that adolescence is a "second chance." She opposed conceptions of development that featured the pre-Oedipal phenomena as all-determinative, no matter whether the conceptions were oriented toward pre-Oedipal instinctual drive and object relations "positions" or toward separation-individuation issues or attachment behaviors. She thought that the various debates among schools of psychoanalysis about what happens pre-Oedipally all neglected adolescence (as well as latency), underestimating critically the degrees and kinds of psychic alterations that can and do come about in adolescence. In the historical reflections she recorded in the 1970s, she again and again stressed both what advances in understanding had resulted from focusing analytically and observationally on the mother-child dyad of the pre-Oedipal period, and how truncated the image of "normal development" had become as the first two years of life dominated all inquiry.

Interestingly, as she reflected on the ideal of a theory of child-adolescent normal development, and as research on developmental issues proceeded in the 1970s at the Hampstead Clinic, Anna Freud shifted her own research focus—and provided as she did a brilliant example of how historical reflection can shape a view of what needs doing. Targeting normal development had helped her bring into focus pathologies *of development,* which are pathologies of arrest, as distinguished from infantile neuroses, which are pathologies of unconscious conflict that produce regression. The developmental pathologies—arrests, traumatic interruptions, unevennesses on different developmental lines, organic or environmental defects or deficits—require special and specific analytic techniques, and discovering them emerged in Anna Freud's mind as a key challenge for child and adolescent analysis. Late in her life, she envisioned two kinds of child and adolescent analysis—one for the infantile neuroses and one for the developmental pathologies, one that had been created, and one that needed creating.

▼ ▼ ▼ ▼ ▼

The third and most complex theme Anna Freud pursued required her to sketch the main psychoanalytic interpretive frameworks or views—the dynamic, the genetic, the economic, and the topographical-structural—and to argue that good practitioners and theoreticians use them in combination, each complementing the others. Historically, however, these frameworks have not, she would note, received equal attention either in practice or in theoretical writing. She was convinced that the genetic view, and particularly its object relations strand, had, by the early 1970s, virtually eclipsed the others in theoretical work, and that the instinctual drive theory, for which the dynamic and economic views particularly account, had fallen into neglect. Even more generally, she felt that psychoanalysis had fissured into two camps, the clinical practitioners and the theoretical researchers, precisely because the metapsychological frameworks had come to be considered so widely and wrongly as *merely* theoretical, not as the very essence of therapy as well.

One particular consequence of this distorted view of metapsychology received her attention again and gain: the failure of analysts to develop diagnosis into a metapsychologically grounded practice. She argued against considering diagnosis simply a cataloging of symptoms, but also against refusing to do diagnosis because symptom cataloging is nonanalytic (in the American context, such cataloging would merely be application of the categories in the *Diagnostic and Statistical Manual of Mental Disorders*).[9] Her stance was related to the one she took toward distinguishing infantile neuroses from developmental pathologies—without a good diagnosis, a child's disorder cannot be assessed, and the right type of treatment cannot, thus, be recommended. In historical terms, Anna Freud had summarized the situation thus in 1965, just as she was beginning to articulate clearly her own distinction between infantile neuroses and developmental pathologies: "to date, [the] revolutionary and adventurous spirit of the child analyst has exhausted itself in the areas of technique and theory, and has stopped short of the important question of the classification of disorders. Here a wholly conservative policy has been pursued, i.e., diagnostic categories have been taken over wholesale not only from the field of adult analysis but, beyond this, from adult psychiatry and criminology. The whole psychopathology of childhood has been fitted, more or less forcibly, into these existing patterns" (6:110).

This third historical theme, which might be called "continually elaborating metapsychology," constituted a plea for a psychoanalysis in which nothing once achieved was ever neglected, or in which everything

▼ ▼ ▼ ▼ ▼

counted but no one thing counted more than others. It was a plea, in effect, for not giving any part of the evolving family of psychoanalytic notions special privileges—the kind of plea one might expect from a youngest child arguing against favoritism or prerogatives of seniority, but also from a scientist well acquainted with the dangers (not to mention the dreary repetitiveness) of reductionist thinking.[10]

The history of psychoanalysis generally over the period that Anna Freud surveyed has been characterized by a great deal of reductionism, or a great deal of what might be called contests for a "most important" prize. Anna Freud's historical perspective, with its threefold stress on the widening scope of psychoanalysis, on the necessity of a developmental approach in theory, therapy, and diagnostics, and on metapsychological complexity, allowed her to assess *psychoanalytically* these various efforts at awarding the "most important" prize. It is to this contribution of hers as a historian that I would like to turn finally.

The field of "most important" reductions Anna Freud cataloged was as extensive as psychoanalysis. All analysts after Freud, for example, acknowledged the importance of sexuality and aggression—if not the dual instinct theory of Eros and Thanatos outlined in *Beyond the Pleasure Principle*—but recently many analysts have asserted that aggression, less explored by Freud than sexuality, is more important in human development and in pathology. All analysts recited that dream interpretation is "the royal road to the unconscious," but many argued that transference interpretation is more important and asserted, in terms of technique, that transference should actively and purposefully be brought into the analytic process, not awaited as a spontaneous product of the process. Reconstruction of childhood events and experiences has been called by some less important than analysis of present events and experiences, the here and now, especially the transference and countertransference here and now. An object relations narrative is said to be most important, or certainly more important than an instinctual drive one. The analyst-analysand dyad is said to be a more important focus of the analyst's attention than the abstractions of metapsychology. And so forth.

Anna Freud considered these claims with two key assessment criteria. The first was that different developmental contexts, especially therapeutic contexts, produce different psychic phenomena, which, in turn, influence psychoanalytic concepts. To cite one example: She noted that conceptualizations of sex and aggression relate to analytic contexts: "While free association seems to liberate in the first instance the sexual

▼ ▼ ▼ ▼ ▼

fantasies of the patient, free action—even if only comparatively free—acts in a parallel way on the aggressive trends. What children overwhelmingly act out in the transference are therefore their aggressions, or the aggressive side of their pregenitality which prompts them to attack, hit, kick, spit, and provoke the analyst . . . Theoretically this linkage between acting out and aggression may produce a biased picture of the proportion between libido and aggression in the child" (6:30–31). Aggression is "most important" in the context of child analysis (and of analysis with adult patients who act out as much or more than they free-associate), but this does not mean that aggression is most important generally (in all people or all pathologies) or theoretically.

Second, Anna Freud understood that interactions of phenomena and concepts are systemic: one change changes the whole system. To cite one example: When the widening scope of psychoanalysis brought the pre-Oedipal period, and thus preverbal communication, to the fore, this, in turn, had an impact on the role of transference in analysis, therapeutically and theoretically. In analyses emphasizing the pre-Oedipal and preverbal, "remembering yields its place to repetition, verbal communication to re-enactment. This explains the heightened significance of communication via transference in many present-day analyses, where transference interpretations are considered the only therapeutically effective ones and where transference phenomena are perforce given preference over memory, free association and dreams, as the only real road to the unconscious" (8:147).

In recent years, as psychoanalysis has been slowly acquiring a conventional textual historiography, diverse theoretical emphases or types of reduction have most frequently been explained as facets of institutional and biographical competition. Competitions among theoretical schools and individual personalities even get stereotyped: Anna Freud, thus, becomes the paternal, Oedipal figure in child analysis and Melanie Klein the maternal, pre-Oedipal one; Freud is the father of analysis and Sándor Ferenczi the mother, and so forth.[11] Rather than this kind of psychobiographizing, Anna Freud was offering as a historian a look at the dynamics of analytic practice (including types of technique) and the setting (including types of patients and pathologies).

In the two decades since Anna Freud wrote her historical papers, much has changed in psychoanalysis. Although the cultural hostility toward psychoanalysis that arose in the late 1960s has abated, a new challenge has arisen during the spectacular shift in psychiatry toward psycho-

▼ ▼ ▼ ▼ ▼

pharmacology: hostility to a treatment so long and expensive. The pace of internal institutional fissuring has slackened a great deal; once feuding contingents—like the Anna Freudians and the Melanie Kleinians—address each other's meetings as all share the feeling of being beleaguered in a changing mental health climate. Certain institutional failings of psychoanalysis—crucially, not offering training to lay analysts and not according equal status to child analysis—have been somewhat addressed or redressed. The Freud biography industry is still flourishing, to the detriment of psychoanalysis, and the historical consciousness in the field is, if anything, I think, less sophisticated than it was twenty years ago and even more organized around the Freud literature.

But the most dramatic new challenge facing (particularly) child psychoanalysis is fundamentally socioeconomic. In Europe and the Americas, as well as in many other parts of the world, the last twenty years have been a period in which children are—generally speaking—more at risk than they have been at any time since the end of the Second World War. In the two eras when child analysis had its most important growth spurts—the decade after the First World War (1918–1928) and the decade around the Second World War (say, 1937–1947)—children were given great priority by progressive, socialist governments and societies, and elimination of poverty was a clearly articulated goal. Now, without much echo of this idealism to be heard, governmental policies and societal attitudes marked by thoughtlessness for the future are allowing children worldwide to sink into poverty in record numbers, and thus they are growing up in family and social circumstances that do not in any way favor normal development. Many children live in war zones, and many live under conditions of technical peace that are warlike, so that they display the environmentally induced problems Anna Freud studied as a young woman in Vienna and then as the director of the Hampstead War Nurseries. Ours currently is a time she would have recognized as in many ways familiar, and she would have argued for research into developmental disorders as of particularly pressing urgency: She would have recognized the need for psychoanalysis to have another responsive growth spurt, to bring its history and tradition to bear on family and social planning agencies as well as on the legal settings she addressed in *In the Best Interests of the Child* and its companion volumes. Had she lived into our present moment, her sense of herself as a historian would, I am sure, have adapted and expanded to become a sense of herself as a social historian for psychoanalysis and its emerging social settings.

▼ ▼ ▼ ▼ ▼

Meanwhile, to speak in the language of fact, not fantasy, Anna Freud's way of being a historian of psychoanalysis has had a very limited influence, and her conclusions—for example, about the need for a meta-pychologically grounded diagnostic—have had their greatest significance for those trained in her manner or at her clinic. But, in my estimation, nothing in the last two decades has made her approach any less relevant or cogent or her historical example as a respondent to social conditions any less important.

▼   This essay, begun in 1992, was rewritten to celebrate the centenary of Anna Freud's birth at a conference at Yale's Child Study Center, December 1995, and then published in *The Psychoanalytic Study of the Child,* 51 (1996): 56–58.

▼ ▼ ▼ ▼ ▼

6

Profile of Anna Freud
as a Latency Woman

Methodological Lacks

Since Sigmund Freud's *Studies in Hysteria,* psychoanalytic case studies and biographies have grown up together, related like step-siblings, from the same father. And they both show his parenting influence, but not in the same way. Case writing has grown with psychoanalysis, becoming more and more sophisticated while incorporating—as Freud's own practice forecast—complex understandings of clinical perspectives, complex theoretical debates, and attention to the historical and social contexts of cases, the environments of diseases. But biography writing has never had a rich tradition of psychoanalytic reflection and methodological sophistication. Its practice still chiefly depends on "content analysis," as *Studies in Hysteria* did; intricacy comparable to that in Freud's five full-scale case studies has largely eluded it.

On the model of Freud's case-writing practice, which he also applied to subjects like Leonardo to produce "pathography," his early followers produced a rich library of caselike biography writing, an achievement that compelled the whole art of biography in the twentieth century toward psychoanalysis, if not directly or doctrinairely, then indirectly, as a matter of cultural osmosis or absorption of the psychoanalytic "climate of opinion." But the genre influence did not flow so strongly in the other direction, and psychoanalysis itself has only recently become biographical—in two senses. First and most obviously, in the late 1950s the history of psychoanalysis began to be written as a biographical history, a history of clinicians and the psychological sources of their theories and practices. Launched officially and monumentally by Ernest Jones, this

▼ ▼ ▼ ▼ ▼

history was a history of Freud biographies, but now it is a burgeoning biographical archive of books, oral histories, and memoirs, of Freudians, former Freudians, and anti-Freudians. Second, within psychoanalysis, clinicians have stepped into their case studies: there they are, telling what they said and did, setting themselves in the history of psychoanalysis, becoming subjects for biography as they explore their countertransferences.

Over the decades of this uneven joint development of psychoanalysis and biography, it seems to me that three methodological roads have appeared and been considered, if not taken. The first road is the most widely acknowledged and the most consistently taken. It is understood that different people looking at or imagining the same subject will see different beginnings of a life narrative and attribute different significances to childhood events and experiences. Appropriators of Freud's theories line up in factions within the fold: some, for example, looking at an infant subject, see the primary narcissistic baby Freud saw, while others see a baby programmed for relatedness; some think that what can be observed can be read as the manifest content of intrapsychic process, while others think that such readings are the readers' fantasies. And everyone is in a quandary because it is obvious that the materials with which a childhood—some version of a childhood—could be thoroughly or deeply reconstructed are *never* available to biographers. Biographers always deal with little fragments, little bases of inference, and are tempted to engage in "content analysis" because they do not have a psychoanalytic situation, a transferential process, to work in and with. Such divisions of opinion and problems of material have had an impact on psychoanalytic biography writing, and particularly on biographical—or autobiographical—writing about psychoanalysts. But there is not yet a literature that approaches multidirectionally the methodological and technical issues raised by complex interplays of subject, biographer, biographer's biography, theory, and theoretician's biography over the question of how to reconstruct and determine the significance of childhood.

The second methodological road can be indicated by noting that all modern biographers work with a developmental line in mind that extends over the course of a life. Each has ideas about stages or phases, key junctures or forks, processes of identity formation, anxieties of influence, meanings of identifications, and, generally, developmental norms and deviations. For most, these ideas are sketchy and full of blanks because they have been acquired piecemeal from a culture in which

▼ ▼ ▼ ▼ ▼

developmental theory in some form is as taken for granted and as unexamined as evolutionary theory. Psychoanalytically trained biographers, by contrast, have developmental ideas that are much more precise and coherently articulated. They, however, suffer from an embarrassment of riches—there are many psychoanalytic developmental theories and each involves many developmental lines. Here, too, as in the matter of childhood, fashions in psychoanalytic biography and writing about biography have tended to follow fashions in psychoanalytic theory and technique, but as camps in psychoanalysis have ramified, so has confusion in the field of biography writing.

A third methodological road is apparent to some biographers, quite unknown to others, both within and outside the psychoanalytic profession. This concerns the way in which biography writing is part of the history of psychoanalysis itself and part of the cultural history in which psychoanalysis lives. Biographies, particularly of Freud, but also of his followers, have agendas as far as psychoanalysis itself is concerned. Those who have wished to undermine psychoanalysis have produced or used biographies that show Freud to be in one way or another pathological and that show psychoanalysis to be a reflection or transcription of that pathology. Freud's own techniques often serve this Freud debunking purpose. On the other hand, those who have wished to promote psychoanalysis have produced or used biographies that appreciate Freud's genius and see it displayed in his science. It is not news, of course, that biographies—like any kind of history—have cultural purposes, but the extent of this problem for the genre and for psychoanalysis has only in the last decade become obvious, because this has been a decade of culture wars generally in Europe and America. In this war time, most of those who might raise their heads to methodological reflection do not; they are down in the trenches. Various camps of Freudians and anti-Freudians go to their own conferences.

Let me give an example of how these different methodological roads come into conjunction. I think that it would become clear to anyone who troubled to read through the vast biographical and biographically oriented literature on Freud that two dimensions of his life and work are consistently singled out for both critical reflection and polemic—although for very different, indeed wildly different, purposes. One dimension could be covered with the rubric "views on female psychology." At least since the 1920s, when Jones coined the term "phallocentric," commentators have noticed that Freud had phallocentric biases, and in the era of early second-wave feminism his biases were magnified

▼ ▼ ▼ ▼

into paradigms of sexism. Freud himself acknowledged that he had limitations, and no answer to the famous question "What do women want?" The second dimension of Freud's life and work that is consistently a focus of attention is his ability—some would say inability—to hear criticism, criticize himself, and relate to his critics as contributors to his science. This is the Freud of the period when psychoanalysis was institutionalizing and the psychoanalytic movement becoming a site of schisms. Now, any psychoanalytically informed person looking at the biographical literature with these two dimensions in mind would realize that a theory of narcissism would be required to approach the views on female psychology and the history of the psychoanalytic movement— these two sorts of problems of "the self and the *other*." But which theory of narcissism? Freud's? Which might be viewed not as a way to illuminate his narcissism but as a product of it. And what inferences about Freud's narcissism could be drawn from the details available about his childhood? His relationship to his mother, to his father—especially in light of criticisms that he left the pre-Oedipal period in relative neglect and hailed the Oedipal one with distorting preoccupation? In the current moment of Freud biographical scholarship, in which Freud's integrity as a theorist (for example, in relation to "the seduction theory") and as an evaluator of others' theories is the focal point, Freud's narcissism is an object of cultural judgment—but do the judges have any idea what assumptions about narcissism subtend their own positions? or why Freud's integrity should be the polemical issue of the moment?[1]

Making the same experiment of considering what has been written about Anna Freud's life and work, I think that two dimensions would stand out to an informed reader as consistent sites of critical reflection and polemic: her emphasis on norms of development—her conviction that there is such a thing as "normal development" in the singular—and, second, her fierce defense of her father's legacy, to which she was heir apparent. She appears to many psychoanalysts and cultural critics as a great conservative, particularly when the concept of normativity is invoked with regard to homosexuality, as it is throughout her *Normality and Pathology in Childhood.*

A psychoanalytically informed reader, considering the normativity emphasis and the filial piety, would, I think, realize that obsessional character traits were at play in Anna Freud's theoretical orientation and proceed to investigate them. But the classic encyclopedic essay on obsessionality in the literature after Freud is by Anna Freud, so the same methodological circle the I noted with respect to Freud on narcissism appears here. However, Anna Freud, in her essay, was summarizing not only her own views but those of the whole psychoanalytic community as that community had been represented at the 1965 meeting of the International Psychoanalytic Association, devoted to the theme of obsessional neurosis. Her life is a life embedded in, not presiding over, the psychoanalytic movement, since her contributions were researched in her clinics, with coworkers, not, like her father's, in the solitary study of Bergasse 19 in Vienna. Her status as legatee is tied to the achieved institutionalization—turbulent as that is—of psychoanalytic research; her biographers cannot fail to be historians of—within—psychoanalysis, with attitudes about conservatism and progressivism in psychoanalysis.

What Might Be Done?

When I wrote *Anna Freud: A Biography* nearly ten years ago, I was aware of these methodological issues, but I did not address them directly, either in the book or in my own ongoing self-inquiry about myself as her biographer. I was struggling with my own position as a relative newcomer—an adolescent—in psychoanalysis, a historian rather than a clinician; and I was trying hard to find the common experiential and characterological ground between my subject and me, the ground for understanding her and not getting confused by our very great differences. I could not make a contribution to thought about biography while I was trying to contribute a biography, even though I knew that my biography would indirectly present my methodological perspective. But I write now from quite a different position. I am no longer a newcomer to psychoanalysis. I am trained and practice as a clinician, which implies, of course, that I am more embedded in the history I study. Most important, however, I am able now to make my own self and my position the site of the methodological and practice problems I formulate, to study through myself. Specifically, I can now allow myself to make comparisons (not just search for common ground) between my subject and myself. I do not subordinate myself, putting myself at the service of my subject, which means that Anna Freud's work can be at my service for purposes different than the ones demanded by my construal of the subtitle, *A Biography*.

Proposing to raise questions of the sort I sketched about the biographical foundations of psychoanalytic theories is proposing a phenomenally complex undertaking. From my present perspective, I am convinced, however, that the only way to address it is to encourage

▼ ▼ ▼ ▼ ▼

biographers to be even more complex and self-conscious about—particularly—the matters of presenting childhood materials, tracing developmental lines, and considering cultural contexts. Specifically, I have been struck, while working as a clinician doing assessments, by the fact that in the course of these evolving interrelations between psychoanalysis and biography the Diagnostic Profiles created by Anna Freud and her colleagues at the Hampstead Clinic, which are the most complexly articulated developmental frameworks in all of modern psychoanalysis, have never been used as biographical instruments, either for subjects of biography or for technical reflection on biographers' methods. They were certainly not applied explicitly by Anna Freud's own biographer—myself. So here I am going to take the biographer's role again, with a larger purpose, offering an exercise in such an application, and along with that exercise making some remarks about myself and my creativity, in comparison to Anna Freud's (or as matters of something like "countertransference"). Although I am going to be working in sketches and gists, not showing you my "clinical" process or working on anything like a full scale, I hope to be able to show you that this biographical method can illuminate a subject's creativity, if the methodological pitfalls I outlined are kept in mind and their resulting cautions applied to the research instrument itself, the Diagnostic Profiles.

Theoretically, my larger purpose is a reflection on—a hypothesis about—what might be called "latency creativity" and a formulation about a phenomenon that I will call "prolonged latency" (on the model of Siegfried Bernfeld's phrase "prolonged adolescence"). To put my project in starkly simple terms, I want to follow a question that I asked myself when writing *Anna Freud* but was, then, unable to answer for lack of self-understanding and perspective on her: how did a person so constrained in terms of her libidinal development and obsessional traits come to have such a powerfully and productively organized creative life? I want to indicate that the answer "sublimation" is much too specific and unidimensional.

Sketches Made with the Profiles

Creativity Arenas

The Diagnostic Profiles developed and used at Hampstead, which were designed to compass and assess pathology, asked a clinician to begin the process of profiling with a description of "symptoms, anxieties, inhibi-

▼ ▼ ▼ ▼ ▼

tions, difficulties, abnormalities, breakdowns in functioning, acting out in the environment, inability to fulfill inherent potentialities, arrests in development leading to faulty ego and superego structuralization, etc." This kind of description displayed a "Reason for Referral." I am going to start my sketch, however, not with a survey of problem areas but with a study of Anna Freud's creative modes—a "Reason for Biographical Study," so to speak—and then come back to a structural reflection on the basis of it.

Let me begin by asserting that Anna Freud had three main creative modalities. First, she liked to work in groups, building institutions. She assembled coworkers, particularly those who wanted training in psychoanalysis, and made settings in which work was also training and training was also perpetuation of psychoanalysis. Her organizations were always divided into smaller units, family-sized, which were responsible for particular types or ages of clients, research tasks, projects, and so on. The organizational whole resembled a family of families, and leadership was thus multiple, decentralized, not concentrated around a (potentially rebellious) favorite or successor: there were many heads of households, many of them male, even though the majorities in her postwar groups were female. The ultimate leadership, hers, could be exercised with great firmness but, because it was diffused through the groups, without the reality or the appearance of authoritarianism, overt aggression, or too-masculine identification. Each of her institutions also had a rank of people on the outside who supplied the funds, who did fund-raising. She did not ever put herself directly in the role of the one who asks; she always had patrons and emissaries to raise money. In her institutions, in sum, she addressed—if she did not always solve—all the Freud family dilemmas that had so affected her: she contained sibling rivalries, provided multiple mothers, and identified herself with her father as the leader but was not patriarchal.[2]

Second, in solitude, Anna Freud composed lectures and essays by making outlines (comparable to lists) and then filling them in, oftentimes after having talked through the outline in a lecture and usually after a considerable passage of time. The fleshed-out final prose product was less exciting to produce than the spare skeleton. These productions were assembled at the initiative of others, especially editors who took responsibility for many of the completely unexciting scholarly components (like bibliographies). Anna Freud's prose was clean, unencumbered, efficient, and close to speech in its vocabulary, lucid; it seems to be studiously unsophisticated—to have a childlike simplicity—and its

▼ ▼ ▼ ▼ ▼

nuances only appear on rereading. She achieved a nearly magical tri-umph over her obsessionality—she made her solitary labor sociable, organized around her, and she made her labor look easy; altogether, a condition in which she was, as she put it in another context, "a law unto herself," omnipotent.

In her organizations and in her essays, Anna Freud's greatest gift was for synthesis—she brought all the parts together. She was a collector. She collected people, research projects and their results, ideas, perspec-tives; her purposes were to make order and to be encompassing, con-solidating, which involved noting in the assemblies she made what was missing so that the missing items could then become the next focus of research or assembly—remedy of lack, which so resembles salving of a narcissistic wound, was also a purpose.

Third, Anna Freud practiced both child analysis and adult analysis, stressing in her theoretical writings the differences between the two types of analysis (while others—like the Kleinians—stressed the similarities). She never wrote a case study that showed her technique in action, and she never wrote a technical treatise, although she allowed interviews with her on technical matters to be published. It can be said generally that when Anna Freud was at her most original, she was creating a new domain—as when she created child analysis (as distinct from her father's practice, adult analysis), when she created nurseries and clinics for treat-ment and observational research, and, late in her life, when she began to create a new specialty within child analysis for treatment of devel-opmental disorders. While she was making new domains, she was not in direct competition with existing or reigning institutions, schools of thought, or people. She moved to new territories by deferral—or what looked like deferral—of parts of old territories to others.

Assessment of Drive and Ego-Superego Position

The Diagnostic Profiles call for intricate history taking on the basis of interviews and assessments of environmental factors, but I am going to skip over these—or their biographical equivalents, which already exist in my *Anna Freud*—and go on to consider the categories called for by the Anna Freudian versions of the drive theory and the structural theory.

Anna Freud's Diagnostic Profile stipulates that, for a woman, there is an ideal adult libidinal position, labeled the "passive feminine one," which involves "no more than the normal admixture in terms of bisex-uality." But it is very unlikely that any women fulfilling such an ideal

▼ ▼ ▼ ▼ ▼

would be subjects of biography—as the history of psychoanalytic biography writing for females and males unanimously attests. A woman in the passive feminine position would be much more likely to be entirely the altruistically surrendering woman described (without questioning) by Anna Freud in *The Ego and the Mechanisms of Defense:* "[Surrender] of instinctual wishes to an object better qualified to fulfill them often determines the relation of a girl to some man whom she chooses to represent her—to the detriment of any true object relation. On the grounds of this 'altruistic' attachment she expects him to carry out the projects in which she believes herself to be handicapped by her sex . . . A man's success in life does, indeed, go far to compensate the women in his family for the renunciation of their own ambitions" (2:132).[3]

Both in general and when one is constructing a biographical profile, it is important to take into account the rigid normativity of Anna Freud's approach that I mentioned before—to treat it as a symptom for describing her own libidinal position rather than as a theoretical last word. So, the first descriptor in this category should be: Anna Freud idealized heterosexuality and, for women, a passive feminine position. This form of idealization, I will suggest later, is a latency achievement.

Anna Freud's elaborations of the libidinal developmental line and her surviving letters, dream transcripts, preadolescent and adolescent poetry and reminiscences (as told to and recalled by others) suggest that she reached the phallic level, engaged in masturbatory activity that continued (at least) into her latency, but had a significant fixation to, and potentiality for regression to, the anal level. She developed two specific types of sublimation to defend against her masturbatory activity: conversion of masturbatory fantasies into literary productions and pleasure in story-telling (including telling life stories, case stories—psychoanalytic narratives); and hand-controlling activities such as knitting, weaving, calligraphy—her handwriting was an art form for her. (But the dynamics of these defenses need exploring—they are sublimations, but they presuppose ego alterations, as I will argue below.) Further, Anna Freud developed versions of the well-known obsessional defenses against the anal-sadistic drives: rituals of collecting, ordering, cleaning, and so forth. The precise, hyperorganized way in which she hoarded and filed her personal and business correspondence can be taken as a general illustration.

Given what the Profiles call "Libido Distribution," starting with "Cathexis of the Self," it is important to note that Anna Freud viewed herself as physically unattractive, never, for example, liking any photographs that were taken of her (except one, in which she appears with August Aichhorn, that shows her only from the waist up—she felt she was bottom heavy—and wearing a scarf that covered her thin hair). Her clothes were always dark, dowdy, unexposing (particularly of her legs); her shoes (she had many pairs) were all low-heeled, dark, and sensible rather than comfortable. Her self-presentation was designed to deflect attention away from her body and from herself as a physical-sexual being; in psychoanalytic terms, this modest demeanor, like her shyness as a girl and reticence as an adult, cloaked a tendency to exhibitionism. The exhibitionism came through, however, in situations that called for it—for example, when Anna Freud was lecturing, she was experienced as riveting, charismatic, her lucidity a marvel.

Anna Freud invested a great deal of libido in her ego and in her superego, which was very strict: she valued her rationality and her moral integrity, sometimes to the point of finding it difficult to admit to misjudgments or moral weakness. Her psychodynamic description of mature morality is, in this connection, very interesting. Going against the view articulated in her analytic generation most forcefully by Wilhelm Reich, Anna Freud set herself up early in her career as a staunch opponent of the idea that the superego is the origin of neurosis since it commands the ego to squelch libidinal and aggressive impulses. True as it may be for many adults that superego anxiety permeates neurosis, she argued, the origins of neuroses should be sought in anxiety stimulated by the outside world: "the infantile ego fears the instincts because it fears the outside world" (2:57) and specifically adult punishment or disapproval. But it may well be, Anna Freud argued, that the origin of neuroses in objective anxiety is less important to their early forms than anxiety induced by the strength of the instincts—ultimately, anxiety about being overwhelmed or annihilated, about ego destruction (2:59). That she could see and articulate these distinctions with such clarity, it seems to me, suggests that she was working on the basis of self-knowledge, that she did not overplay the role of the superego (and guilt or anxiety of conscience) in the formation of neuroses because she recognized in herself the role of defenses responding to objective anxiety and dread of the strength of the instincts and to the shame or anxiety she felt when comparing herself with others.

Anna Freud took as developmentally normal the superego's turning of aggression on the self, and she found both praiseworthy and clever the moral integrity she so valued in herself:

▼ ▼ ▼ ▼ ▼

There are also some exceptional individuals whose moral demands on themselves are higher and stricter than anything which the environment expects from them or would impose on them. They acquire their standards by identification with an ideal image of the parents rather than by identifying with the real persons of the parents and they enforce them via a superego that is excessively severe owing to the turning inward of almost all the available aggression. Such individuals feel secure in the internal judgment and regulation of their own behavior which they know to be above and beyond the common norm. In the indirect, circuitous way of extreme (and often obsessional) character development they have succeeded in becoming once more what individuals set out to be as infants, namely, a "law unto themselves." (6:184)

In terms of "Cathexis of Objects," it is important to note that Anna Freud did not (as far as the biographical record yields) choose a sexual partner or seek to have her object needs met by a sexual partner, although she did, in a specific way, achieve what she calls "the attitude necessary for motherhood"; she was quite maternal toward the children she cared for in family settings and in her nurseries and clinics. She cannot be said to have outgrown her infantile Oedipal relationships, particularly not the one with her father. Other than her father, her most important adult tie was to Dorothy Burlingham, with whom she created a kind of family life that included Dorothy's four children, whom Anna Freud both mothered and treated analytically. This relationship does not seem to have been homosexual in the narrowly sexual sense, and Dorothy Burlingham seems to have been a figure who was important for Anna Freud primarily neither for her femininity nor for her masculinity, but for her allegiance to Sigmund Freud, who had analyzed her, for her commitment to psychoanalysis, for her maternal capacities, and for her own search for a twin. The relationship had a large ingredient of latency girl bonding in it, and of choice of partner on a narcissistic basis (a characteristic of latency choices), and it can be usefully seen against the background of Anna Freud's description of object choice in latency. Latency object choice she saw as a move away from the "phallic oedipal period [that] foreshadows more closely than at other times [a person's] future inclinations regarding sexual role and choice of object." As she noted:

> When entry into the latency period is made, this particular [phal-
> lic] aspect of the child's libidinal life disappears once more from
> view. There are, of course, at this time, unmodified remnants of

the Oedipus complex which determine the attachments, particularly of the neurotic children, who have been unable to solve, and dissolve, their oedipal relations to their parents. But apart from these, there are also the phase adequate aim-inhibited, displaced or sublimated tendencies for which the sexual identity of the partner becomes again a matter of comparative indifference. Evidence of the latter are the latency child's relationships to his teachers, who are loved, admired, disliked or rejected not because they are men or women but because they are either helpful, appreciative, inspiring, or harsh, intolerant, anxiety-arousing figures. (6:188)

Just as the Profiles ask that "Libido Distribution" in relation to self and objects be assessed, they ask that "Aggression" be described. In the overt picture of Anna Freud's personality, very little aggression was apparent. What was apparent got channeled into the cause of psychoanalysis—in fighting for its survival, its purity (as she conceived that), and its extension into new areas of work—and into working for the purposes of her protégés and colleagues. Very little was employed on her own behalf or directly. Her aggression does not seem to have been of the predominantly anal-sadistic sort; rather it was phallic—sublimated in forms resembling knight errantry. She had a sharp wit. She did not direct aggression against her body, but, when directing it against herself went (as she put it on the Adult Profile) "through the superego to the ego"—that is, she was self-critical: she unrealistically complained of herself that she did not do enough, she was not assiduous enough in the cause of psychoanalysis, and so forth. In the psychoanalytic world, she fought by keeping her enemies out of her own oasis, her clinic, not to the point of direct censorship, but nonetheless, in reasonable tones, decisively.

In terms of defense activity, she sublimated her aggression. But she also employed reaction formation, turning aggression into supportiveness for the cause and people she believed in. She could delegate fighting to others, especially to men, behavior that can be construed as a variant on the defense that she called "altruistic surrender," which involves signing over libidinal interests to others and then enjoying their activities at a distance, as a promoter or supporter.

About the ego and the superego, it can be said, first, that Anna Freud's ego functions serving perception, memory, mobility, and so on, were prodigious. She had an especially remarkable memory—for her cases, for all of the cases in her clinics, for business details—and also very great curiosity, patiently and carefully deployed. Curiosity is, as she

▼ ▼ ▼ ▼ ▼

always stressed, particularly associated with the phallic stage and inquisitiveness about sexual matters.

Her thinking was very reliant on personification. She tended to imagine psychic structure dramatically, as though it were a play with a cast of three characters—id, ego, and superego—talking to each other or engaged in struggles with each other. (The only other psychoanalyst I know of who used this kind of personification to the same extent was Otto Fenichel, and his, too was a cataloging, collecting mind.) Like a concrete-thinking latency child, she imagined psychic life as a field of conflicts in which battling was normal. And it is certainly a very easy step to conclude that she unconsciously imagined herself as the child, ego, standing between indulgence and conscience—the Oedipus complex of the latency child.

When I look now at Anna Freud's creativity modes and assess her in Profile developmental terms, I do so thinking comparatively as I go, and asking what my own creativity type allows me to see with the Profile lens. I survey the terrain as a person who likes to work alone, conducting an imaginary conversation with one other, or conversing in two-person partnerships, with my phallic phase—as the Profile has it—very much in evidence. I seek an other, like myself, but also to complement myself, make myself more capacious, so that I am able to be encompassing or synthetic in quite a different way from the way an encyclopedic collector is. I like to make maps of intellectual territories, guide tours; to be the one who gets there first, before any rivals (to be the one, for example, who writes the first biography); to be the one who is the best and is comprehending, who wins love by being understanding (especially of the loved one, or of the admired—maternal—biographical subject). I need to win Oedipal competitions against parental and sibling rivals, both in the negative (predominantly) and positive Oedipal modes, androgynously, but to do so modestly (or, with reaction formations against self-advertisement). I do not, like Anna Freud, avoid direct Oedipal triumph (especially with the father, over the mother) by moving into asceticism and altruistic surrender and filial piety, enjoying the triumph by indirect means, and I have had to guard against judging her psychic strategy to be too cautious, unthrilling, and—considering her late adolescent psychoanalysis with her father—self-sacrificing. I have learned from considering her and myself a great deal about the difference between desiring to be neither sex, or staying in relative sexual undifferentiation, and desiring to be both, as I learned about the difference between being spurred to creative effort by a fantasy of living in an oasis

▼ ▼ ▼ ▼ ▼

of latency—a prelapsarian fantasy—and being spurred by a sense of always having failed the (bisexual) ideal, of not having done quite enough to win the love, to be the everything. In sum, proceeding comparatively, I can see the mode of Anna Freud's creativity as less restless and stormy than mine, more ego driven while less erotically charged, and wider in informational reach because it was team oriented. Indeed, she is a paradigmatic example of how team creativity can flow from latency creativity—which prompts me to turn once more to her own analyses to understand her.

Latency Creativity

Anna Freud saw—schematically—two extreme outcomes to the ascension of libidinal drives in adolescence: in the battle waged between the id and the ego, the id could win and the "entrance into adult life be marked by a riot of uninhibited gratification of instinct," or the ego could win, "in which case the character of the individual during the latency period will declare itself for good and all" (2:149). One variant of the victorious ego scenario, I want to suggest, is a condition—"prolonged latency" it might be called—in which the character of latency is continued throughout adolescence as the defense organization, so that the key tasks of adolescence, finding love objects outside the family and reaching libidinal organization under genital dominance, are not carried out. There is latency fixation.

But a person with a latency fixation can, to make a further distinction, be a person whose ego is victorious primarily through repression— that is, someone whose latency character is a texture of inhibitions—or a person whose ego is victorious by employing defenses which allow for or even sustain creativity. The first is a person Anna Freud described in this way: "Apart from the resulting crippling of the instinctual life, the fact that the victorious ego becomes rigidly fixed is permanently injurious to the individual. Ego institutions which have resisted the onslaught of puberty without yielding generally remain throughout life inflexible, unassailable, and insusceptible of the rectification which a changing reality demands" (2:151).

The second way for the ego to be victorious is to permit creativity. In *The Ego an the Mechanisms of Defense*, drawing on her self-understanding as well as her clinical practice, Anna Freud made a study of alternatives to inhibition or stifling of ego functions and thus creativity. First, she distinguished inhibitions, involving repression, from ego restrictions. A child who becomes inhibited wards off prohibited instinctual impulses, unacceptable wishes and desires, and becomes unable to do or say or think something that is associated with or substitutes for those impulses, wishes, and desires. The inhibition, then, is impervious to environmental influence. By contrast, a child who avoids an *external* situation in which he or she feels anxious or humiliated or diminished by comparison or competition with others restricts the field of his or her ego activities, without becoming impervious to environmental influences. Away from the disturbing situation, such a child may find his or restricted activities flourishing again; and, similarly, such a child very frequently is able to develop ego activities other than the ones restricted. Anna Freud offered as an example a girl who, without the fear of punishment or anxiety of conscience that might produce an inhibition, gives up clitoral masturbation, "thus restricting her masculine strivings." "Her self-love is mortified when she compares herself with boys, who are better equipped for masturbation, and she does not want to be constantly reminded of her disadvantages by indulging in the practice" (2:101). This girl might, then, take up a substitute activity—a manual activity like knitting, initially, then a broader field of activity like excelling at intellectual tasks. Creativity in the new domain can actually be given a spur by ego restriction, whereas inhibition has only a negative, rigidifying effect. But, to keep the ego restriction in place, it may well be necessary to rule out the forbidden striving—masculine striving in this case—by many means. And one of those means could well involve idealizing theoretically the passive feminine position and heterosexuality. In general, notions of normativity can function to secure ego alterations (as well as to secure repressions)—whether these be notions of normal heterosexuality, normal homosexuality, or normal bisexuality, normal passivity or normal activity. (Each of these tactics is, of course, well represented in gender theory, and I tend to idealize normal bisexuality.)

A second defense alternative to repression and inhibition is assigning prohibited libidinal and aggressive impulses that arise internally to another person, "altruistic surrender." Let me return to this defense one more time by citing Anna Freud's description of a governess, a woman with a superego too severe to permit her gratification of any of her wishes—for a penis, for children, for displaying herself naked before her father—who made over her wishes to her female friends. "She gratified her instincts by sharing in the gratification of others, employing for this purpose the mechanisms of projection and identification" (2:126).

In each of Anna Freud's creativity modes—her creation of new families or teams, her manner of making solitary activities into magically sociable ones, her assignments of tasks to others, her development of manual activities, and so forth—there is apparent, in her own terms, not repression but alterations of the ego, in relation to the id and also in relation to the strong superego (so often represented in her self-understanding by her father or her father's superego). Alterations of the ego are, I think, the essence of latency defense—as opposed to splitting of the ego, which is much more characteristic of Oedipal and especially pre-Oedipal defensive structuration. They are, in effect, equivalent to obsessional behaviors and traits (as opposed to a fully manifest obsessional neurosis), so serviceable for a well-ordered, efficient life in which external challenges and rivalries remain external, distanced from the oasis of order, even downgraded. Anna Freud's defensive style was restriction, which meant concentration of resources, intensification in a special, select arena—psychically and socially.

I find that assessing Anna Freud's creativity in the manner of this essay, using her Profile and using my profile, provides a way to stay away from the normativity that is characteristic of her Profiles. The emphasis falls on similarities and differences between and among people—on pluralities of developmental lines—rather than on normality and abnormality. This emphasis, in my case, arises from my one-to-one conversational thinking style—and, for this piece of writing, from my pleasure in having another imaginary conversation with my subject, Anna Freud.

▼   This essay is based upon a lecture on biography and psychoanalysis delivered to Division 39 of the American Psychological Association in New York, April 1996. My thanks go to the lecture organizers and to those in the audience who offered their comments. It will be published in 1998 in *American Imago,* in a special issue on biography and transference.

▼ ▼ ▼ ▼ ▼

7

A History of
Freud Biographies

Psychoanalysis is unique among the sciences for many reasons, but certainly the most important is its completely exceptional mode of transmission from one generation of practitioners and researchers to the next. It is the one science, even the one type of psychology, that is practiced upon its future practitioners as the key ingredient of their training. Not simply a course of study or even an apprenticeship is required of the future practitioners, but insight in the science's own terms, and self-alteration. Psychoanalysis is not learned; it is incorporated and an identification is formed with it.

In their training all analysts must, in effect, or perhaps one should say in affect, recapitulate both the analysis of the founding father, which he, uniquely, conducted upon himself, and their own analysts' analyses. They all know that a self-analysis cannot, considered in light of Freud's own theory as well as his practice, be complete; so they are all automatically supercessors, better trained than their masters' master, but they are all also, nonetheless, lesser, for Freud is the unsurpassed genius.

This last observation brings me to a second reason why psychoanalysis is unique among the sciences (including other types of psychology). That is, the founder has never been made historical by a successor, never been equaled or even approximated as a contributor to psychoanalysis. There is no Einstein for this Newton. On the contrary, in their contributions to psychoanalytic method, theory, and metatheory, psychoanalysts for now some six generations have had, before they can truly begin, to go back and confront the master's vast opus, and, as they became available, his almost equally vast correspondence and, eventually, even large libraries of commentaries on his person and his work. It

▼ ▼ ▼ ▼

is not surprising, therefore, that psychoanalysis is a science that not only cannot hold up the banner of progress with any confidence, but is full of rebellions—frustrated rages, in fact—against the very patriarchal achievements without which it would not exist. During Freud's lifetime, schisms and reassertions of the true—if not fixed or far-followed—path alternated, and since Freud's death the patterns of these possibilities have been replayed again and again. But in the replaying decades there has, of course, been no Freud, but only claimants to his legacy to point the true path, and, further, the process of identification has become progressively less and less with Freud's science (in a personal sense) and more and more with a literature about Freud.

For a related reason, psychoanalysis is—third—unique among the sciences as the one without major contributions to its own history as a science, and also without major contributions to the history of its own history—without any historiography.[1] What I mean is not just that psychoanalysis after Freud's death in 1939 has no history—although this is certainly true; but the more striking fact is that the history of psychoanalysis that has so far been written is not really history: it is biography, a subspecies of history, and, further, much of it is the type of biography which Freud himself originated: psychobiography.[2]

Let me indicate briefly what this state of affairs implies by noting that the first history of psychoanalysis was written in 1914, entitled without ceremony *On the History of the Psychoanalytic Movement*, and penned by Freud himself. With this book the history of psychoanalysis began as a type of autobiography, and so it continued until Freud's death, as the title of his next history, *An Autobiographical Study* (1925) shows. Later, when history writing fell to the first generation of heirs, it became a type of biography—of Freud. Ernest Jones's *Life and Work of Sigmund Freud*, the most fully documented and the most official of the first generation's histories, became, in turn, the precipitant for a third type of history: critiques of Jones's biography, or what might be called second-order biographies. In these subsequent biographies, written with increasing frequency by nonanalyst historians, Jones's idealization of Freud has been rejected, and, particularly in the medium of psychobiography, a much more contextualized and conflicted and complicated founder has emerged.[3]

Biographies of Freud, both of the Jones vintage and of the later more critical sort, have had a greater role in the development of psychoanalysis since the Second World War than biographies of seminal figures have ever had in the development of other sciences. Freud's life and the life

▼ ▼ ▼ ▼ ▼

of psychoanalysis were and still are intertwined in a unique way. This is so for the reasons I have been noting: Freud made his discoveries partly by analyzing himself; his autobiographical writings, which conveyed his self-created image of himself, were consequently key texts in the intellectual and organizational history of his science; and, finally, he established psychobiography and the psychoanalytic theory of creativity. Among these factors, however, the first remains key. The most written-about and debated moment in the history of psychoanalysis remains the moment declared to be the origin of psychoanalysis: the period in and around 1900 of Freud's self-analysis, of *The Interpretation of Dreams,* and of his letters to Wilhelm Fliess. The whole of psychoanalysis, in Freud's lifetime and after, seems to rise up out of the legendary beginning, the moment of founding. And it is no exaggeration to say that each and every Freud biographer has based his or her assessment of psychoanalysis *tout court* on an assessment of the originary period.

The story of this phenomenon in the cultural history of science began after the Second World War, when psychoanalysts in Europe and America began to turn their attention to how their science, without its founding father, should be prepared for its second half-century and transmitted to new generations, particularly after the great damage done to its followers and its aspirations during the *Nazizeit.* Analysts who had known Freud personally in Vienna or Berlin wrote textbooks for the extra-familial analysts who were founding training institutes in London, New York, Boston, Washington, Buenos Aires, Delhi—all around the world. Otto Fenichel produced *The Psychoanalytic Theory of the Neuroses* (1945), Frieda Fromm-Reichmann reached out to nonanalytic practitioners with *Principles of Intensive Psychotherapy* (1953), Hermann Nunberg revised and expanded his 1932 *Principles of Psychoanalysis* (1955), and Robert Waelder slowly assembled the materials for his *Basic Theory of Psychoanalysis* (finally published in 1960), which includes a revealing "List of the Most Common Misunderstandings of Psychoanalytic Concepts."[4]

Between 1945 and 1960, the production of textbooks was meant both to teach and to prevent misunderstandings. The biographical studies of Sigmund Freud written by analysts during the same period—to which I will return in a moment—had the same two purposes.

But it is important to realize that the first postwar analytic textbooks and biographies were launched into an atmosphere created by a spate of nonanalytic popular biographies. Helen Walker Puner, an associate edi-

▼ ▼ ▼ ▼ ▼

tor at *Parent's Magazine,* wrote *Freud: His Life and His Mind* (1947) for her magazine's audience, and Emil Ludwig, a prolific journalist, wrote his *Doctor Freud* (1947) for a similarly uninformed general audience.[5] Only the first of these two books had a significant afterlife, but both were works suited to that period of American arrogance in intellectual and technological matters. Puner assumed that most of Freud's work was already outmoded and that more recent psychoanalysis was more scientific, both less like a religion and and less reflective of the personal faults of the founder, a man as "fallible and frail as other men," a man possessed by secret father hatred and repudiation of his Judaism. The combination in Puner's work of celebration and debunking condescension became quite typical of the non analytic biographical literature, as did her tendency to psychoanalyze Freud with amateur versions of his own techniques.[6]

Works like Puner's and Ludwig's struck fear into the communities of Viennese émigrés in England and America, particularly those associated with Anna Freud, who had assumed the role of chief protector of her father's memory. After Freud's death in 1939 and through the period of these first postwar popular biographies, Anna Freud had stood strenuously opposed to any kind of biographical inquiry into her father's life. But 1946 had also brought a challenge to her convictions. Marie Bonaparte came to London bearing a packet full of Freud's letters to his friend and fellow explorer of biological-psychological territories, Wilhelm Fliess, letters written during Freud's "self-analysis" in the originary decade of psychoanalysis. Despite her fear that the letters would be misunderstood and misused, Anna Freud decided, in consultation with her siblings, that the letters should be published. Ernst Kris, one of the Viennese trainees, was designated the editor and assigned the task of a thorough biographical introduction.[7]

Working with Kris richly informed Anna Freud about the complexities of biographical writing. Kris had to work on himself, in a self-analysis and in analysis with Anna Freud, as he wrote, and others involved in the project were similarly unsettled by the difficulties of being objective about their hero. Max Schur, Freud's physician during 1938–39, vacillated frequently between the idea that Freud's physical symptoms at the turn of the century were psychosomatic and the idea that they were not. Siegfried Bernfeld, another Viennese colleague, contributed important material from his series of historical essays on Freud's prepsychoanalytic neurological work, but he grew restive when confronted with Anna Freud's anxieties and discretions.[8] Wilhelm Fliess's

▼ ▼ ▼ ▼ ▼

son Robert sometimes expressed to Kris the opinion that his father was a paranoiac and sometimes backtracked to protect him. The only one of Freud's associates who wrote biographically in relative isolation from the Anna Freudians and the Fliess project in these years was Hanns Sachs, a member of Freud's original circle whose two studies, *Freud: Master and Friend* (1944) and *Masks of Life and Love* (1948) are among the most interesting—obviously partisan, but understated and unpretentious—works of the period.[9]

While the letters to Fliess were being prepared for publication, the Puner and Ludwig biographies appeared—without so much as a mention between them of Freud's crucial friendship with Fliess. The Freudians could see clearly that keeping letters out of the public domain would increase the distortion and reliance on anecdote in biographies, but they could also see that an irresponsible biographer might use the letters sensationalistically. Finally, without enthusiasm, Anna Freud came to the conclusion that an authoritative full-scale biography might forestall future falsifications. An additional advantage would be that one person, a sifter and a winnower, would act as recipient for all who wanted to tell their anecdotes about Freud, thus preventing betrayals or civil wars among the Freudians. Discussions about such a biography and possible biographers began in the Freud family circle even before Ernest Jones, one of Freud's earliest associates and the preeminent member of the British psychoanalytic group, was approached for the task by an American publisher.

Despite the Freud family's misgivings about Jones's past hostilities toward Freud, Jones became the biographer designate and began work in 1951, just as James Strachey was launching upon the monumental editing and translating project later called *The Complete Psychological Works of Sigmund Freud* (in twenty-four volumes, 1953–1974). Both the biographer and the translator, who exchanged information as they worked, had to develop the basic ingredient of scholarly biography: a detailed, reliable chronological frame. Their joint work, together with Kris's on the Fliess letters, set the standard for future biographies, and also established a key feature of them: all the researchers considered the founding decade of psychoanalysis, 1895–1905 (and especially 1896–1897) to be the crux of biographical inquiry, and it appeared in their standard-setting works as both the great creative period and the great "psychoneurotic period" (in Jones's phrase), the psychoanalytic *mysterium tremendum*.

As he worked, Jones took enormous (and rather self-deceiving)

▼ ▼ ▼ ▼ ▼

pride in his accuracy, and he keenly pointed out in his voluminous correspondence with Anna Freud how inaccurate other biographers—including Ernst Kris—had been. Gradually cured of her skepticism, Anna Freud complained to Jones about Siegfried Bernfeld's loose interpretations in a paper on Freud's cocaine use, and about a hated piece on Freud's "Irma dream" by her Vienna trainee and fellow child analyst Erik Erikson: "it should be your role to silence all the other 'biographers' who have to invent half their facts" (to Jones, September 19, 1952).[10] She became more and more deeply absorbed in Jones's work, feeling, as he sent her chapter after chapter, that she was discovering her father: "I thought that I knew my father better than anybody, but I do not think it any more," she told Jones (to Jones, February 14, 1954). Jones relished her praise and enjoyed spending paragraphs demolishing inferior works like Puner's. Together the coworkers even indulged in a little humor about the stream of other biographical work, which continued unchecked by Jones's efforts. "I wonder if a book entitled 'Lies about Freud' would sell? It would be easy to concoct." (Jones to Anna Freud, December 3, 1957).

The Jones biography, which eventually ran to three stout volumes, was a collaborative venture from the start. Martha Freud supplied memories and some of her husband's courtship letters, the Freud children read the manuscript as it evolved (the oldest, Martin, was even inspired to pen his own work, *Sigmund Freud, Man and Father,* 1958),[11] and all participated in delicate discretionary decisions, including one that resulted in a version of Freud's death that completely protected Max Schur from any possible charge of euthanasia for administering a lethal dose of morphine when Freud was *in extremis.* But it was Anna Freud who most clearly assumed the role of biographer *manqué* and also *grise.* She had many times refused importuning publishers who had wanted her to write about her father, insisting that this was the last thing in the world she either could or would think of doing, but in the role of conscience to Jones, to whom she had (in her own technical term) "altruistically surrendered" this self-forbidden work, she was so comfortable that she agreed to translate his first volume into German.

Jones's pages are vivid with details only his direct sources could have supplied about Freud's domestic and work routines, his friendships and working relationships, his organizational tribulations and his travels. Protecting the family's privacy produced some strange disbalances—there is almost as much about Freud's dogs as there is about his children and grandchildren; the reader gets no real sense of the complexity of the

Freud family and household and the many crises and strains weathered while the children were growing up; Martha Freud becomes more and more enigmatic as the story unfolds. Jones's own feelings about others of Freud's colleagues produced some distortions (for example, no inquiry into the nature of Sándor Ferenczi's mental condition in his last year, which Max Schur had told Jones was probably an "organic psychosis" linked to pernicious anemia); and the institutional history of psychoanalysis is very lightly filled in, while the episodic schisms are covered in the kind of strategic (as opposed to theoretical) detail Jones, a great combatant himself, enjoyed. There is a compelling history of Freud's unfolding discoveries, but not much sense of how his mind worked, the character of his thought, or the intensity of his often lonely battle for his cause. In the first volume, which ends as psychoanalysis has been created, the life and work dimensions are carefully interwoven, but this achievement is lacking in the later volumes, since Jones elected to alternate between life sections and work (or thematic) sections. Unrealistically, Jones tended to see Freud's struggle and growth as completed by the end of the originary decade, and after that he often idealized his subject as a serene, always composed patriarch.

It is, nonetheless, one of the great virtues of Jones's massive work that it is a psychobiography, but a very restrained one and one that does not lose sight of the current historical contexts (as do so many works by analysts who are recapitulating psychoanalysis in the manner I noted before). Jones had such an abundance of material that he did not suffer the temptation to invent or to speculate at each step of the way, but he also had so much that he knew clearly how much he lacked, how much was missing, lost, or unavailable. He wrote as a historian, without the idea, so common among later psychoanalyst-biographers, that biography writing and doing analysis are similar kinds of activities. He did not, for example, interpret blanks in his documentation as secrets or resistances; he knew that many of the most important things in people's lives are never recorded and also that many records vanish for reasons that have nothing to do with the biographical subject's unconscious life. Occasionally, he felt that he was in the presence of a secret, as he noted of Freud's adolescence, but he was content to say so without trying to cut a keyhole in the closed door.

As soon as Jones's biography was completely available (1957) and both it and Freud's centenary (1956) had been celebrated in an outpouring

▼ ▼ ▼ ▼ ▼

of small biographical speculations, some by others of Freud's early associates, a new phase of biographical study began. From about 1961, the publication date of a selection of Freud's letters, edited by his son Ernst Freud, until the mid 1970s, every biography both set out from and contended with Jones's biography.[13] This was a reactive period and not one of new discoveries or interpretative innovation, for the materials available to others were fewer than those known to Jones. In New York, a Sigmund Freud Archives was set up under the direction of a Viennese analyst named K. R. Eissler, and most materials not available to Jones went into the closed archives, out of the reach of biographers not sanctioned by the Freud family or Eissler. The field was, thus, divided into insiders and outsiders, a situation bound to foster resentment.

Although it was not published until 1972, Max Schur's *Freud Living and Dying* is the ultimate insider's biography of the late 1960s, the period when Schur began work. Schur had prepared a lengthy medical memorandum about Freud for Ernst Jones, and he had been drawn into the biographical arena while he negotiated by mail about Jones's use of the memorandum. What fascinated Schur was Freud's attitude toward death, which Schur tracked from the period of the Fliess letters on into the 1920s, when Freud formulated the theory of the death instinct, and up to the year of Freud's dying. The biography is very uneven—Schur himself did not live to finish it—but it contains some of the most insightful reflections ever recorded on the influence of Freud's personality on his theories. And it also contains a sampling of Freud's letters, cited only in German, as an appendix—another sign that the Freud circle gave special documentary access to its own.[14]

During the fifteen years or so after the Jones biography, when Schur was the only biographer with further access to documents, the main biographical mode was "assessment of influence." In this mode, the outlines of Freud's life were taken as a settled matter, and interpretation of his personal and intellectual significance seemed the job in need of doing. And assessing Freud's influence became one of the key modes—the other was assessing Marxism's (not Marx's) influence—for portraying the course and meaning of the twentieth century in its third quarter, its period of prolonged Cold War and of booming consumer culture in America and Western Europe.

Lionel Trilling's *Freud and the Crisis of Our Culture* (1955) was a brilliant, distinguished harbinger of this phase, but the title of the book by Frankfurt School Marxist Eric Fromm, *Sigmund Freud's Mission: An Analysis of His Personality and Influence* (1959), was much more typical

▼ ▼ ▼ ▼ ▼

in its polemical purposes and tone. (For his main historical argument, that Freud's psychoanalysis became a religious movement for a secularized and disoriented and consumption-driven urban middle-class elite, Fromm acknowledges his debt to . . . Helen Walker Puner.) Of this vast assessment literature, however, the one book that has lived on and is kept in print is Philip Rieff's *Freud: The Mind of a Moralist* (1959).[15]

Rieff's work has not had its staying power, I think, because of its portrait of "the mind of Freud," which is a portrait too admiring to be acceptable in any American reading atmosphere since the early 1960s, even though Rieff explicitly distinguished it from Jones's idealization (Jones, he said, "was too near his subject"; "he compelled the reader to venerate the man as well as respect the ideas"). Rather, what has remained challenging about Rieff's work is the ardor and compellngness with which he sought "psychological man," an ideal type whom Rieff hoped would show himself courageously able to live a truly liberated life, a life free from all constraints of authoritarian community life (whether religious or political) and from external moral imperatives, a life of unsentimental autonomy. Even while he insisted that Freud was not a moral messenger, Rieff nonetheless felt compelled to set Freud up as the very model of this modern man, and to "draw the implications" (his own recurrent phrase) of Freud's personal and scientific example for a new morality, nondoctrinaire and stemming from analytic introspection. Rieff's image of Freud demanded—in contrast to Fromm's— that Freud be considered apart from the psychoanalytic movement he founded and apart from the popular expropriations of Freudianism that had, actually, prepared the way for "psychological man" to emerge as a possibility. For Rieff, every man had the potential to be his own cultural hero. And it seems to me that there is such a deep affinity between this idea and the individualism (of the rugged sort or the more refined Emersonian sort) of American mainstream culture, that Rieff's vision of "psychological man" could reverberate, even among those who had far less admiration than he for Freud, right into the quite different sort of extreme individualism and nonmoralistic moralism that now goes under the name postmodernism.

The general "assessment of influence" cultural-historical approach to Freud became more intense as the 1960s unfolded in all their upheaval and torment, and Freud's cultural speculations, particularly *Civilization and Its Discontents,* attracted much more nonanalytical interest than his clinical and more technically metapsychological contributions. For many of the rebellious "baby boom" postwar generation, Herbert

▼ ▼ ▼ ▼ ▼

Marcuse's *Eros and Civilization* (1955, but only in mass market paperback after 1961), with its invocation of "polymorphous" sexual liberation, was more compelling than any assessment of Freud's influence, any text of Freud's own or any image, like Rieff's, of Freud the man.[16] For these rebels, biography in general was too "role model" oriented. But during this period of ferment two important tributaries of biographically focused critique did arise and branch off from the growing Freud assessment literature. One concerned Freud's Jewishness and the influence of his religious heritage and national character on his work, and one focused on his psychology of women. The latter was fed by one of the most widely read books of the mid-1960s, Betty Friedan's pioneering *Feminine Mystique* (1963), but it did not really swell into a rushing torrent until the end of the decade.[17]

The Jewish stream, however, was mingled with an intense Jewish identity quest that became more articulated during the Eichmann trial in 1961 and gathered momentum through the 1967 war in the Middle East.[18] The progenitor of this stream is David Bakan's 1958 work *Sigmund Freud and the Jewish Mystical Tradition,* which was reissued as a paperback in 1965; many works followed until a slackening was signaled by the reemergence, in the mid-1970s, of images of Freud as a Jewish self-hater, exactly the character who had starred in Puner's popular postwar volume. But this whole stream of inquiry then had a revival in the 1980s, and typical of this new era is D. B. Klein's *Jewish Origins of the Psychoanalytic Movement* (1981).[19] The literature is very repetitive in its claims about the importance of Freud's Jewishness for psychoanalysis, but recently emphasis has shifted to the biographical question of whether Freud's upbringing had actually been as Reform or unreligious as he liked to present it. The historian and future biographer Peter Gay argued that it had been in *A Godless Jew* (1987), while two works that focused on Freud's late work *Moses and Monotheism,* Emanuel Rice's *Freud and Moses* (1990) and Yosef Yerushalmi's *Freud's Moses* (1991), took new information about Freud's parents into account and presented him as more shaped by Orthodoxy than the gentile Jones or the Freud children—or Freud himself—had admitted.[20]

The second wave of Jewish-influence biographers has tended to focus on Freud's later years, the years of Hitler's prewar power and promulgation of anti-Semitism. But this was precisely the period in Freud's life that a small but vociferously critical group began, in the later 1960s, to see as the period of Freud's deradicalization. Critics who admired the early Freud, the id theorist, the pioneering discoverer of the unconscious

▼ ▼ ▼ ▼

whose complex genius was so clear in the massive volume by Didier Anzieu called simply *L'auto-analyse* (1959; 1986 edition in English), found his later work, with its growing emphasis on ego psychology, too conservative.[21] These critics, mostly Kleinians (in Britain and America) and Lacanians (in France) among analysts, mostly radical Marxists among nonanalysts, set up "ego psychology" and the progressive bureaucratization of psychoanalytic societies as the twin signs of an anti-liberationist turn in psychoanalysis, and they held Freud's own alleged retrenchment in his last years responsible for the turn.

As this critical spirit was gathering force, Henri Ellenberger published a huge tome called *The Discovery of the Unconscious* (1970). Many of the biographical claims in Ellenberger's work have now become staples in Freud portraits. Chiefly, thanks to Ellenberger, the milieu into which Freud launched his psychoanalytical studies on hysteria is now generally thought to have been both more ready for psychoanalysis— that is, there were more precursors of Freud's ideas abroad than Jones had acknowledged—and less monolithically disparaging or critical than Jones maintained. Ellenberger gave tremendous impetus to a mode of Freud biography that flourished ten years later, one that stressed contextualizing Freud, putting him in his intellectual milieu, showing his influences and debts, questioning Freud's own and Jones's versions of the history of psychoanalysis and even of particular cases. Ellenberger was a very respectful critical historian, but not hindered by the Jonesian conviction that the psychoanalysis which appeared in the miraculous discovery decade of the 1890s was completely *sui generis*.[22]

In the mid-1970s, the revisionary period forecast by the late 1960s critiques of Freud and of psychoanalysis began in earnest. There were two ruling assumptions in this period. The first was that Freud was an authoritarian who suppressed dissent in his movement and induced in his followers a spirit of orthodoxy. The second assumption, really a corollary of the first, was that the Freudian biographers of Freud were also authoritarians who had been keeping secrets about the master or idealizing him, suppressing his weaknesses as a person and as a psychologist. This second assumption was reinforced as publications of Freud's correspondence appeared in German and then in English (with Oskar Pfister in 1963, Karl Abraham in 1966, Arnold Zweig in 1968, Lou Andréas-Salome in 1972, and Carl Jung in 1974) and also when two other key sets of correspondence, with Ferenczi and Jones, did not appear. The published collections were both biographically stimulating and frustrating for their glaring omissions of letters and deletions within letters. The Sigmund Freud Archives in New York came to be perceived more and more widely as the institutional equivalent of the protective, idealizing Freud family: both were reactionary and dedicated to embalming both Freud's story and the story of psychoanalysis, particularly of the heretics and dissidents within psychoanalysis who, had they not been crushed by the orthodox believers, would have made psychoanalysis a progressive force.

A particular battle exemplified the conflict: in 1969 Paul Roazen, a young Harvard-trained historian, published *Brother Animal,* a book dedicated to showing that Viktor Tausk, one of Freud's early disciples, had been a genius whose unorthodox views Freud had repudiated and whose very sanity he had helped destroy. This book was a more focused version of an argument that Roazen later made more diffusely in *Freud and His Followers* (1975), a book that both beneficially headed the business of biography writing toward the second generation of Freudians (where it eventually flourished in the 1980s) and established a tone of aggrieved outsiderdom combined with slipshod scholarship that had a baleful influence on future nonanalytic and non–Freud-circle biographers.[23] Kurt Eissler responded to the Tausk study with a book twice as long, called *Talent and Genius* (1971), in which Tausk was shown to be merely talented, Freud got the designation genius, and Paul Roazen was made out to be a charlatan. (Eissler made many rich contributions to the Freud biography literature, all of them, strangely enough, in the form of replies to allegedly and sometimes actually charlatan biographers and other ignorants, and his work is, unfortunately, skewed by its defensive function.)[24]

Debunking had, of course, always played a role in the Freud biographical literature, particularly in the popular, amateur ranges, where Helen Puner had set the postwar tone. But the debunking of this period was done not by journalists but by academics, many of them trained in history and the social sciences, and it was connected to the larger cultural phenomenon of the baby boom generation, those who went to graduate school in the late 1960s, and proceeded to deconstruct and reevaluate the historical work of the elders who had dominated intellectual life in the 1950s and 1960s. The most significant biography of this sort was Frank Sulloway's *Freud: Biologist of the Mind* (1979), which contains an elaborately constructed argument that Freud, far from being an isolated and lonely heroic genius, was a man in step with the biological and evolutionary thought of his time, a man whose theories, in all their deep

▼ ▼ ▼ ▼ ▼

contradictoriness and inconsistency, bear within them all the fallacies of nineteenth-century natural science. Sulloway's work is both enormously informative about the history of science and quite tone-deaf to psychoanalysis—it willfully reduces Freud's work to its biological dimensions and then calls the impoverished result "psychoanalysis."[25]

Much more publicly important—and, eventually, important for the internal reform of psychoanalysis—was the debunking done in the the late 1960s and early 1970s by feminists. Kate Millett's attack on Freud throughout the pages of *Sexual Politics* (1971), for example, set a standard for rejection of psychoanalysis among radical feminists. Freud's views on female psychology, read as a function of Freud's supposed misogyny, became targets for many polemics, and older works like Simone de Beauvoir's *The Second Sex* (1949) and Viola Klein's *The Feminine Character* (1946) were rediscovered and reissued to increase the attack and to hammer home the basic claim that Freud had conflated "sex" (the biological or anatomical) and "gender" (the social) in female development. From many different angles, the "phallocentrism" (a word originally coined by Ernest Jones) of Freud's views was noted, and, generally, the period of infant development prior to the differentiations Freud described, the pre-Oedipal, came to be the only period feminists judged uncorrupted by Freudian misunderstandings. Not coincidentally, the pre-Oedipal period became the focus, then, of feminist efforts to find a time of innocence, and thus of fresh possibility, prior to what came to be called "the social construction of gender." Eventually, however, this important but sometimes wild critical assault was tempered, and by the late 1970s Freud was being read with much greater appreciation—and in a way that actually moved psychoanalytic practitioners to a major reconsideration of Freud's views on female psychology and that also exploited rising psychoanalytic interest in the pre-Oedipal period.[26]

But it is interesting to note that, although the vast preponderance of biographical work on Freud is by men, feminists have seldom used the genre for their critique. There were, however, three biographical speculations by women in this period: two were French, Marthe Robert's *From Oedipus to Moses* (1974; English, 1976), and Marie Balmary's *Psychoanalyzing Psychoanalysis* (1979; English, 1982), and one German, Marianne Krüll's *Freud and his Father* (1979; English 1986). These works shared with Helen Puner's postwar volume the assumption that Freud hated his father and also hated being a Jew, the son of a Jewish father. But the assumption played out differently. For example, Robert felt that Freud, trying to free himself of a paternal "mediocrity who did nothing to overcome the confinement of his existence within the intolerable limits of inferior birth," wanted to be a self-created man, "the son not of any man or country but like the murdered prophet [Moses] only of his work." And she felt that his failure was reflected in his clinical doctrine of the Oedipus Complex. But Marianne Krüll felt that Freud had succeeded, that in his last book he had settled accounts with his father and with his secret wish not to have been born a Jew. This late triumph left the Oedipus Complex doctrine unrevised, however, and Krüll viewed it as an impediment to a truer psychoanalysis, one which would be more attentive to the importance of "the social environment in the socialization of man" and less fixated on intrapsychic conflict.[27]

Krüll noted in the preface to the 1986 translation of her book that she had not been a feminist in 1979, when the German edition was published. But she had since been converted—by her good friend Sophie Freud, Sigmund Freud's granddaughter—and had realized in retrospect that "I unconsciously took a woman's stand against the extremely patriarchal Oedipus theory. I also believe that my picture of Freud as a frightened and bewildered, yet courageous and curious, little boy is a view not easily reached by most men, and also not by those women who accept their subordinate role in our male society." This supposedly feminist view of Freud embroiled in his father rivalry and denigrating women as a consequence has its counterpart in the trend that appeared in this period among male biographers. While the female expositors were focusing on Freud's relationship with his father, the men argued that Freud's relationship with his mother had been misconstrued by Jones, Schur, and all other orthodox Freudians. As Peter Homans, a Chicago-based sociological expositor has said in summary: "Jones's exclusively Oedipal interpretations of Freud's relationships and conflicts have made it difficult to introduce the idea of earlier developmental lines into the study of Freud's life, such as the persistence of maternal motifs in his intimate dealings with other men."[28] (I think one can see—in retrospect—a foreshadowing within this contra dance of biographical concerns much of the 1980s general cultural ferment over who is to blame for *la condition masculine*—indulgent mothers or unsatisfactory, uninvolved fathers. Since this debate was also common in the early 1950s under the popular title Momism, it is not surprising that there is an underground channel, so to speak, connecting the two eras in the specific little domain of Freud biography.)

Devotees of the "self psychology" espoused by the Chicago analyst Heinz Kohut, including Kohut himself, have developed the idea that

▼ ▼ ▼ ▼ ▼

Freud's creativity was a matter of his narcissistic transferences and displacements, which carried over into his entire creation of his bond to his adoring mother.[29] The pre-Oedipal motif has been worked out by Kleinian expositors such as Richard Wollheim in *Sigmund Freud* (1971), and from thence it has filtered into the work of Peter Gay, whose *Freud* (1988) will be considered below. Among French biographers influenced by Jacques Lacan, Sigmund Freud's first two years of life with his mother are floridly imagined, but there is also a very clear and interesting, somewhat Lacanian work of the period, Octave Mannoni's *Freud* (1968; English 1971). Mannoni's book is quite unusual for its freedom from chronology; it does offer a narrative of Freud's life, but its order is really thematic, and it makes a truly rare and admirable effort to show how Freud thought his way from one facet of his evolving system to another, how and why he revised his ideas so frequently.[30]

In general, it can be said of this third period in the history of postwar Freud biographies that every school of psychoanalysis—and this was a period of proliferating schools—had its Freud biography and that each sectarian Freud biography showed how Freud could best be understood in the terms of the school. Just as the proliferation of schools and the consequent battles among and splittings within psychoanalytic institutes encouraged abundant polemics, it also stimulated reworkings of almost every important item in the history of Freud biography. Dreams from *The Interpretations of Dreams* many times written about were written about again; Freud's case studies were raked over and reanalyzed from new perspectives; all the schisms in the history of psychoanalysis were rediagnosed by the latter-day schismatics and schism-haters. Similarly, the trend established by Paul Roazen in the late 1960s of writing about Freud's followers grew in this period, and many early analysts were treated biographically, with their adherent or schismatic relations to Freud figuring largely in their stories.

The political and polemical agendas behind psychobiographies became quite widely recognized by the late 1970s, when deconstruction, embraced as a dispeller of illusions about objectivity, took over as the critical method of choice in universities. Also helping to raise consciousness about the battle over Freud were various types of hermeneutical views of psychoanalysis itself, visions of it as a symbol system and as a method for culture decoding rather than as a type of natural science. The key methodological problem of psychobiography was also widely recognized—although such recognition has not yet informed a major historiographical work on psychoanalytic biography and history writing.

▼ ▼ ▼ ▼

That problem is that all types of psychobiography, no matter what their brand of theory, are rooted in the research that relates to childhood, and childhoods, particularly ones lived in eras when childhood was not subject to the sort of study Freud and his followers developed, are notoriously wrapped in obscurity. For Freud's own childhood, the source is Freud himself in the medium of his self-analysis. Birth records may show the number and ages of his parent's children, but only the analyst of himself could say, "I welcomed my one-year-younger brother (who died within a few months) with ill wishes and real infantile jealousy, and . . . his death left the germ of guilt in me."[31]

In the 1970s, revisionists trained their detective skills on the next best thing to new material about Freud's childhood experiences: they sought out archives in Moravia and Vienna to unearth facts about the Freud family during Freud's childhood. On the basis of such facts as the existence of a third woman (perhaps a third wife) in the life of Freud's father, Jacob, many speculations were built. When letters from Freud revealing his infatuation at the age of fifteen with a girl named Gisela Fluss (and with her mother) surfaced, his adolescence became a new focus of interest; and biographers, according to their theories, saw in Freud's letters to two adolescent friends, Emil Fluss and Eduard Silberstein, replays of Freud's pre-Oedipal or of his Oedipal psychodynamics.[32]

The one good product of the search for new facts, particularly when it has been combined with a growing recognition of how difficult it is to reconstruct a nineteenth-century childhood, has been a growing tendency to place Freud in his historical contexts more carefully. Writers with this kind of methodological sophistication are often indebted to the work of Henri Ellenberger or to the methodological critique of the French philosopher Paul Ricoeur in *Freud and Philosophy,* but the most important progenitor of this tendency among historians was Carl Schorske, whose essay collection *Fin de Siècle Vienna* (1980) was extremely influential. Recently Schorske's follower William McGrath, who published *Freud's Discovery of Psychoanalysis* in 1986, has provided important information and interpretation about Freud's relation to liberal political currents in his day and about his search for a political place to stand in the rising anti-Semitic tide of the 1890s. McGrath's notion that Freud tended to reduce political perplexities to psychological dilemmas and fashion theory out of his retreat from the political perplexities strikes me as unsupported by his careful exegesis, but his work is nonetheless important for this salutary contextualizing trend.[33]

Ronald W. Clark's *Freud: The Man and His Cause* (1980), the first

▼▼▼▼▼

full-scale biography to incorporate the new Freud family data and Freud's adolescent letters, is eight years older than Peter Gay's *Freud: A Life for Our Time* (1988), which benefited from the new research and documentation but also suffered from the atmosphere created during the intervening decade by the escalating debunking trend. Clark's book, thus, lacks the magisterial set-everything-right tone of Gay's encyclopedic book, but it did not, on the other hand, conduct an unspoken argument with the *dramatis personae* in a media event like that precipitated by Janet Malcolm's *In the Freud Archives* (1984). This volume by a New York journalist tells the story of how Kurt Eissler at the Sigmund Freud Archives took under his patronage a young psychoanalytic candidate, Jeffrey Masson, to make of him the future archives director, and then was astonished when Masson turned into a Freud detractor and eventually wrote *The Assault on Truth* (1984), whick argued that Freud intentionally suppressed his early "seduction theory" (the idea that Oedipal love stories represent stories of real, not fantasized, incestuous relations) because of a "personal failure of courage."[34]

Also in the cast of this melodrama, which was magnified in the manner of the 1980s media, so preoccupied with scandal and celebrity-making, is Peter Swales, a young Welshman with no formal connection to psychoanalysis and no university training, an autodidact, who has developed quite a reputation both for his remarkable archival detective work and for his debunking biographical speculations. Swales, who is determined to prove that Freud and the Freudians were and are, simply, crazy, wrote a series of papers, most of them privately published, which now turn up in all biographical studies, where they are either dismissed as wild, as they are in Gay's book, or treated with a kind of reverence, as they are in J. N. Isbister's *Freud* (1985), a dreadfully bad volume in which hostile speculations about Freud that had been mounting up since Helen Puner's time are simply asserted, without evidence, but with Swales cited as the authority. The two key interpretive ideas of Puner's work—that Freud hated his Jewish father, and that he made of psychoanalysis a new religion, a religion of sexuality—appear in Isbister as facts. The book is full of ponderous absurdities like this: "Psychoanalysis was for Freud a means whereby he could vicariously enjoy sexual gratification with women."[35]

Peter Gay's *Freud: A Life for Our Time* begins with a list of biographical problem areas, and solves each one as judiciously as possible. As far as evidence can show, no, Freud did not (*pace* Swales) have an affair with his wife's sister Minna; no, the libido theory is not indebted (*pace*

▼ ▼ ▼ ▼ ▼

Swales, again) to Freud's cocaine use; and so on. Like the Jones biography, but written after the end of Anna Freud's reign as biographical conscience, the Gay biography is dedicated to accuracy and to overcoming the Helen Puners of its day. Also like Jones, Gay is an insider biographer, with more access to the archives than those whose hashes he set out to settle, which makes him—depending on the assessor's point of view—more reliable, more beholden, or more resented.

Building on his treasure of sources and using his own previous studies of Freud and of psychoanalysis, Gay presented a Freud who is fallible but basically a son of the Enlightenment, a rigorous scientist, a rationalist with uncanny insight into the irrational. He is a son, also, of his mother, and Gay says (in the manner of all biographies by men after the late 1970s) that he was chiefly limited by being "unconsciously eager to leave some of his ambivalence about his mother unanalyzed" while he concentrated on his father and his Oedipus Complex.[36] This is Jones's Freud brought up to date in terms of the evolving biography literature, the evolving psychoanalytic concern with the pre-Oedipal period, and the evolving debunking tendency—but this last in a very curious way. Gay's *Freud* is not focused on the originary decade of the founding of psychoanalysis. Indeed, it took Jones a third of his pages to arrive at 1900 and *The Interpretation of Dreams*, but Gay gets there in less than a sixth of his. And this is not because Gay has made an argument to the effect that concentrating on the discovery of psychoanalysis is, in some way, distorting the whole story or falling into the genetic fallacy. Rather, it seems to me, his pace acknowledges that the 1890–1900 terrain has become too polemic-strewn and contested for strolling narrative passage. Gay traveled by train, photographing through the windows, outlining, and then conducted his quarrel with preceding biographers indirectly, in the long bibliographic essay situated at the end of his trip. But this tactic entailed that he did not get to the level of querying why the founding decade of psychoanalysis has become so critically embattled, or, even more specifically, to querying why we are now, for example, hearing accusations that Freud, by abandoning "the seduction theory," and psychoanalysts by following him, neglect seduction and child abuse; why we are now hearing charges that a frustrated or mother-fixated Freud overplayed or made a religion of sexuality, which is certainly not as important as he said it was; and so forth.

The result of Gay's attitude is that he does not rise to the level of interpreting the possible meanings of his own subtitle, *A Life for Our Time*. And the unexamined shadow of the Freud debunking in the early

▼ ▼ ▼ ▼ ▼

1980s that falls so heavily over the key first chapter and the rapid first part of Gay's book also marks it off decisively from Ronald Clark's opener, written a decade earlier. But, in general, the two biographies show clearly what different biographical methods and priorities can reveal of the same subject. Clark, who is not analytically trained, lingers over the details of the recent archival research into the Freud family in Moravia and Vienna, devoting two pages to the newly discovered second (perhaps) wife of Jacob Freud; Gay, who is analytically trained but lacks the restraint shown by Jones, simply states that Jacob had three wives and moves right along past family matters to get to the kinds of analytic themes he relishes—Freud's deep ambivalence toward Vienna, Freud's many "mistakes in remembering his childhood" (alleged on p. 11 without documentation). Clark devotes four pages to Freud's infatuation with Gisela Fluss and his inexperience with women, citing many letters; Gay disposes of the Gisela episode in two brisk paragraphs, asserting flatly and blandly that it was a "belated Oedipal infatuation." Clark is very knowledgeable about the history of science, so when he introduced Freud's cocaine experiments in the early 1880s he gave background about the drug and cited Freud's letters about how it affected him; Gay concentrates thematically on how Freud displaced his annoyance at failing to discover cocaine's anesthetizing properties onto his fiancée, who drew him out of his laboratory at the wrong moment. Clark quotes an ebullient letter of Freud's about his joy on receiving a stipend to study in Paris with Jean Charcot and his anticipation of a six-week stay en route with his fiancée; Gay remarks on the visit to Martha Bernays in passing and gets his affectless Freud to Paris as quickly as possible.

In short, while Clark enjoyed Freud's family and love relations, as well as his scientific development, and looked always for the affective side of his subject, Gay was quick and perfunctory on both love and science while he built up his psychodynamic picture. Clark quoted Freud when he wanted to show Freud's feelings, while Gay went straight past feelings to alleged unconscious complexes, offering one-sentence quotes as evidence. But the balance in these books begins to shift as Freud's life unfolds: Gay is better informed about psychoanalysis after the originary decade, and he gives a richer clinical and theoretical picture of its unfolding than Clark is able to provide or than had been provided by any biography adopting Jones's method of treating life and work separately.

These two full-scale biographies of the last decade show, I think, that the limitation upon Freud biographies is no longer chiefly a matter

▼ ▼ ▼ ▼

of materials—of unavailable or unrecovered documents and letters—or a matter of sectarian theories circumscribing portraits. Good Freud biography requires, like any good biography, accuracy without defensiveness (which means both using strict evidentiary rules and analyzing as a cultural historian, not just reacting to ongoing polemics). But in this case it also requires relinquishing the idea that theories—much less a whole science like psychoanalysis—can be explained by or reduced to motivations, as though a theory and a symptom were the same thing. The great weakness in the whole of the Freud biographical literature, in my estimation, is that it is all skewed in the same two ways. First, it is focused on the originary decade of Freud's science to the neglect of his later work and to the neglect of a sense for the evolving whole of his work; and second, the originary decade is itself constantly read simplistically as a record of or a product of Freud's childhood, which has meant that Freud has not emerged as a character, a man with an adult character, a man who could be *portrayed,* not just analyzed with more or less sophisticated versions of his own theories. Both of these limitations are reflected in the persistent idea that Freud's "self-analysis" was confined to the period of the Fliess correspondence and *The Interpretation of Dreams,* whereas it seems obvious that self-analysis was Freud's constant mode and that his later work was as deeply indebted to his *changing* conception of himself as it was to his continued clinical experience. But important self-analytical results from Freud's later years have consistently been overlooked by his biographers.

For the history of psychoanalysis, the fixation on Freud himself and, even more particularly, on the originary decade of Freud's discoveries, has meant that later developments, during Freud's lifetime and especially since, are virtually without history. One can hope that Gay's biography, so encyclopedic and yet so superficially responsive to the moment with which its subtitle—*A Life for Our Time*—seeks to link it, will simply signal that in our time we do not need more biographies of Freud. What we need is a much higher degree of self-consciousness among cultural critics about why and in what changing terms Freud has been so fought over, and fought over with such clamor that it is nearly deafening to turn an ear—analytic or otherwise—on the battle-scene.[37]

It is not surprising, of course, that the man who gave theoretical formulation to the phenomenon of "transference"—to the capacity all people have for playing out upon a later stage their earlier, and often quite unknown, dramas of love and hate and love-and-hate—should be a "transference object" for the particular class of analyst and nonanalyst

▼ ▼ ▼ ▼ ▼

biographer-historians and also much, much more generally across our polysemic culture. We need a history of this transference object. The history might be called $F\_\_\_d$ to acknowledge that this figure is so familiar that any literate person can fill him in acrostic fashion, with a flourish of feeling—positive, negative, in-between, or studiously indifferent; but also to acknowledge that this figure is unknown, a space onto which innumerable stories of individual and cultural desire have been projected, a palimpset so run together that each layer of stories carries an imprint of all the others. Such a history would be very valuable as a deep sounding of how twentieth century people have wanted to understand themselves and to be understood. But more narrowly, $F\_\_\_d$ might help psychoanalysis's history dissolve its Oedipus Complex and develop beyond biography.

▼   This essay was requested by the editors of *Discovering the History of Psychiatry* (New York: Oxford University Press, 1994) edited by Mark S. Micale and Roy Porter; used by permission of Oxford University Press, Inc. It was also published in *Studies in Psychoanalytic Theory,* 1 (1992): 3–21.

8

Hannah Arendt
among Feminists

During Hannah Arendt's last decade, until her death in 1975, feminists of the "second wave" responded to her work as Kate Millett did in *Sexual Politics:* they took up her conceptualizations of such political phenomena as power and violence and employed them for the project of women's liberation. They did not ask that she be a feminist, or assert that there is a womanly way of thinking that she should have achieved; they also did not appropriate her work for considering feminism critically. Arendt herself was certainly aware of the developing feminist movement, but she did not respond to it publicly. She did not think of herself as a feminist and she was deeply skeptical of any single-issue political movement, especially one that brought into question the distinction she drew between the private and the public.

Since Arendt's death, not particular conceptualizations, but the whole terrain of her work and of her life have been thick with feminist commentary and controversy. Panels dedicated to Arendt and feminism appear on the programs of the annual professional meetings of the political scientists and the philosophers; international conferences on the theme have been held in Italy, Germany. In 1995, the twentieth anniversary of her death was being marked with a collection of thirteen American feminist essays followed by an annotated bibliography citing thirty-two pieces in English and many more in German, French, and Italian. As my contribution to a more general collection of essays on Arendt's work published in 1996, also to commemorate the twentieth anniversary of her death, I offered a brief overview of the feminist responses in order to raise some questions about how Hannah Arendt had become both a magnetic figure for American feminist political the-

▼ ▼ ▼ ▼

orists and an exemplum of feminism's current struggle for theoretical direction.[1]

In the first phase of post-1975 feminist writing about Hannah Arendt, which lasted until the late 1980s, Arendt's distinction between the private realm of the household and the public realm of speech and action, the political realm, was lifted out of the broad range of her political theoretical concerns and targeted. Most feminists found this distinction, particularly as she articulated it in *The Human Condition,* to be a hateful legitimation of the relegation of women to the household's "separate sphere." Arendt's firm distinction seemed a kind of Victorian sexism made out of Aristotelian materials. Male citizens, Arendt seemed to be saying about the ancient Greeks, acted in public, creating and sustaining public spaces, having been given freedom from necessity and freedom to enjoy political life, to be actors, by the women and slaves and other noncitizens who performed the domestic labor and produced the offspring in households. She also seemed to be saying uncritically that this state of affairs—a politics predicated on domestic slavery—was the truly human human condition.

Actually, the household or private realm which Arendt distinguished so sharply from the public realm was characterized in *The Human Condition* in a number of different ways, and with quite different valuations. As a realm of production and necessity, it was clearly a lesser realm. But, more positively, it was also the realm of privacy, of intimacy, of protection from the harsh struggle of public life; a place for important prepolitical processes like the education of children, and a place for crucial extrapolitical activities like critical reflection and judging, for the peacefulness needed to engage in the interiorized "life of the mind," the interior dialogue of thinking. As in many dimensions of Hannah Arendt's complex political theory, which is a texture of distinctions, evaluation depends upon where you stand to evaluate. From the point of view of a person concerned to praise and celebrate the political realm, the household is inglorious, determined, mute. But if the private realm disappears or is absorbed into social and economic processes, or into the political realm itself, the conditions for tyranny or authoritarianism and, in the modern world, totalitarianism are present. Totalitarianism, as Hannah Arendt analyzed it in *The Origins of Totalitarianism,* is the form of government in which there is no action or persuasive speech in public spaces—that is, in which politics has been eliminated—and in which there is also no privacy. Even the most intimate bonds of family are

▼ ▼ ▼ ▼

corrupted or disrupted by a totalitarian regime that tries to lodge itself everywhere, driving right into the genealogies, the minds, and the hearts of its subjects.

The Human Condition was, I have argued in my biography of Arendt, written under the shadow of the analysis in The Origins of Totalitarianism, and it offers the private/public distinction—recommends it—as a bulwark against the totalitarianizing character of the modern world. In On Revolution, Arendt went further, and offered the distinction as a bulwark against the self-destructive, self-devouring potentialities of modern revolutions. Revolutions that focus on addressing the realm of necessity, "the social question" of how necessities are produced, supplied, distributed, or the social-justice question of how different groups are employed and organized, that is, revolutions that do not focus on the political question of how a union of people is to be constituted for the possibility of continually renewing political speech and action, will be revolutions that eventually lose their meanings as new beginnings and succumb to depoliticization—sclerosis, as it were, of the political. They can become pretotalitarian.

Arendt's perspective can be compassed more generally by saying that she was trying to point out a vast modern political dilemma—a potentially or incipiently tragic dilemma. The modern industrial-technological possibilities that have been slowly changing the way in which the necessities of life are supplied and the generations raised and educated are doing two things at once: they are progressively rendering slavery—of subject peoples and of women—obsolete, and they are destroying the boundaries between household realms and public realms. Emancipation or universal citizenship for the formerly enslaved or marginalized is the great good of the modern revolutionary period; but the great danger in this period, in Arendt's estimation, is the emergence of a hybrid realm, neither private nor public, in which necessities are supplied in ways that cannot be independent of governance—they cannot be separate, unregulated—and that require laboring activity that infringes on any other form of life. So modern political theory has been organized by a deep quarrel between those who think conservatively that government, for the sake of endless increase, should be as little involved as possible in the emergent social realm and those who think liberally or socialistically that government should control this realm so that it can be made as equitable as possible, so that it can be a realm of social justice. But Hannah Arendt subscribed to none of the range of positions on this basic question because she thought that economic processes could and should be contained and controlled by economic means, that is, administratively. Politics, for her, was something else again—not administration, but "words and deeds."

The feminists who approached Arendt's work in the 1970s, looking to her as a major political theorist and as a woman—the only European or American woman other than Rosa Luxemburg, Simone de Beauvoir, and Simone Weil who wrote philosophically about politics at the "classic" level—approached as liberationists. Their emphasis was on breaking the bonds of discrimination that kept women, despite their attained rights as citizens, in households and in the roles of domestic laborers and mothers, not on pointing to the dangers to either the private realm or the political realm of modern economic and social conditions. Their desire was to see women become fully and equally political and also free from the subordination of the household realm itself, where "the personal is political." And from this point of view, of course, Arendt's emphasis—although she certainly had no trace of conservative opposition to the modern movement for equality—seemed misplaced, even perverse.

And those of this liberationist generation who criticized Hannah Arendt for ignoring what the sway of the household and the development of "the social" meant for women were certainly correct. She did not ask how the conversion of households in the process of industrialization and urbanization from productive, economic spheres into "separate spheres," not productive but only reproductive—motherhood spheres, as it were—affected women, either those pushed into the working class or those defined only by their mothering roles in households. She did not ask how "the social" shaped life in households, setting the subordination of women there more on a specifically sexual and reproductive basis, less on a laboring basis. "The personal is the *social*" was not her topic, even though she was quite aware of the social *Frauenproblem*, as a book review she wrote in 1933 makes quite clear.[2] In that review, she outlined sharply the complexities of the German situation then, in which women had achieved many political rights but were still trapped in social contradictions as mothers and as second-class workers. But she also agreed with the socialist position, the one also taken by Rosa Luxemburg, that a "women's movement" (or a women's political party) was inappropriate because it would be too abstract, too focused on specifically women's issues and not focused enough on the larger issues facing the working class as a whole. This position, which is, of course, still the position of many socialists, did not, however, inform any of Arendt's later political

▼ ▼ ▼ ▼

theorizing. Or, one might say, it did not break through her overriding concern with the household sphere as a sphere of protection against the continued expansion and extension of the social.

Her stance was, in fact, so resolute that when she applied its terms to the scene of American race relations in the 1950s, she ended up alienating another group seeking liberation. Considering the civil rights movement's school-integration effort in Little Rock, Arendt objected to children being asked to do political work and to educational institutions being selected as the sites for political action, because children and schools were, in her terms, part of the private sphere, prepolitical. She later used similar arguments against politicizing universities and specifically against "open admissions" to bring in more disadvantaged young people. For these judgments, as well as for her criticism of the 1960s Black Power movement and its debt to the theory of violence in Frantz Fanon's *Wretched of the Earth,* which she thought implied destruction of the political realm, Arendt has been sharply criticized by African American intellectuals, most recently by a younger generation of feminists.[3]

After the early 1970s, as the American feminist movement itself evolved, the theoretical aspiration for supporting liberation as equality began to become overshadowed theoretically—if not in terms of practical politics, and if not among either socialist feminists or feminists of color—by a search for ways of addressing sexist denigrations of the particular traits that being raised by women and kept in the household sphere had inculcated in women. So-called cultural feminism or gynocentric feminism aimed to celebrate womanly virtues—the ability to sustain relationships, mothering or caretaking skills, emotional richness and freedom from the distortions of patriarchal behavior and thought—with the hopes that achieving equality would not imply the loss of those virtues and that embrace of these virtues would give the feminist movement much-needed solidarity. Political participation and equality were less important theoretically to cultural feminists than the cultivation and promotion of female virtue—the triumph of these virtues was, in effect, envisioned as women's liberation. Cultural revolution superseded political revolution. Arendt's work, then, seemed to be not only underappreciative of emancipation and of the social question, but totally unappreciative of the specificities of women's lives and virtues and cultural possibilities. Arendt seemed as unconcerned with women as any patriarchalist.

Among the cultural feminists who criticized Arendt as a woman who thought like a man there was a shared—sometimes tacit, sometimes

▾ ▾ ▾ ▾

explicit—assumption that women should and naturally do think in gyn-ocentric terms and always within the fundamental framework of sexual difference. Women's categories are FEMALE and MALE, with FEMALE being the "good" category, and all other differences being lined up with this fundamental one. PRIVATE, in this perspective, is valued as a female realm where virtues of caretaking and forming relationships are nurtured, and PUBLIC is a realm in which struggle and violence are corrupting, where machismo and harsh manipulation of others reign. Arendt's distinction, then, looks like a retrograde and patriarchal celebration of just this deval-ued masculine public space.

In most of the feminist literature on Arendt from the mid-1970s to the mid-1980s, there is a theme of castigation and lament.[4] How could a woman entertain a distinction that seemed to have no liberationist potential whatsoever, a distinction that could and did and still does serve both sexism and political conservativism more generally? How could a woman subscribe to a distinction that completely foreclosed the strong feminist insight that "the personal is political" and called for keeping the personal resolutely away from the political? In an often cited essay, the poet Adrienne Rich called Arendt's *Human Condition* a "lofty and crip-pled book" and claimed that it "embodies the tragedy of a female mind nourished on male ideology."[5]

Rich's assessment can stand as a marker for the cultural feminist attitude that a next generation of feminist theorists slowly and ambivalently rejected.[6] The women of this cohort, who began to write in the mid-1980s, saw things differently when they approached Hannah Arendt's work. They could, first of all, appreciate that even though she did not consider the situation of women explicitly, she had understood quite well the special virtues that inhere in people who have been denied access to the political realm, who have been kept in service or in par-iahdom. But she had come to this understanding as a Jew and as a his-torian of European Jewry, not as a feminist. Arendt's first book had been a biography of the Berlin salon hostess Rahel Varnhagen, and this book became a touchstone for the feminists who wanted to understand Arendt's relation to "identity politics" (as the phrase of the early 1980s put it).

Different marginalized and scapegoated groups, Arendt had shown in *Rahel Varnhagen* and in *The Origins of Totalitarianism*—where she had compared turn-of-the-century Jews to homosexuals, using Marcel Proust as her example—are characterized by different social character types and

▼ ▼ ▼ ▼ ▼

different historical types of exclusion from politics. Further, people in such groups are often in other groups as well; their identities are plural—they are women and Jews like Rahel Varnhagen, for example—and they thus look at the political realm from diverse perspectives. These Arendtian insights were taken up by feminists who criticized "cultural feminism" for overgeneralizing about women, for saying that all women—regardless of class, race, ethnicity—share the same womanly virtues. In these debates, American feminism itself became a field of controversy as women described by different adjectives, often many different adjectives, struggled to determine whether they had anything culturally in common and to find ways to talk across their differences of background and purpose. They brought Arendt into the multiculturalizing moment of feminism by acknowledging that she had—for reasons that she had articulated quite self-consciously and politically—written her major works of the late 1940s and 1950s as a Jew.

"When one is attacked as a Jew," Arendt had said retrospectively in a 1964 interview, "one responds as a Jew." And then she had, later, during the controversy that erupted over her *Eichmann in Jerusalem* (1963), made it just as clear that her "as a Jew" identification was not a matter of love of the Jewish people—because love, she said, was something she felt for individuals, in private; it was, rather, a matter of public, political choice. She was, thus, distancing herself from a range of ideas about identity as based on "nature" or on loving identification (of the sort implied by the phrase "woman-identified woman") that cultural feminists had adopted and that cultural feminism's feminist critics described, in quite Arendtian terms, as falsifying, essentializing, and sentimental. Neither the strictly biological nor the cultural-mystical definitions of "woman" are adequate to the political complexities of being a woman and being a woman in a context, from a context with many more identity possibilities in it than FEMALE and MALE.

This younger generational cohort of feminists also reassessed Arendt's private/public distinction. The importance of protecting a private realm from the encroachments of the social or the political was more apparent to this group because hard-won protections of privacy, particularly the 1973 Supreme Court decision in Roe v. Wade, were then under assault. And, more generally, the increasing sexualization of the social realm, including the expansion of the pornography industry into new technological media, had impelled some feminists—under the theoretical leadership of Catharine MacKinnon—to call for increased regulation of the private sphere as well as qualifications of First Amendment

▼ ▼ ▼ ▼ ▼

rights, and a deep quarrel had opened between these feminists and those who objected to the antipornography campaign's attitude toward protection of privacy. That antipornography feminists could make alliances with far right political activists who were sexist and homophobic, and anti-choice on the abortion question, shocked theorists into reconsidering the private/public distinction and newly appreciating its Arendtian function—its function as a bulwark against totalitarianizing trends, in general and as advocated by feminists.

The younger generation of theorists also recontextualized Arendt's private/public distinction in the larger texture of distinctions that make up *The Human Condition*. They noticed that Arendt did not generally operate with binary concepts, that the private/public distinction is, in fact, unusual in her work and it is, further, tied to the third concept of "the social" as a hybrid modern realm, a threat to both the private and the public. Attention was turned to the fact that the main axis of distinctions in *The Human Condition* contains the troika labor, work, and action (and speech), three modalities of activity, and that there are also six "conditions of human existence," which Arendt named life, natality, mortality, earth, worldliness, and plurality. The last three of these are, respectively, the preconditions for the activities: labor is a process on and of the earth, a "metabolism of nature"; work is the fabrication of the things, the artifacts, the cultural objects, that make up the world; and action requires a plurality of human beings (since action is not possible if human beings lose their distinctiveness, as they do when they live in a mass society or, more horribly, when they are reduced to the torture of concentration camp existence). Feminists who have reflected on these Arendtian categories of activity and condition have generally been more receptive than others to Arendt's overall approach.

But some have also tried to adapt this overall approach to feminism and its particular concerns, and for that purpose the concept of natality has often been singled out. Natality, which Arendt used to emphasize both the new beginnings of the human generations and the new beginnings represented by political action, has seemed to feminists to be the quintessential female contribution—so it is, indirectly, a celebration of motherhood—and also an antidote to the masculine imagery associated with politics as action and speech. In effect, the concept of natality has been used to make Arendt's private realm into the realm of motherhood and the font of all politics—to revalue it positively. Arendt becomes a kind of feminist, or at least not a sexist, in this expansion of the cultural feminist frame into the larger domains explored in *The Human Condition*.

▼ ▼ ▼ ▼

But not all of the commentators who have focused on the overall approach of *The Human Condition* have tried to appropriate Arendt for feminism by singling out the natality concept and extolling motherhood. Mary Dietz, for example, has noticed that *The Human Condition* presents a vast modern dilemma unfolding along with the one I highlighted above.[7] In addition to the titanic conflict between the social and the political, propelled by modern industrializing and technologizing in the domain of labor and by the instrumentalizing of life in the domain of work, Arendt noted that this same alliance of labor and work to defeat action contains an antagonism of labor and work. The industrializing and technologizing that has elevated labor and laboring people ("animal laborans" in Arendt's terms) into dominance, threatens work and people who do work ("homo faber" in Arendt's terms). Laboring, processing the earth's resources into life necessities, grows like a jungle and makes fabrication, the creation of artifacts and cultural products, inefficacious, obsolete. Making furniture for the world, including the monuments and memorials that tell the stories of political action, becomes less and less possible as a consumer culture focuses on the pursuit of abundance, on nondurable goods, planned obsolescence, automation (and now telecommunications). Dietz argues that Arendt presented not the private/public distinction but *this* struggle in gendered terms—women are associated with the laboring process, men with the fabrication—and that Arendt understood the way in which the "battle of the sexes" is played in and through these domains. Dietz also suggests that by contrasting both labor and work with action Arendt was presenting action as beyond gendering, as a domain in which all people can be free. Action is, as Dietz puts it "beyond the phallocentric:gynocentric divide."

As I look back over the territories of these contestations and appropriations, it seems to me that there are three major questions that were raised not so much in this history as by it; questions that can be articulated by treating this history as itself an exemplum. And, specifically, I will treat it as an exemplum that offers possibilities for feminist reflection on Hannah Arendt's work that I would like to point out, gesture toward—possibilities that are marked in Mary Dietz's essay with the phrase "beyond the phallocentric:gynocentric divide."

Let me start with the question raised by the cultural feminist critique of Arendt. What does it mean to claim or to believe that women think differently than men, that women's experiences—even if they have

▼ ▼ ▼ ▼ ▼

great diversity across ethnic, racial, and class groups—have a commonality that is expressed in the method or form or the content of their thinking?

It seems to me that Hannah Arendt's life and work show that the cultural feminist claim that women think as women and gynocentrically, putting women at the center of their concern, is overgeneralized. I think that the most that can be said about women's thinking is that it will have a strand in it that is determined by being a woman, and that this strand may for some women be the major strand, while for others it will be subsidiary to other strands that arise from other ingredients of experience and condition. For some women, thinking will be relatively genderless—as Hannah Arendt, in *The Life of the Mind,* claimed that *all* thinking is. My differentiating conclusion could be said more succinctly in psychoanalytic terms: all thinking occurs on a narcissistic basis to some degree—so men think as men and androcentrically (which usually means phallocentrically), women as women and gynocentrically, to some degree. The narcissistic bases for the two sexes will always be different, to individually varying degrees. Further, women's narcissism, under conditions of sexism, will always be reactive to the oppressor's narcissism, while male narcissism, although it may be reactively wounded or warped by the conditions sexism produces, will not be reactive *because it is oppressed.* Different historical and cultural situations will promote or inhibit differently the narcissism of one sex or the other or both.

Hannah Arendt thought more as a Jew than as a woman—history demanded that of her, so to speak—but the narcissistically feminine strand in her thought does not seem to me a difficult matter to identify, since it is of a piece with the insight that she said Rahel Varnhagen had come to at the end of her life about her Jewishness: she accepted, even celebrated her Jewishness and said that she would on no account have wanted to miss what being Jewish had meant for her.[8] Arendt often stated—most clearly in her essay on Rosa Luxemburg—that her own position on the *Frauenproblem* was, basically, "Vive la petit différence!" What this meant was: Celebrate who you are in your distinctiveness, in your not-that, not-the-other; do not try to *be* or *become* the other. Plurality, the precondition of action, includes among its possibilities plurality of sex/gender identities, and this plurality, like others, should be respected.

Distinctiveness means nonconformity, which Arendt presented as preserved in thinking itself by dialogue—what she called "the dialogue between me and myself." It was not the orientation or the content of

▼ ▼ ▼ ▼ ▼

thinking that Arendt considered crucial to it, but its interactivity, its internal mobility and freedom from rigidities of ideology or received ideas. Thinking is the quintessentially human internal-mental activity, just as the quintessential external activity is being political, speaking and acting, opening political spaces; and both of these activities are, in Arendt' view, more important *qua* activities than in the specificities of their content because it is as activities that they perpetuate themselves, renew themselves. Further, thinking's activity in the modern world, as Arendt understood it, cannot rely on tradition, much less on received ideas or ideology, because historical realities have rendered these useless, obsolete, out of touch. She imagined thinking as a process of gathering up the fragments of broken traditions and assembling them anew, in something new.

This reflection suggests a second question: How and why has sexual difference come to operate like a received idea—a fixation point—in feminism, and must it remain so? This question has been raised by historians of feminism within the last several years—it is the focus, for example, of Carol Lee Bacchi's *Same Difference: Feminism and Sexual Difference* (1990), which argues that "perceiving issues in terms of women's sameness to or difference from men" is "politically unwise," because it "diverts attention from the inadequacy of social institutions"[9] Such histories make it clear how the political contexts of Anglo-American feminism have promoted the sameness-difference focus and reinforced the alignment of feminists with either "cultural feminism" (stressing difference) or radical feminism (stressing future possibilities for sameness). And it is certainly appropriate psychologically to argue that the question of difference reflects the basic narcissism of men and women, both being threatened by the difference of "the other." But I think that the exemplum of feminist commentary on Hannah Arendt shows something further.

Theorists working within movements of liberation think initially from within particular experiences of oppression—nationalists from within experiences of national oppression, people of color from within experiences of racism, Jews from within experiences of anti-Semitism, women from within experiences of sexism. But the measure of their movement's longevity and vitality is the extent to which they then come to think more broadly, both in terms of others' experiences of oppression, for the sake of coalition building, and in terms of historical grasp, for the sake of freely imagining the future, imagining the future to be as free of repetition compulsion as possible. Arendt's work is a vivid example

▼▼▼▼▼

of how someone initially politically identified with the Jews and with Zionism pushed outward.

Arendt's political philosophy could be said to have arisen out of her reply to the the anguished question that every Jew of her generation was compelled to pose by the Holocaust—why the Jews? Her reply reached out across the nineteenth century, into the history of imperialism, the rise of "the social" as capitalism expanded relentlessly, in geographical terms and into the political realm; as European states became businesses and extended their enterprises around the world; as the modern nation-states, so intolerant of their own minorities and so prejudiced against their colonials, were instituted. But her reply was also explicitly framed as a *political* reply, ultimately an analysis of a novel *form of government,* because she felt that the European Jews of her parents' and her own generation, being politically inexperienced and failing to distinguish between their social lives and their political lives, had misestimated the threat of political anti-Semitism. Specifically, they had sought social acceptance, assimilation, not realizing that this would be worth nothing unless their rights were politically and legally secured; they did not grasp that the real threat to their community lay with a political party that put itself above the law, saying "the Führer's will is the law" and thereby destroying law as that which should be above all individual citizens and groups.

Arendt's analysis was, I think, historically the most rich and illuminating of any produced in response to the Holocaust. But I also think that it is not generalizable to other types and historical courses of oppression—to racism, to sexism. Each time Arendt used her framework to discuss these prejudices and their courses, she missed important differences between them and anti-Semitism; the analogizing of the prejudices blocked her view. Her feminist critics have noted this problem again and again, but not given it the analysis it calls for. For Arendt, all oppressed people were oppressed like the Jews. For many of her critics, all oppressed people are oppressed like women. The differences between the prejudices falls out of the theoretical picture either way.

Feminism has begun to extend its theoretical reach, but it is still tied, repetitively, to what Mary Dietz called "the phallocentric:gynocentric divide." It is tied to the categories male/female, masculine/feminine. It cannot yet see sexism as part of a much larger picture of prejudice types and a much larger set of questions about why people need prejudices, what functions they serve. When the frame is broadened in this way, a third question appears on its horizon. The conclusion that extrap-

▼ ▼ ▼ ▼ ▼

olating from one experience of prejudice and discrimination to another, analogizing the prejudices, is problematic has only been drawn on the basis of realizations that victim groups' self-understandings are not being taken into account—black women's feeling that racism, not sexism, is their main problem, for example. But the problem of analogizing the prejudices and the experiences of victim groups has not been clearly formulated theoretically. What is there in the specificity of sexism as a prejudice—held by individuals and vastly institutionalized—that distinguishes it from anti-Semitism, from racism, and that distinguishes the experience of its victims? What is it that makes the private/public distinction central to feminist theory, while it is not central to current Zionism, to Black Pride or Afrocentricity, to other forms of single-group (defensive) self-assertion?

The key to pursuing this question, it seems to me, is an initial admission that not all prejudiced people are prejudiced alike—there is no such creature as "the prejudiced personality" and no single psychic or social dynamic underlying all prejudices. I would argue—on the basis of psychoanalytic characterology—that there exist fundamentally different character types, each of which uses a particular type of prejudice as part of its defensive structure, as what might be called its social mechanism of defense. The major character types seem to me to be three in number, and I will call them in clinical shorthand obsessional, hysterical, and narcissistic.[10] The rigidly, conformistically structured obsessional type, commonly quite paranoid, is suited to hold prejudices against groups construed as international commericial conspiracies of infiltrating, dirty, or polluting secret agents who can burrow into the obessional's fortressed self. All such groups—especially immigrant commercial groups—are "Jewish." Hysterical people, volatile, chameleonic, theatrical, and typically divided or split psychically into an eroticized self and a chaste self, are prejudiced against groups construed as hypersexual and threatening "from below" the bulwarks of civilization and the natural hierarchies of human society. Finally, narcissists, arrogant and unempathic, who imagine themselves as their own living standards of measurement, are prejudiced against groups construed as sexually other, threatening to the coherence of narcissistic bodily and mental ideals and transgressive of gender identities, and in need of rigorous control to keep them from asserting their otherness, to keep them in the role of mirrors, enhancing to the narcissist's sense of self.

A model like this, even sketched in such quick strokes, without theoretical rationale, can raise important questions about the ways in

▼ ▼ ▼ ▼ ▼

which anti-Semitism—the prejudice Arendt dissected so brilliantly—and sexism—the one she could hardly see—differ in terms of their service as psychic defenses. But this kind of distinction-making can also run along more political theoretical lines—less psychological, more Arendtian. The main danger of sexism—or rather the phenomenon that marks its dangerous ascendancy—is not collapse of the private/public distinction. This was the danger of anti-Semitism as it grew into totalitarianism, which entailed a complete erasure of privacy, even of the privacy of people's thoughts. Such a collapse, as I implied before, could, given the material precondition of drastic socioeconomic decline, very well follow upon sustained, progressive erosions of First Amendment rights such as those being mounted now, with which antipornography feminists are unfortunately associated. But this kind of arena, fundamentally anti-state, is really an arena made for people whose prejudices resemble anti-Semitism, obsessional people who see infiltrating conspiracies everywhere, who fear penetration of the fortresses of their defenses by polluting agents. The main danger of sexism, by contrast, is complete separation of private and public and assignment of women to the private, an extrapolitical realm where law does not reach, rights cannot be secured, and only the master's will orders life. Essentially, such a domain has historically functioned as an arena for the control of reproduction, either by permitting men to insist that males are really the agents of reproduction or by permitting them to control the bodies of women.[11]

For the sake of further comparison, it is important to note that neither separation of the private and the public nor collapse of the distinction has been central to the theorizing of victims of white racism. Neither the New World descendants of African slaves nor the descendants of colonialized Africans think in these categories. They have been oppressed by people who have thought of them as servants—as naturally fitted for being servants—in households and in larger entities imagined as vast households, societal households, national households, indeed, imagined as what Hannah Arendt called "the social." Their oppressors' main psychological need is for male and female servants who care for them, support them, give them inside or alongside their households a second family, which can be the quasi-familial object of their desires while at the same time being not-family, not being incestuous parental or sibling objects of desire. Racist ruling elites and less successful racists imaging themselves as elites are *patrons,* no matter what the size of their real or imaginary, rural or urban estates. Racism is most dangerous when this expansionary vision of households with natural servants is strongest,

▼ ▼ ▼ ▼ ▼

so the liberationist rhetoric of racism's victims focuses on fighting free of the master's house—whether that is a single family dwelling or a nation.

The analytical categories that different victim groups need and find to present the nature of their oppression and organize their resistances and rebellions are not the same, and should not be. Feminists who recognize this stand at the edge of a complex theoretical problem of integrating perspecitves, both for political coalition building and for taking into account the complex experiences of people who are mulitiply victimized—Jewish women, black women, for examples—and people who are suited to be victims for any type of prejudiced person—homosexuals, for example, who can be targeted for their "Jewish" qualities, for their hypersexuality, or for the threat they pose to gender identity. The future of feminist theory, I think, lies in these territories.

I do not think that Hannah Arendt's political theorizing is going to be very helpful in this project—although it has been and will continue to be crucial for understanding anti-Semitism in itself and as the ideological centerpiece of Nazi totalitarianism. But, on the other hand, the encounter that the current generation of feminist political theorists has had with Arendt's work has certainly helped dislodge the feminist theoretical fixation on the question of sexual difference and the single-minded view of the public/private distinction as in every way—for every group—a distinction to be overcome. The encounter with Arendt has helped feminism in this way because she would not fit into the feminist frameworks the theorists tried to apply to her. In her intellectual greatness, Arendt has had her greatest value to feminism, I think, precisely because feminists have said clearly "*she* was not one of us" and proceeded from there to an examination not of her but *of feminism* in light of her life and work.

▼ This essay was requested for *Hannah Arendt: Twenty Years Later* (Cambridge, Mass.: MIT Press, 1996), edited by Lawrence May and Jerome Kohn.

▼ ▼ ▼ ▼ ▼

9

The Exemplary Independence
of Hannah Arendt

Since Hannah Arendt's death in 1975, three generations of American commentators on her life and work have contributed to her reputation. They have produced a shelf of books, many dozens of scholarly articles, and myriad book reviews for the volumes of her writings that have appeared posthumously. Off the publishing stage, the archive of graduate seminar papers and doctoral dissertations grows, and conferences are convened. Even without a school of proponents or any prominent epigones, Hannah Arendt stands out among the "public intellectuals" in her European émigré cohort as a figure still to be reckoned with when serious talk turns to the political and moral condition of our nation and our world. Passions flow over her oeuvre, her legacy, as they once used to flow over the statements she made as a presence, a unique personality.

The first generation of Hannah Arendt's posthumous commentators was made up of her longer-lived and her slightly younger European émigré and American contemporaries. Even before they commented on her legacy, many who had made Arendt's acquaintance with *The Origins of Totalitarianism* (1951) joined in the campaign waged twelve years later against her *Eichmann in Jerusalem* (1963). They had advanced from the left and from the right on the hard-to-locate territory of her independence, and they kept up their maneuvers straight into their memoirs. The second generation is of an age to have been her students in the late sixties; they now chair departments, go to conferences, edit magazines, contemplate celebritydom, fight cultural wars, and still mull over their old questions about the way things should be in a democracy, about the topics of Arendt's *On Revolution*. The third generation, in kindergarten and elementary school when Hannah Arendt died, now twentysome-

▼▼▼▼▼

things and thirtysomethings, is comprised of the much discussed and worried over inheritors of the sixties generation's hopes and, especially, disillusionments. By e-mail they communicate about selected statements by Arendt on identity, appearing in public, natality.

Over the course of the two decades of accumulating Arendt commentary, it seems to me, three interrelated themes in her work have been magnets, each for one of the generations, and each with the eventual result of a particular distortion. Similarly, an image of her as a person, a persona, has dominated each generation's collective imagination and the result here, too, has been a particular distortion. In this essay, I briefly tour these territories, which I visit only as ideal types, not by reviewing individual contributions or noting exceptions to the types.

But my main purpose is different. As Arendt's former student, one from the late sixties, and as her biographer, but also as an intellectual situated now, uneasily, worriedly, in a world-historical moment that I think she would have found strange, I want to reflect on her character and on elements of it that have been exemplary throughout the postwar period, across waves of change, and that are available to us now, all intervening distortions not withstanding. I want to think along the terms of a project that her teacher and friend Karl Jaspers was making sketches for just before he died in 1969: a meditation, focused on Arendt's life and work, about what conditions subtend, permit, and promote independence of thought or independent-mindedness, what is known in German as *Selbstdenken*. This is a project that, in quite different terms, became Arendt's own in the unfinished "Judging" section of *The Life of the Mind*.

Understanding Totalitarianism

In *The Origins of Totalitarianism*, Arendt first articulated her most fundamental thought—as an alarm, a dire warning. She claimed that politics—in the sense of citizens speaking and acting in a "world," a public space, variously allowed by different forms of government and secured by their laws—appears only under certain historical conditions, and can disappear. Further, a form of government can come about—as she knew as a "stateless person" and a survivor of the Twelve-Year Reich—that has the unprecedented and hideously contradictory consequence of making politics disappear *completely*. Totalitarianism, a novelty among forms of government, is not, like tyranny, the atrophy of politics; it is the radical elimination of politics brought about by methodically eliminating the very humanity of, first, a selected group and, eventually, any group, by

▼ ▼ ▼ ▼ ▼

making humans superfluous as human beings. Such is totalitarianism's "radical evil."[1]

This profound chord of Arendt's thought provoked the commentators of her generation, but only in a very partial and, ultimately, deleterious form. Her argument that Nazi Germany and the Soviet Union under Stalin were instances, despite their very great differences in evolution and ideological origins, of fundamentally the same form of government, totalitarianism, precipitated a quarrel from the political left and great abuse from the political right. Her analysis got caught up in Cold War polemics, and, among her contemporaries, it has stayed there even after the Berlin Wall came down.

From the political right came acceptance of Arendt's analysis because anticommunism could be very effectively promoted as antitotalitarianism: opposing not just the Soviet Union but Marxism as an ideology took on the moral rightness of opposing Nazi Germany and Nazism as an ideology. Arendt realized very soon after the 1951 publication of her book that the mainstays of anticommunism in America were people who had been communists—"the ex-communists"—and whose rigid intellectual mode was, in their new allegiance, unchanged. The mainstays were characterologically ideologues, who could change causes without dislocation and whose diktat was, simply, that the end justifies the means. The end of victory for democracy over totalitarianism justifies any means for promoting democracy—including totalitarian means. And it is no exaggeration to say that this intellectual mode, one that forbids independent thinking, has been the greatest detriment to our national political life since the 1950s: it has helped make moralistic "patriotic" crusading for democracy into such a norm that it can hardly be recognized any more as the aberration from American constitutional traditions that it is.

On the left, communists and socialists objected both to Arendt's disregard of their idea that a fascist regime is the very opposite of a Marxist revolution, and to her disregard of their argument that the Soviet Union under Stalin was a betrayal of Marxism. This leftist perspective made it virtually impossible to appreciate Arendt's attention to the *elements* of totalitarianism and the *anti*political processes by which these elements had crystallized and might again crystallize. She seemed from this perspective to be incapable of seeing that the Soviet revolutionaries were idealists with a vision of social justice.

Arendt herself had great respect for Marx when she wrote *The Origins of Totalitarianism,* and she also made a clear distinction between

▼ ▼ ▼ ▼ ▼

Lenin and Stalin. But she, unlike her critics on the left, became steadily more deeply probing about Marxism as she worked her way in the early 1950s toward *The Human Condition* and *On Revolution*. The result of Hannah Arendt's critical journey is immediately apparent in her portrait of Marx as the theorist of labor—neither work nor action—in *The Human Condition* and in her strident attack throughout *On Revolution* upon Marxists who elevated concern with "the social question" over political action, the principles of the French Revolution over the principles of the American Revolution. But the course of her thought is perhaps starkest in the passages in her correspondence with Jaspers in which he challenged her to reconsider Marx himself.

Their exchange began in 1951 when Arendt praised an essay of Jaspers's on Freud and Marx and he wrote to her: "You speak favorably of Marx's passion for justice, which links him to Kant . . . Marx's passion seems to me impure at its root, itself unjust from the outset, drawing its life from the negative without an image of man, the hate incarnate of a pseudo-prophet in the style of Ezekiel." She replied to this by defending Marx not as a scholar or a philosopher, but as a "rebel and a revolutionary" who had really understood what she called the "de-naturing of man and of nature by the economy of commodities." Jaspers held his ground and spoke about Marx's "intolerance, indeed terror [as] exemplified in his personal character. There is an unbroken continuity from him to Lenin . . . He is probably a figure of destiny, like Luther, not as important for his ideas as for the character that carried those ideas." After this, Arendt went on a reading program and came to agree: "The more I read Marx, the more I see that you are right. He is not interested either in freedom or in justice."[2] She had come not just to a shared criticism of Marx's ideas, particularly "Marx's obsession with the social question and his unwillingness to pay serious attention to questions of state and government," as she wrote in *On Revolution*, but to a different sense of the importance of character as the carrier of ideas.

In the years after *The Origin of Totalitarianism*, Hannah Arendt became a dedicated critic of Marxism, and her preoccupation with the right—with the ex-communists and McCarthyites in America—receded. The forces needing challenging on the world political stage were less shaped by Nazi-like ideologies centering on a group like the Jews than by Marxist-like ones promoting social revolutions. Her shift also reflected a shift in her own feelings: the advent of hopefulness after years of horror. But she did not leave behind her own character as the carrier of her ideas. On the contrary, she came to appreciate it and understand

▼ ▼ ▼ ▼ ▼

it better as she shifted. She knew that her book had been written in deep fear and even deeper rage that had occluded her own feeling of being at home in the world. She had fearfully felt the world suspended between freedom and totalitarianism, and she struck out. Her writings were acts of preventive retaliation against murder wreaked upon the Jews of Europe—her people—and against betrayals of freedom by so many in two generations of European intellectuals, her own and that of her teachers, people of the ideological right and of the left. In 1948, Karl Jaspers, writing to Arendt about her essay on the concentration camps, expressed what her nonideological, independent contemporaries experienced again and again when reading her: "Yes, the fear in which you live, not fear for yourself but for humankind, gives you great clarity of perception. And you recognize the danger of people not wanting to accept these facts [about the camps], pushing them aside, not comprehending them, not believing they exist in the real world. You think the logical consequences through to the end. And what you reveal can truly make one's blood run cold. Yes, you ought to alert people, only by way of this knowledge can we prevent such things 'from ever happening again' " (p. 105).

After the war, as Hannah Arendt's thought continued to mature, as the world situation she was responding to evolved, she became clearer about how her own character encompassed the desires that were partially reflected in the views of those to her left and to her right. Her character encompassed deep conservatism in combination with radicality, an impulse to preserve and protect the world and all the natural and cultural things that make it up, along with a love of novelty, new beginnings— desires that seemed to others contradictory. People whose imperatives make them sheerly traditionalists or sheerly innovators feel to the independent-minded like extremists. As Arendt once remarked: "Man's urge for change and his need for stability have always balanced and checked each other, and our current vocabulary, which distinguishes between two factions, the progressives and the conservatives, indicates a state of affairs in which this balance has been thrown out of order."[3] In both characterological and political terms, the distortions in understanding of Arendt and her work that were typical of the Cold War era reflected this disbalanced state of affairs.

"The Council System"

The theoretical writings Arendt produced after *The Origins of Totalitarianism* years, when she had stepped back to pose the reflective question

▼ ▼ ▼ ▼

implicit in her magnum opus, were the ones that commanded the attention of the sixties generation. These readers returned and keep returning again and again to *The Human Condition, Between Past and Future, On Revolution, On Violence,* and to the unfinished "Judging" section of *The Life of the Mind.* In these works, they found Arendt's attention turned not to totalitarianism per se but to the catalog of deeper trends and ideas that constituted, in her understanding, the preconditions for totalitarianism, the elements that could crystallize into totalitarian forms—but not inevitably, unpreventably.

Her experience in the United States in the early 1950s, during the Korean War and as Joseph McCarthy rose to prominence in American politics, pointed up for Hannah Arendt the specificity of the European totalitarianisms and the fact that totalitarian elements do not necessarily lead to totalitarianism. In her adoptive country, she saw some of the elements of totalitarianism appear, but with two of the key ones missing and without a full crystallization process. There was no "movement" in McCarthyism, no swell of support coming from adherents in group after group, class after class, uniting in a vast abandonment of self, an ecstatic conformity, an anti-state fervor. And there was no group-targeting ideology like anti-Semitism espoused by a leader, to provide the unifying vision, the common enemy in the form of the international Jewish conspiracy controlling the government. McCarthy's power group included many Jews and was not anti-Semitic, and his supporters did not come from the whole spectrum of American groups. "What I see," Arendt noted to Jaspers in 1954, "is totalitarian elements springing from the womb of society, of mass society itself, without any 'movement' or clear ideology" (p. 249).

In her European fearfulness, Arendt overreacted to McCarthyism and underestimated the resilience of American political life, which is so baffling to Europeans because so shifting on the surface, so blown about by winds of opinion, so subject to change, and so unballasted by ideologies of the left and the right other than those of its intelligentsia. She wrote to Jaspers in 1955 that the whole McCarthyism phenomenon seemed to have disappeared in a blink of public opinion: "The atmosphere in the country is again what it was before, hardly changed at all. The political tradition of the country has come through again; and we—thanks and jubilation be to God—were wrong."

Her admiration for American traditions reinforced, Arendt started writing enthusiastically about American history and political theory; but also, on a deeper level, she experienced a confirmation of a healing process that had been taking place in her in the years since *The Origins of Totalitarianism* was published—a mellowing, a youthful exuberance and joy in the world, a diminishment of the anguish, the fear, and the rage. Jaspers, anticipating a visit from her that would bring him and his wife "the wide world," heard the new note clearly from her after having remarked it himself several years earlier.[4] "Yes," she replied, (p. 265), "I would like to bring the wide world to you this time. I've begun so late, really only in recent years, to truly love the world, that I shall be able to do that now. Out of gratitude, I want to call my book on political theories 'Amor Mundi' " (p. 265).

It is this strand in Arendt's character, her *amor mundi,* that underlay her enthusiasm for "the council system," the political form she considered the antidote to totalitarianism, the form for genuine political life, for action and for reasoning speech. She studied the American town meetings, wards, and voluntary associations, the 1871 Parisian Commune and popular societies, the Russian extra-Party workers councils, or soviets, which appeared in 1905 and again in 1917, the *Rätesystem* of the German revolutionary period of 1918 and 1919, and the councils that sprang up in Hungary during the 1956 revolution. These were, in Arendt's words from *On Revolution,* "spontaneous organs of the people, not only outside of all revolutionary parties but entirely unexpected by them and by their leaders."

Arendt began to think that the gravest danger in American political life was a kind of thoughtlessness, and very specifically a lack of historical memory of America's revolutionary origins and of its constitutional tradition, which protected its council formations. She noted in *On Revolution* that American political life was suffused with fear of revolutions on the model of the ones that did not aim at constitution making, particularly the French and the Russian. "Fear of revolution has been the hidden leitmotif of postwar American foreign policy in its desperate attempts at stabilization of the status quo, with the result that American power and prestige were used and misued to support obsolete and corrupt political regimes that long since had become objects of hatred and contempt among their own citizens."

Lacking any sense of their historical political traditions, domestic policymakers of both American parties were focusing on socioeconomic goals, not political processes, valuing free enterprise over freedom. The progressive Democrats, she felt, were engaged in promoting centralization in ways that crushed local initiatives, while the Republicans were busy sponsoring capitalism regardless of its consequences. Americans

▼ ▼ ▼ ▼

generally, she thought, failed to understand that free enterprise, capitalism, except in a situation of natural abundance and relative lack of class structure, leads only to unhappiness and mass poverty. They do not suspect that even in such an optimal situation capitalism may well eventually produce unhappiness and regions of mass poverty—as it is doing now in America: "Economic growth may one day turn out to be a curse rather than a good, and under no conditions can it either lead into freedom or constitute proof for its existence."

Very few of Arendt's sixties readers noticed this critique of capitalism in Arendt's *On Revolution*. They concentrated instead on Arendt's distinction between "the social question" and politics, some accepting the distinction, some rejecting it. The acceptors fastened enthusiastically on her hopefulness about the council system and applied it to their own enthusiasm about grass-roots or participatory democracy. The rejecters, from a Marxist angle, raised questions about the way in which she found obsession with "the social question" to be the doom of revolutions, first of the French Revolution and then of all its legatees. Her critics thus questioned whether a distinction between the social and the political of the sort that Arendt drew made her, in effect, antirevolutionary in their terms. And they questioned how being obsessed with "the social question" came to stand in Arendt's work as characteristic of social utopian "compassionate zeal," a rhetoric about power to the people that she believed was ultimately about promoting the power of zealots.

In effect, the Marxist critics of the sixties generation repeated the critique of Arendt launched by their elders, but their emphasis was different. They were not fighting over whether and how the Soviet Union was totalitarian or about whether a Marxist revolution had ingredients of totalitarianism built in. The central debate was about how to take up "the social question," which Arendt's critics posed as a *moral* question, even a question about whether violence was *morally* justified to bring about social justice, to help the downtrodden. Her sharp distinction between "the social question" and political action seemed to them to condemn the victims of social injustice to waiting upon politics for their next meal, much less for their triumph over the bourgeoisie. This criticism, then, came to have great weight even among Arendt's appropriators, who wanted grass-roots organizations to address "the social question" as a matter of urgency.

This distortion of Arendt's thought haunted the kindred problem of the relation of morality and politics, which she took up in her reflections on the controversy that erupted over her *Eichmann in Jerusalem* and in

▼ ▼ ▼ ▼ ▼

her reflections on the American tradition of civil disobedience during the Vietnam War. To question the relationship between morality and politics, she considered cases of men who were evil and men who were good in relation to their societies and states. In these considerations, she assumed that morality has to do with conscience and that conscience is an individual matter. In the European tradition, the exemplary man of conscience is Socrates, who was concerned with whether or not he could live *with himself* if he did this deed or that. Morality becomes political only when people of conscience act together, at which point, Arendt argued, it is transformed: "In the market place, the fate of conscience is not much different from the fate of the philosopher's truth: it becomes an opinion, indistinguishable from other opinions. And the strength of opinion does not depend on conscience, but on the number of those with whom it is associated—'unanimous agreement that "X" is an evil . . . adds credence to the belief that "X" *is* an evil.' "[5] Arendt had been very impressed when Eichmann showed at his trial that he was capable of telling right from wrong—he had a conscience—but the problem was that his conscience told him to obey his Führer, and in the society in which he lived obedience to the Führer's will was right.

Arendt argued that the civil disobedience of significant numbers of Americans in the late 1960s was a continuation of the nation's tradition of voluntary associations, councils. She praised it as such, and even hoped that a constitutional amendment might one day be proposed to cover the right of association. But she was very well aware that voluntary associations at that time were also—as lobbies, pressure groups, and special interest organizations—working against political action. So her criterion for judging the worth of voluntary organizations was political, not moral. They become dangerous "if the original contractual model of the associations—mutual promises with the moral imperative *pacta sunt servanda*—should be lost. Under today's circumstances, this could happen if these groups, and their counterparts in other countries, were to substitute ideological commitments, political or other, for actual goals. When an association is no longer capable or willing to unite 'into one channel the efforts of divergent minds' (Tocqueville), it has lost its gift for action. What threatens the student movement, the chief civil disobedience group of the moment . . . is the growing infection of the movement with ideologies (Maoism, Castroism, Stalinism, Marxism-Leninism, and the like), which in fact split and dissolve the association."[6] To those for whom an association is a vehicle for a moral cause, Arendt seemed to be saying flatly that there are no right and wrong causes, there

▼ ▼ ▼ ▼

are only right and wrong ways of associating or being political. In this distortion of her meaning, she seemed amoral.

Behind this distortion of Arendt's position and meaning stood her refusal to accept moralistic ideologies or enthusiasms, to be predetermined by the role of the moral judge. Anyone thus predetermined becomes unable to experience directly or concretely as well as unable to reflect freely on experiences. Independent thought is mobile—free in the most elementary sense. For those lacking independence, everything is prepackaged, but they do not recognize the abstract quality of their thought because they are so impressed by the buzz or the charge that they feel in anticipation of actual experiences and in their possession of a prefabricated language to impose upon experiences. Among the sixties *moralistes* who criticized Arendt and whom Arendt criticized, the most common prefabricated script featured violence justified. She felt that their scripts completely prevented young people from recognizing the novel realities of the world-historical moment that these very same young people had created with their moral fervor. Arendt marveled to Jaspers over a member of the German Gruppe 47 who had visited with her in Chicago: "still so young and already totally incapable of learning anything. Sees in everything only more support for his prejudices, can't absorb anything concrete, factual anymore" (p. 639).

Politics and Identities

The currently emergent intellectual generation has grown up in political conditions that look in many ways like those obtaining at the turn of the last century—nation-states are everywhere consolidating, contesting their borders, oppressing their minorities, rediscovering or dreaming up national traditions, while supranational movements with world-domination ideologies, often religious ones, offer nationalists even wilder dreams. In the nationalistic and supranationalistic parties, as well as within the camps of persecuted ethnic minorities, there is a pervasive malaise about modernity that also resembles turn of the century anti-modernism, a key ideological ingredient of fascism; however, there is also great turmoil and fracture in the camps of counterclaiming ideologies that elevate progress into a law of history. But the world now is also colored by mid-century events—by the specter of totalitarianism—and all the intervening developments of globalizing organizations and technologies and communications, vastly increased populations and ecological threats, spreading mass poverty. In the intellectual life of "the West"

▼▼▼▼

there has evolved an atmosphere in which Arendt's thought is of great interest to the emergent generation because it is not traditionally ideological. But she is also being made to serve a key quest—for identity—for which she had no sympathy whatsoever.

Now it is neither the instrumental utopianism of the postwar rightist and leftist intellectuals with their end-justifies-the-means thinking nor the moralism of the sixties generation, but a self-referentiality, a particularism of identity—*my* ideas, *my* group, *my* fiefdom—that dominates the intellectual atmosphere. In an era in which the possibilities for action have become very limited as vast party bureaucracies come more and more thoroughly to control representational processes, a type of intellectual has appeared who is the successor to both the leftist ideologues and the antirevolutionary think tank "new mandarins" of policymaking that Arendt castigated in the 1960s. These are the pundits, who operate via the evolving communications technologies—the opinion-conveying technologies—sending out bright ideas, trying to distinguish themselves, which means achieve celebrity status, by the appeal of their life stories. People enter into political life now with their autobiography in hand, not their ideological manifesto.

In this atmosphere, many younger intellectuals without particular defining political allegiances of the left or the right have tried to co-opt Hannah Arendt as an exemplar of their form of identity politics. Theoretically, they question whether Arendt's basic categories from *The Human Condition*—the existential-situation ones (natality, mortality, plurality, world), the activities distinctions (labor, work, action), and the domains (the private, the public, and the social)—can be appropriated or used critically to articulate a concept of identity. But they also read her biography of Rahel Varnhagen, a famous German Jewish salon hostess, to consider Arendt as a Jew, or her correspondence to consider her as a woman, often, in both cases, finding her way of being a Jew or her way of being a woman challenging but unsatisfactory. Most of these approaches, it seems to me, come up partial or distorted because they do not compass the way in which Arendt herself approached the question of identity; they do not consider her philosophically, socially, and politically—three dimensions that did not always fit together logically or comfortably in her life or her work.

Philosophically, she valued the internal dialogue of thinking that she referred to as "a conversation between me and myself," and she held that having an identity implied having your mind be a monologue, not keeping up the endless back and forth, questioning, searching, rethink-

▼ ▼ ▼ ▼

ing project of thinking. In this sense, she rejected having an identity as a state of being or a way of life. Socially, she valued the creative tension of being at once a private and a public person, and assumed that this tension would not exist if a person had *an* identity and was reliant on having that identity confirmed in public. She could have said of herself what she said of the Danish writer Isak Dinesen in an essay full of autobiographical themes: "she had discovered . . . that the chief trap in life is one's own identity—I will not be one person again." In Dinesen's case, the trap "was not so much writing or professional writing as taking oneself seriously and identifying the woman with the author who has his [sic] identity confirmed, inescapably, in pubic." Socially, Arendt felt that taking oneself seriously and identifying the private person with the public person—in whatever terms, professional, cultural, ethnic, or gender—signaled a private lack of what she called "the supreme confirmation of one's existence which only love, mutual love, can give."

Politically, Arendt's reflections on identity were closely tied to analyses of particular historical-political situations, as her many essays on Jewish identity make clear. From the mid-1930s until after the war, she spoke and wrote as a Jew, having very carefully—painstakingly, through several revisions—clarified for herself what "as a Jew" meant. She was culturally—most basically, linguistically, literarily—a German; and Zionism in its pre-1930s forms had not been part of her youth. But she became *politically* a Jew, and in the manner of the Zionist critique of assimilation, in response to a specific form of anti-Semitism, which she called political anti-Semitism. She admired Jews who were self-declared pariahs, and she was harsh about parvenus, by which she meant people who tried to live divided lives, Jews at home and gentiles in public. Her nonassimilationist stance meant never repudiating her origins (for example, by conversion); but it did not mean never marrying a non-Jew. It meant supporting the establishment of prewar Jewish settlements in Palestine and in 1948 defending the existence of the state of Israel as a political necessity, but criticizing the equation of religious affiliation and citizenship in the state. Her political identification as a Jew was at its height when it needed to be, defensively, while later, particularly in the 1960s, she thought of herself, as she thought of Jaspers, as more of a citizen of the world, and she traveled back and forth between America and Europe in that role, as something like an intellectual interpreter between America and Germany. After the period of persecution, which she held was governed by the principle "one can resist only in terms of the identity that is under attack," she considered that identifying herself first and foremost as a Jew would "seem like a pose."[7]

The complexity of this picture only deepens if Arendt's private attitude toward religious institutions comes into account—an attitude in which the philosophical and the political intersect. When Arendt considered herself religiously, she counted herself among those who are—as independent-minded people typically are—respectful inheritors of a great religious tradition without being institutionally religious. She trusted in the existence of a higher power, but she refused to name or idolize or make any claim upon or even to have faith in this God. "I make my way through life," she wrote to Jaspers in 1951, "with a kind of (childish? because unquestioned) trust in God (as distinguished from faith, which always thinks it knows and therefore has to cope with doubts and paradoxes). There's nothing much you can make of that, of course, except be happy. All traditional religion as such, whether Jewish or Christian, holds nothing whatsoever for me anymore." She then added a remark in her political vein: "I don't think, either, that it [religion] can anywhere or in any way provide a basis for something so clearly political as laws" (p. 166).

About being a Jew, Arendt's thoughts were complex; about being a woman, they were simpler—and thus much feminist commentary has been dedicated to showing the complexity that Arendt did not see for or in herself. She simply did not wish to have a public side to her being a woman, and she rejected every effort made to understand or publicly recognize her as a woman. She did not feel herself to be attacked as a woman; nor did she feel herself part of a group, "women," being attacked and needing to defend herself as a woman. She subscribed to feminism as a type of political action concerned with suffrage, equality of opportunity, and equal rights, but she did not support the idea of a feminist political party or movement and she did not think of sexism as central in American politics: She once referred in her essay "Civil Diobedience," for example, to the failure of the American Congress to consider a constitutional amendment directly addressing the situation of the African Americans, the legacy of slavery, as "striking in light of the overwhelming vote for a constitutional amendment to cure the infinitely milder discriminatory practices against women." Philosophically, she marked the boundary between what is and ought to be private and what public with the maxim she imagined Rosa Luxemburg adopting in objection to the advocacy of her friend Clara Zetkin for the women's emancipation movement—Vive la petite différence!

▼ ▼ ▼ ▼ ▼

From Arendt's political point of view, what is at issue in this matter of identity is a judgment about whether the identity "as a woman" is called for, in her particular case or generally. Arendt herself clearly felt that legal redress was all that the situation of women called for. She did not see around her the sexual equivalent of political anti-Semitism—that is, a political sexism in which sexism becomes the organizing ideology of a political party or movement—which would have called for the equivalent of Zionism. Arendt understood the question of discrimination against women as similar to "the Jewish Question."[8] But it is important, I think, to argue that sexism is not at all the same type of prejudice as anti-Semitism, because sexism discriminates against a majority of the population, without a group history, much less a history of group separateness or clannishness. Sexism affects a population living in the households of its oppressors and bound to them by ties of sexuality and reproduction. This means it is a prejudice that exists in households and grows out into the public domain, rather than the reverse; there is no private space in which to get away from it—thus the feminist maxim that "the personal is political."

In order to learn from or adequately criticize Hannah Arendt's reflections on identity, her readers would have had to take a broad view—compassing different discourses, historically contextualized, and comparative across types of identity—and this has, so far, not happened. The way in which this generation of Arendt commentators poses questions of identity—or embraces the idea of having an identity—has limited its collective view.[9] Only the political dimension of having an identity has been at issue, and at issue in a moment when having an identity often substitutes for acting, since the possibilities for acting have grown less and the antipolitical forces more pervasive in the contemporary world.

Preconditions of Independent-Mindedness

I have been tracking three types of approaches to Hannah Arendt's life and work, each coming for the most part from a specific generation for whom independent-mindedness was difficult to achieve or sustain for specific reasons, and for whom her independent-mindedness was difficult to appreciate for the same reasons. I want to turn now directly to independent-mindedness and inquire about its preconditions and characteristics. In the political-theoretical parts of this inquiry, I am going to use Arendt as an exemplary figure and draw upon Jaspers's reflections on her character. The psychological strands will grow from my assumption, for which I am not going to make an argument here, that lack of

▼ ▼ ▼ ▼ ▼

independent-mindedness correlates with salient narcissistic character traits while independent-mindedness requires, fundamentally, a healthy narcissism, or, phrased developmentally, an ego ideal that allows a person the capacity that Hannah Arendt called—not at all psychoanalytically—*amor mundi*.

Let me begin with the claim that the first and most elemental precondition, necessary but not at all sufficient, for independence of thought is vitality, by which I mean physical vitality: energy—perhaps it should be called renewable energy—and drive and concentration of physical resources, but also a reflexive love of vitality, an enjoyment of vitality, an ability not to cut oneself off from what Freud called the ego and sexual instinctual drives. Vitality in this sense *is* growth and plea-sure; that growth and pleasure which Hannah Arendt, writing about Lessing, defined as "fundamentally the intensified awareness of reality, [which] springs from a passionate openness to the world and love of it."[10]

Very closely related to this necessary vitality is a reflexive sense that one's appearance in public is a pleasure to oneself and attractive to oth-ers.[11] Such attractiveness is, of course, less a matter of specificities of figure and features than of the reflexive attitude toward figure and fea-tures, toward bodily existence in general; it is an attitude of self-worth—self-esteem in the current jargon—rooted in enjoying appearing before and being with others, being appreciated, distinguishing oneself. In psy-choanalytic terms, what I am indicating could be called normal bodily narcissism, and it should be understood as a precursor for normal mental narcissism, a sense of growth in and pleasure in mental activity, espe-cially mental activity with others, in the same way that autoerotic and alloerotic curiosities are precursors for (or, in other terms, are sublimated into) intellectual curiosity.

Very seldom is the attractiveness of an independent-minded per-son conventional, for conventionally beautiful people are usually spoiled in their youths by admiration directed only at their beauty, attention they then come to need too much or despise too vehemently. Most independent-minded people, on the contrary, have had to discover and interpret their own attractiveness precisely because it is not conven-tional. This revelation, then, not usually an achievement of youth or even of early adulthood, connects them to the beauty of the natural world and the world of human creations, culture, of which they feel themselves a part, where they feel at home, both when they are in their homes and when they travel.

▼ ▼ ▼ ▼

Hannah Arendt was quite well aware, especially as a reader of Kant's *Critique of Judgment,* that there is a connection between aesthetic judgment, with its roots in the elementary sense or taste judgments "I like this" and "I dislike this," and political judgment. These are the worldly and world-loving judgment modes. Subjective enjoyment of oneself—taking pleasure in one's pleasure and in one's self, tasting one's self—can, of course, be a type of alienation from the world, as it is among hedonists and aesthetes of the sort that baffle historians of Nazism—the lovers of Beethoven who ran crematoria. But enjoyment of one's self can also be the ground for an enjoyment of the world that supplies the pleasurable things among which the enjoyer feels at home, kindred, alike, a world that, therefore, the enjoyer wishes to preserve and protect. World alienation as self-absorption, which ultimately is an inability to tell the difference between self and world, virtually forbids any real political judgment, any judgment that is really focused on and concerned for the world. Political judgment arises out of engagement with and receptivity toward the world, worldliness.

There is a common idea that sickness or ugliness or some traumatizing sense of default or deficit—a narcissistic wound in psychoanalytic terms—provokes people into world alienation; they retreat from their fallible bodies and the world of appearances into some kind of philosophizing, sometimes with great prejudice against what they have left behind—a misanthropy or a *Weltschmerz.* And this seems quite right for at least some kinds of sickness and ugliness and hurt. However, philosophizers are not, by that criterion, independent-minded. Withdrawal is not independent-mindedness. On the contrary, withdrawal results in dependence upon being withdrawn; it fixes the mind not on the world but on ideas that praise and protect being-withdrawn. The worldly Greeks and Romans—not the unworldly philosophers among them—were the peoples responsible for an aphorism about this condition that would strike a Christian as cruel: *monstrum in fronte, monstrum in anima.*

Rebelliousness against the world is a condition similar to withdrawal in that it is dependent—dependent upon what is rebelled against—as is revealed by the fact that rebellions, particularly successful ones, often entail or are followed by tyrannical behavior or collapse. In her critique of revolutionary "compassionate zeal" focused on social injustice, Hannah Arendt was recognizing how frequently this means zeal for power; or how typically it does not mean commitment to equality in the future political order. Chronic rebelliousness or indiscriminate rebelliousness or rebelliousness for rebelliousness's sake are also states

▼ ▼ ▼ ▼ ▼

that forbid independent-mindedness because they involve constant referencing to or absorption by a fixed image of the world as disordered and disordering.

Alienation from the world as self-absorption can also take another form, quite different from withdrawal or rebelliousness, that forbids independent-mindedness and manifests itself as an inability to tell the difference between self and world. A person of this type is driven by a sense of entitlement and expects provisions from the world both in the abstract and from those with worldly goods and favors to offer. Grandiosity, or what Nietzsche once described, speaking of philosophers, as "swelling up to the macrocosm," is a form of world alienation in which the world is, as it were, swallowed, not rejected or withdrawn from. People of this sort may not lack vitality or attractiveness, but their sense of their vitality or attractiveness is insecure and they are always in need of ratification or reassurance.

Both those who lack vitality and attractiveness and those who are ruled by a sense of entitlement are susceptible to the hope that either ideas or self-serving alliances with other people will—to use the language of our day—empower them. They seek empowerment, which is something completely different from solidarity; they wish to be inflated, to have their self-esteem improved or sustained, their individual existences intensified or given a kind of charge; they are not looking first and foremost for communicative bonds with natural or cultural things or with others. Public life is expected to supply what such people feel they cannot attain or keep on their own—being loved, which is, in their experience, indistinguishable from flattery. That is, what they feel is not love, but an ersatz version of the self-love known to the secure. Those who use ideas, like people, as boosters—prizes, adornments, distractions, cover-ups—can never live without their aids; they are ultimately dependent.

The independent-minded are, by contrast, much more likely to have needed ideas and people in their youths to curb them, contain them, temper them, give their ego ideals guidance capacity, than to empower them. Hannah Arendt's contemporaries at all the phases of her life experienced in her presence as in her work her vitality, particularly as it was manifest as passionateness, a tendency to exaggerate and overstate, which required anchoring. As she became close to her mentor Jaspers after the war, he became her main anchor, the key teacher figure in her ego ideal. She had lacked a similar figure in her university years, when she involved herself with two very narcissistic characters, Martin

Heidegger, a man of considerable genius, and her first husband, Gunther Stern, an aspiring genius, whom she seems to have married hoping to create a rarefied world of intellectuality. For loving her second husband, Heinrich Bluecher, her truly democratic partner in philosophical conversation, she was prepared by a large dose of hard reality—persecution and exile—as well as by a sustained meditation in her biography *Rahel Varnhagen* on the folly of trying to construct a life at odds with realities.[12] She could well have been writing about herself when she later described how Isak Dinesen was prepared for her *grande passion* in middle age— with a man of the First World War's "lost generation," like Bluecher— by learning that it is self-destructive to try to overcome a futile youthful love, like Arendt's for Heidegger, by making your life into a work of art or to go "interfering with life according to a preconceived pattern, instead of waiting patiently for the story to emerge." This was Rahel Varnhagen's mistake as well. "Wisdom is the virtue of old age," Arendt said about Dinesen, "and it seems to come only to those who, when young, were neither wise nor prudent."[13]

That securely felt vitality and attractiveness are the underpinnings of independent-mindedness—in and of themselves constituting, of course, neither wisdom nor prudence—is more obvious in some circumstances than in others, and in the dark times of Europe in the late 1930s and during the war years it could not have been more obvious. In 1946, speaking of refugee life in France during the war, Arendt described to Jaspers the apathy-inducing, devitalizing conditions in which her friend Walter Benjamin had taken his own life:

> This exhaustion, which often went along with a reluctance to make a big fuss, to summon so much concentration just for the sake of this little bit of life, that was surely the greatest danger we all faced ... This atmosphere of *sauve qui peut* at the time was dreadful, and suicide was the only noble gesture, if you even cared enough to want to perish nobly. In our time, you have to hate murder a lot to escape the seductive power of suicide. (p. 40)

Suicide as a mode of perishing nobly is, when vitality fails or is rendered nugatory, the path to restoration of humanity and—momentarily, in the gesture—the possibility of human communication arising from the depths, fundamentally.

Conditions in which being at home in the world is physically impossible or nearly impossible reveal—as it were, like a negative—how being at home in the world bodily, physically, is the ground for the com-

▼ ▼ ▼ ▼ ▼

munion or communicative being at home with people that is the essential precondition of independent-mindedness. Only those who have a basic trust in themselves and in others, who meet others on a plane of equality, mutuality, can be free of any tendency to dominate or to submit, to seek empowerment in either the mode of domination or the mode of submission to another's power. Further, they enjoy freedom from "social connections," to use Hannah Arendt's terms, by which she meant the temptations of modern "society," "the social." Then, as a matter of self-confidence, freedom from the social means not having a need to compare one's self, positively or negatively, with others, to make scores or rankings for justifying dominating or being dominated. Both dominators and dominateds in the realm of the mind—as more generally—are dependent on their others, locked into a predetermining attention to them that makes impossible a pleasurable "intensified awareness of reality," an immediacy of experience, a concreteness of observation.

Communicativeness as the Crucial Characteristic of Independent-Mindedness

One rule of thumb that follows from these descriptions is that the most independent-minded people are the least hostile to politics, even if they are not temperamentally suited to be political actors, as Hannah Arendt was not. They relish the give and take of discussion in political forums because of their basic trust in the rationality of people. Their security—their normal narcissism, to speak psychoanalytically—suggests to them that many, even most, others are like them in their rationality and their independent-mindedness. Neither people nor their actions, of course, always or even usually justify such trust, and the independent-minded can easily find themselves in trouble for having failed to anticipate irrational reactions to their ideas, but vital independent-minded people grow rather than wither with experiences that wound or challenge their trust. They maintain an anger of disappointed expectation that protects them from collapse or cynicism. Jaspers once remarked to Arendt, "We always assume that people are rational, and that is what gives rise to our great mistakes and then to our harshness. You are much less prone to that than I am, however. You have mercy in concrete situations with specific individuals" (p. 594).

Those who operate in modes of domination or submission are the ones who think of politics as domination and submission, or who conceive of power as an instrument of rule based on some kind of instinct for domination and for violence as a means for getting and keeping and extending power, a manifestation of power. But although the idea that power is rule or command (and a form of government is a form of rule, law is a form of command) is widely taken for granted, Arendt insisted in *On Violence* that "there exists another tradition and another vocabulary no less old and time-honored." She referred to the Greeks, who called a city-state constitution an isonomy, to the Romans who spoke of their *civitas,* and to the men of the eighteenth-century revolutions who looked to the Greeks and Romans as they invoked a republic, "where the rule of law, resting on the power of the people, would put an end to the rule of man over man, which they thought was a " 'government fit for slaves.' " Citizens are equals before the law, and their governments are based on opinions and the exchange of opinions, which requires trust. The specifically political precondition for independent-mindedness—the corollary to the psychological condition of communicativeness—is equality, or the aspiration to equality among those to whom it has been denied.

Theory can be learned from historical examples, but the impulse to look to those examples rather than others comes from sources closer to home in the lives of the independent-minded. The independent-minded learn from the independent-minded. Hannah Arendt, in a rare moment of introspective psychologizing, attributed her trusting capacity directly to her mother. She was describing in an interview the prewar Jewish communities, which were relatively removed from social life (by decree, not by intention), being neither national nor part of German society: "it was something very beautiful, this standing outside of all social connections, the complete open-mindedness and absence of prejudice that I experienced, especially with my mother, who also exercised it in relation to the whole Jewish community."[14] She experienced a variation of this quality with Karl Jaspers, but she understood that his standing outside of social connections was more individual, a matter of his "difference" as the son of an old German Protestant family who could not, because of a chronic illness, simply exist in his family tradition or his profession. His marriage to a Jewish woman further distinguished him.

The independent-minded are acknowledgers of their debt to a model—or more than one—of independent-mindedness, and they treasure friendship as the medium in which they appreciate the model and in which they play out their ideas. Friendships—or friendly marriages like Arendt's and Bluecher's—give them a little world that allows them

▼ ▼ ▼ ▼ ▼

worldliness combined with intimacy and in which their trust is not disappointed. Jaspers is, in the twentieth century, the great philosophical appreciator of and explorer of communication, which he experienced first with a friend of his youth—in the tradition that began in the modern period with Montaigne's friendship with La Boetie—and then with his wife. Thinking as an activity of partnership, not of solitude—although it may be conducted in solitude, with the partner in imagination or in interior dialogue, what Arendt called the "me and myself" type of thinking—is experienced by the independent-minded as a creative tension. In it, the dialogists do not produce arguments and counter-arguments, like boxers, but experience a tension that allows fresh looks and outlooks.

The creative tension of thinking as partnership has its corollary in a restlessness and need to go from one focus to the next, to grow, always taking fundamental ideas and commitments into fresh arenas, topics, media, cultural fields, or parts of the library. The independent-minded are foxes, to use Isaiah Berlin's Shakespearean analogy, not hedgehogs; they are explorers, not so much interdisciplinary as extradisciplinary, and the charge most frequently brought against them is that they venture into specialized areas without being specialists, that they are dilettantes, which they are, except that their freshness and lack of any sense of possessiveness over the territory usually puts them on a level far beyond what most experts achieve. Jaspers's historical model of ceaseless growth was, of course, Goethe; an American might gravitate toward Emerson.

Beneath their exploratory activity deeper chords of thought will resound again and again in the independent-minded, but these chords are characteristically experienced as common in the sense that they seem to belong to the community of rational people, that they are not private property. Arendt, considering with Jaspers the characteristics of the literati, those they defined as without independence of mind, expressed the matter this way: "From a purely technical perspective, the key thing seems to me to be the 'bright idea.' If you have some degree of talent, there is absolutely nothing about which you can't have a bright idea. And once you've had the bright idea, even if you have it at somebody else's orders, then it becomes 'my bright idea,' . . . What troubles me so much about all this is the alienation from reality, that people ignore reality in favor of their bright ideas" (pp. 592–593).

Psychologically, a bright idea is an idea that makes the person who has it feel bright, brightened—as cartoons say it, a light bulb goes on above the haver's head. Not illumination of reality, but illumination for

▼ ▼ ▼ ▼ ▼

the haver of bright ideas is what matters—so, of course, the more bright ideas the better. And quantity of bright ideas is, then, mistaken for influence because the haver of these ideas inevitably aspires to influence—being dependent upon being noticed in his or her illumined state. Reflecting on Voltaire, who was a fine example of a person with some of the preconditions of independence but without its healthily narcissistic characterological foundation, Jaspers admired the *philosophe* for his remarkable vitality, "his abundance of ideas, his power of formulation, his instinct for creating effects, his feel for French taste," but then argued that he was a paradigm of the "literary type" that has brought modern discourse to its sad state. "Voltaire represents in modern humanity that literary element that is in its very core as inhuman as possible, in reality mean-spirited, but that is responsible for the moralistic tone, the grand gesture, the voice of protest, and so on that have remained so much a part of discourse until today" (p. 590).[15]

Voltaire's was a voice of self-assertive polemic, polemic that calls attention to the polemicist, as opposed to the kind of polemic Arendt admired Lessing for practicing, which is not self-assertive but world-protecting, world-concerned. The difference has to do with bringing talent to a topic and displaying the talent, as opposed to coming to a topic out of inner necessity and concern for the world. Intellectuals who are self-assertively polemical feel themselves to be activists, people of action. They are relieved in their self-display of the suspicion—a curse upon any sense of entitlement—that they are beside the point, useless, irrelevant to the march of events. Their bright ideas both make them feel brighter and make them feel influential, privy to power (in the sense of rulership). As possibilities for action in the modern world continue to diminish, the temptation to self-assertion and violence of speech, as well as to violence itself, grows.

Hannah Arendt could veer off in a Voltairean mode of self-assertion—I think she did so in *Eichmann in Jerusalem,* not in the content of her very challenging, independent-minded argument, but in its tone, its distanced, ironic "I speak the truth" style. But she seldom did so, and only—I think—in relief at finally having gotten clear about something that had troubled her deeply, burdened her emotions and thoughts, baffled her understanding. Her self-assertion was like a manic defense, to speak psychoanalytically, against the anxiety of keeping at the project of understanding, and it operated in the mode of her own youthful tendency to exaggeration. She protected herself against sentimentality or pity with a certain harshness, but generally, her independent-mindedness

▼ ▼ ▼ ▼ ▼

was more secure. And this in the sense that it was, finally, dedicated to preserving its own conditions and companions. She wrote of Lessing, an example for herself, that "his thinking was not a search for truth, since every truth that is the result of a thought process necessarily puts an end to the movement [and thus the freedom] of thinking. The *fermenta cognitionis* which Lessing scattered into the world were not intended to communicate conclusions, but to stimulate others to independent thought, and this for no other purpose than to bring about a discourse between thinkers."[16]

▼   This essay was begun as an address for an October 1995 conference at the Graduate Faculty of the New School for Social Research called "The Legacy of Hannah Arendt," and is published for the first time here.

PART II

FEMINISM AND PSYCHOANALYSIS

10

Rereading Freud on
Female Development

As Sigmund Freud developed his view of female psychology, he indicated areas where he thought his conclusions were quite trustworthy and others where his insights were either untested or still tentative. A pattern has emerged in the criticism of Freud's view that has developed over six decades: where be felt most secure, criticism has been most vehement, sustained, and consensual; where he felt hypothetical or tentative, there has been lack of consensus and conceptual tangle.

This battle of sexuality theories is much too long and full of fronts for review in one essay. What I would like to do is pursue a particular angle, inviting you to follow an exercise in what-might-have-been. Specifically, I will offer a review of the questions that Freud's theoretical revisions after 1920 might have raised had he reconsidered his views on female psychology in light of those revisions. This is only an exercise in historical-biographical reconstruction and theory construction. I am writing not as a clinician on the basis of clinical experience, but as a historian. I do think, however, that this approach can illuminate current psychoanalytic thinking about female psychology.

The area of Freud's views on female psychology that he assessed as most secure was articulated clearly in 1905 in *Three Essays*.[1] He claimed, first, that human beings are psychologically (and also biologically, in some as yet unexplored way) bisexual creatures who develop through two periods of libidinal upsurge—during the Oedipal years and during puberty. Their bisexuality remains as they become adults, but usually under the aegis of either a preponderantly feminine or a preponderantly masculine mental sexual attitude (or what is now called gender identity).

▼ ▼ ▼ ▼ ▼

Second, Freud held that, regardless of what their adult psychosexual balances are, all women experience as girls some degree of "penis envy" when they discover that males possess what they lack. "Penis envy," Freud argued, reinforces girls in their Oedipal-period father love because they hope to get from their fathers the penis they envy and because unconsciously they equate the penis they desire with a baby. It also makes them hostile toward their mothers, whom they hold responsible for their lack.

"Penis envy" specifically and the bisexuality thesis more generally have been met all through the decades of controversy with two counterclaims by psychoanalytic critics. The first counterclaim holds penis envy to be a derivative phenomenon rather than a central, determinative one. The second holds that femininity is not a slow, uncertain achievement but rather a biological given, the predetermined goal of which is motherhood. Karen Horney, for example, argued that girls develop penis envy only when their Oedipal loves for their fathers are inevitably disappointed; they do not need to be reinforced in their father love, however, for they are, as feminine beings, headed in the direction of heterosexuality and reproduction from the start. Melanie Klein, from quite a different angle, also found that penis envy "covers in some measure [the girl's] frustrated desire to take her mother's place with the father and receive children from him." The girl has "feminine desires" from the start, and is enmeshed in a rivalry with her mother; she feels "the impulse to rob her mother of the father's penis and babies."[2] Without using a biological argument about primary femininity Clara Thompson and others argued that penis envy is a derivative of sociocultural prejudice: the penis symbolizes the power and privilege men have, and derogation of the female genitals—which the theory of penis envy implies—is part of that power and privilege.

In the face of criticism from Horney, Klein, and others—notably Ernest Jones—Freud held firm on the importance of penis envy for women and on the universal-bisexuality thesis, which was, to him, the centerpiece of his work. His convictions were deepened after 1925, when he shifted away from the idea that a girl's first love is for her father. As he focused on the girl's original love bond with her mother in the period called "pre-Oedipal," Freud emphasized that a girl's love for her mother becomes active, so that she is her father's rival before she comes to love him. This "negative Oedipus Complex" may remain dominant in a woman who turns toward her father only incompletely or temporarily, and it will always lend its passion to a father love that is very intense

▼ ▼ ▼ ▼ ▼

and becomes intricately woven through with father identification. Indeed, it was in women, like his own daughter, Anna, whose father love was very striking, that Freud first discovered the pre-Oedipal mother-bond. As he increased his appreciation of how strong and long-lasting this mother-bond could be, penis envy as a means for overcoming it became both more important and more complicated: it is a crucial ingredient of a girl's hostility to her mother, but also of her desire for her mother; it is a crucial ingredient of her desire for her father, but also of her identification with him.

I think that Freud's analysis of his daughter was very significant as confirmation for the area of his thought he considered secure—bisexuality and penis envy—and as a challenge for the more tentative extension of his inquiry into the pre-Oedipal period. Anna Freud's was a lengthy analysis, comparatively and for the time: in several segments, it went on from 1918 to 1925. "A Child Is Being Beaten" (1919) and "Some Psychical Consequences of the Anatomical Distinction between the Sexes" (1925) probably, I have argued in Essay 4 above, report on Anna Freud's analysis. The two summary essays "Female Sexuality" (1931) and "Femininity" (1933) probably have debts as well to this analytic work, in addition to their more obvious debts to the work of the child analysts who joined Anna Freud's seminars at the Vienna Psychoanalytic Institute after 1924. But the evidence presented by Anna Freud's analysis and the evidence garnered from early work by child analysts did not prompt Freud to review the full range of his earlier work on female psychology. Indeed, when he returned to the topic in his last essays, like "Analysis Terminable and Interminable" (1937), he reverted to his old emphasis on bisexuality and penis envy as though the new look at the pre-Oedipal years in females had never taken place.

Historically, this lack of retrospection was defensive. Freud was protecting his views of bisexuality and penis envy from his critics. In effect, he was stating—I think quite correctly—that his critics were deriving their views of pre-Oedipal female development from their critiques of bisexuality and penis envy, not from clinical considerations. He wanted to block this kind of theorizing, which constructs the first years of life on the basis of predetermined life courses—Klein's sequence of schizoid and depressive positions, for example. The consequence for later psychoanalysis of such theorizing is a story in and of itself and a very important one. But it is another story—a might-have-been story rather than a so-it-was story—that I want to track here: the lack of retrospection in Freud's own work meant that his late tentative ideas about the female's

▼ ▼ ▼ ▼ ▼

pre-Oedipal years became the focus of later debates without their implications for his overall theory ever having been assessed by Freud himself.
And the same condition is characteristic of three other areas of Freud's
work that he treated as less sure than the domain of bisexuality and
penis envy. Let me give short-hand designations to these three areas in
the form of questions, and then I will take them up one by one in might-
have-been terms:

Are all women masochistic, or more likely than men to be masochistic; is "feminine masochism" more common in females?

Are women more likely to be narcissistic in object-oriented terms
than men, whom Freud called "anaclitically narcissistic"?

Are women less likely to develop firm superegos in the process of
"dissolution of the Oedipus Complex"? Does this mean that women are
ill-suited for sublimation, and thus for cultural achievement, which
Freud linked to capacity for sublimation?

In preparation for taking up these questions one by one, I would make
two simple observations about the way Freud's late work evolved.

The first is that Freud's case studies of females date predominantly
from the period of his work on hysteria: most of the female psychology
in the *Three Essays* that Freud himself thought quite secure was fash-
ioned with reference to hysterics. The only full case study of a female
who was not a hysteric, the 1920 case of a homosexual eighteen-year-
old, was also written before Freud turned his attention to the girl's early
mother-bond, which is only foreshadowed in that case. It may be that
Anna Freud's case lies behind the later work on female psychology, but,
even if this is so, her case is only alluded to in "A Child Is Being Beaten"
and the late essays on female psychology, not studied in detail. There is
no equivalent in Freud's female psychology to the kind of pre-Oedipally
(or "primal scene") referenced case study he did on the Wolf Man or to
the kind of retrospective review of earlier material (Little Hans, the Wolf
Man) that he conducted in *Inhibitions, Symptoms, and Anxiety* (1926).

Second, it is important to note that the three huge innovations in
Freud's late work—the dual instinct theory first offered in 1920, the
structural theory of 1923, and the 1926 theory of anxiety—were none
of them explored or tested or illustrated with full cases studies of either
males or females. The dual instinct theory is crucial for understanding
Freud's concept of masochism as he articulated it in "The Economic
Problem of Masochism" (1924), where he speaks of "feminine masochism" but builds his inquiry on cases—none presented in any detail—

▼ ▼ ▼ ▼ ▼

of male homosexuals. The structural theory is crucial for understanding the formation of the superego, and for interpreting Freud's claims about the superego in female development. But there is no case focused on superego development in either males or females, although, because Freud constantly referred to males in *The Ego and the Id* and related papers, his meaning is clearer for them. Finally, the theory of anxiety offered in his 1926 essay involved a reconsideration of narcissism as it relates to castration anxiety, and for this reconsideration (as I noted before) Freud referred to Little Hans and the Wolf Man. He mentions in this essay that women do not have the castration anxiety so crucial for males' normal and pathological developments, but the whole topic of what early anxieties women *do* have was not taken up until the 1931 essay "Female Sexuality"—which contains not even a mention of female narcissism.

What these two observations indicate is that Freud's evolving view of female psychology was, comparatively, thinly illustrated, and also not reviewed in light of the developments after 1920 in his metapsychology. Large issues deriving from the dual instinct theory, the structural theory, and the anxiety theory were at stake in the 1920s, and they quite overshadowed issues specific to female psychology; and when female psychology did come back into Freud's focus, it was not in the context of the larger metapsychological issues, but only—importantly, but only—in the context of his new look at pre-Oedipal mother-daughter bonds.

With this much preliminary framing, let me try to show what a retrospective stance taken from within the terms of Freud's own thought might yield in the way of questions and problems for his view of female psychology. I turn first to the issue of "feminine masochism" and to the two essays in which masochism is the central topic, "A Child Is Being Beaten" (1919) and "The Economic Problem of Masochism" (1924).

In the first of these, Freud argues that beating fantasies are "the essence of masochism" and discusses masochism as sadism turned on the self under the influence of a sense of guilt. The female cases presented—including, as I noted, what seems to be a disguised version of Anna Freud's case—involved fantasies of being beaten in which girls took on male roles to fend off the incestuous desires for their fathers that Freud considered crucial to their lives. They were sexually ascetic, the fantasies substituting for their sexual lives while serving as their punishments. By contrast, the "feminine masochism" Freud discussed in 1924 is a derivative of a primary masochism, called erotogenic masochism, which is not sadism turned against the self. Erotogenic masochism is that part of the "death instinct" which remains bound in the organism, and involved in all libidinal stages, after another part of the death instinct has been expressed as aggression. "Feminine masochism," which Freud says involves fantasies of being beaten, being copulated with, giving birth, depends, then, very crucially for its form on the degree and libidinal stage of the underlying erotogenic masochism. (Because this 1924 discussion preceded Freud's emphasis on pre-Oedipal events, oral masochism, or fantasies of being devoured, are not mentioned.) All that can be said about feminine masochism generally is that it is most likely to be found in people who were unable as children to express their aggression, who were more erotogenically masochistic than femininely masochistic. Women especially fall into this category, Freud argued, because, for constitutional and social reasons, they are less aggressive— they project less of their death instinct outward sadistically.

It might have followed from Freud's general theoretical orientation in the 1924 essay that a detailed reconstruction of feminine masochism at each libidinal stage would have revealed differences between feminine masochism in men and feminine masochism in women—comparable to the differences in types of beating fantasies revealed in the 1919 essay. But the 1924 essay offers no discussion of differences, by libidinal stage or by gender. As I noted, Freud indicates that feminine masochism involves fantasies of being beaten, being copulated with, giving birth, but he does not indicate that any masculine role playing is included in women's fantasies of being beaten—indeed, he insists that "feminine masochism" in both men and women specifically involves only fantasies of being feminine, not the fantasy of being masculine that he had formerly held to be typical of girls. He does note that "feminine masochism" fantasies arise in the context of guilt-producing incestuous desires for the father and that they are punishments, but they are not said to combine with asceticism in women.

There is a third type of masochism, called moral masochism, which involves desexualization of masochistic fantasies, but Freud does not consider whether such desexualization occurs differently in women and men—even though the 1919 discussion of female asceticism certainly raised the possibility that female desexualization involves assuming a male role vis-à-vis the father in fantasy. There is a clue, too, in this discussion about one type of sublimation, and thus of cultural production, common in women: in a male guise—under a male *nom de plume* in male dress, with a male companion as alter ego, in the medium of a

▼ ▼ ▼ ▼ ▼

male character in a novel, and so on—the female producer stands for moral rectitude in the form of self-sacrifice. This type of sublimation, which is Anna Freud's type, is of course only one type, but discussion of it might have opened the way for considering other types.

Let me summarize this complex matter another way: It seems to me that the 1919 and 1924 discussions of masochistic fantasies do not fit together as far as women are concerned—though they do as far as men are concerned. There was a problem here that never got addressed, and it seems to me that the problem was only exacerbated by the fact that Freud did not return to the discussion of masochism after he began to stress girls' pre-Oedipal history. This blank in the accounts does nothing to illuminate the vexed topic of the female's superego development.

Freud offers two quite different ways to understand how the superego is built up. One was laid out in *The Ego and the Id* (1923) as part of the presentation of the new structural theory, though it has its roots in the earlier text "Mourning and Melancholia" (1915). The superego is said to be made up of identifications with parental figures. It is a legacy of lost loves—people abandoned or lost as love objects are kept on as imagoes in the mind, like a kind of Greek chorus representing the ancestors, immediate and phylogenetic. It is in the context of this story that Freud presents the girl child as relatively without a superego, for she does not suffer castration anxiety and "dissolution of the Oedipus Complex" in the masculine manner. Her castration complex introduces her into the Oedipus Complex by reinforcing her father love and turning her away from her mother. Since her Oedipus Complex does not dissolve or break up she may stay in it for the rest of her days, more or less.

It seems plausible on Freud's own terms that rather than being relatively without a superego, the girl in her sustained Oedipus Complex, having abandoned her mother for her father, should have a superego made up largely of her maternal identification. Half a superego, as it were, rather than none. But this possibility was not considered, even though in 1923 Freud did carefully correct his original statement that the superego is paternal by saying that it is parental—that is, he clearly acknowledged mother identification as an ingredient. Later critics of Freud's theory have argued that the girl's superego should not be disparaged as undeveloped or infirm but acknowledged as speaking "in a different voice" (to use Carol Gilligan's phrase), but even these theorists have not suggested that this voice might be dominated by maternal identifications.[3] Another complexity arises if the situation of girls with intense father identifications is contemplated. Intense father identifications come about, Freud had argued in "A Child Is Being Beaten" when a girl protects herself from incestuous feelings for her father by identifying with him, taking on a masculine role. But father love need not be abandoned here; it is only sublimated—and the result is that she may remain in the Oedipus complex, but with a strong superego. This seems to be how Anna Freud developed. And it is interesting to observe that creativity can in this way, as in the way noted before, be strongly sustained through a masculine fantasy role that might be described as "fealty in the service of a moral ideal."

Noting the situation of the masochistic females studied in "A Child Is Being Beaten" brings me to the second story about how the superego is built up. This one was offered in "The Economic Problem of Masochism" (1924) when Freud was engaged in the project of knitting together theoretically the structural theory and the dual instinct theory. This economic story essentially says: When aggression is not or cannot be projected outward, it is turned inward, and this "destructiveness which returns from the external world is also taken up by the super-ego and increases its sadism against the ego," (19:170). The economic story makes it possible to understand how a child who has unsevere parents from whom to take its identifications can nonetheless end up with a very severe superego and be too rigidly good for its own good. It also makes it possible to infer that girls, who do not, according to Freud, express their aggression as much as boys, should have relatively *more* severe superegos. But this result is exactly the opposite of the result of the first story, which was that the girl can be relatively without a superego.

The tension between these stories might be resolved if we imagined one kind of superego as a legislature lacking much capacity for enforcement of its laws and another as a militia accustomed to using force without much regard for whether there are laws or not—the types could be called Law and Order, for short. But this possibility might also alert us to the fact that in psychoanalysis the same term can often cover two—or more—very different developmental stories. "Narcissism" is a case of particular importance.

Freud did carefully distinguish forms of narcissism by distinguishing two types of object choice, anaclitic and narcissistic. But he did so in 1914, a decade before he began to reconsider his views on female psychology. And in the late essays on female psychology there is no return to the distinction, no new look, and particularly no new look at anxieties specific to females that might be compared with the new formulation of castration anxiety and male narcissism Freud offered in his

▼ ▼ ▼ ▼ ▼

1926 text on anxiety. There is, however, a hypothesis in this text that suggests that females are more anxious about loss of love than boys, who focus on loss of their genitals. We can take this hypothesis as a starting point.

Most men, Freud had argued in 1914, tend to choose their objects on an anaclitic basis, attaching their sexual desire to objects—beginning with the (usually maternal) caretaker—who serve their self-preservation, their ego instincts. They worship their objects, making over their self-regard to them. (Other men may not take this route, but rather homo-sexually love versions of themselves, that is, love as their mothers once loved them, a variation on the anaclitic choice in which they identify with their mothers.) By contrast, most females, in puberty and in social conditions that inhibit their range of action and choice, do not transfer their self-regard; rather they love themselves exclusively, choosing others not to love but to be loved by, and they remain in this state until a child is born to them and converts them, like a little missionary, to object love. In "On Narcissism," Freud said nothing at all about girls before puberty.

Freud did not later fit together his 1914 picture of male and female types with his constant emphasis on the great female narcissistic wound—the discovery the girl makes as a child that she is without a penis. (He had spoken of women who love according to the masculine narcissistic type, "who develop some way along masculine lines" [14:90] before puberty, but he had not explicitly said that these women were longing for a penis.) The later work on female psychology indicated quite clearly that girls are as attached to their mothers as boys are, and that in the "negative Oedipus Complex" they love them as boys do, actively; but there is no consideration of whether this pre-Oedipal attachment fostered future anaclitic object choices, or, if not, why not. The prepubertal story of female narcissism was not opened for exploration.

From what he does say, it is obvious that Freud did not think that Oedipal girls make over to their objects their ego-preserving self-regard and overvalue their objects accordingly. When girls discover that they cannot win their caretaking maternal figure (in part for lack of a penis), they either go right on trying—a formula for perpetual childhood or illness—or they become ascetic, or they turn to their fathers. But Freud does not ask whether or under what conditions the fathers might then be loved or worshipped anaclitically or loved for their protection and nourishment—becoming the new caretakers, successors to the mother. This is after all what is implied by Freud's late insight that girls—like

his daughter—who are intensely attached to their fathers have trans-
ferred to the fathers an even more intense early love of their mothers.

Along these lines, however, it is important to note that Freud was
in his last years apparently reconsidering in the light of child analytic
research his old idea that the girl unconsciously develops her wish for a
baby out of her wish for a penis. Ruth Mack Brunswick reported in 1940
that, with fuller understanding of how both girls and boys pre-Oedipally
desire to make babies with their mothers, it became clear to Freud that
"the baby wish" precedes a girl's turn toward her father. But as the girl
makes this turn, she "understands" that the baby wish and not the penis
wish is the wish both possible and permissible for her.[4] There is ego
instinct support in this realism, and it also means that she is going to be
a recipient again—of the penis in coitus—which she can certainly feel
qualifies the man as a new and better caretaker, an anaclitic object choice
who serves both self-preservation and the self-regard that the mother
did not serve. (This would make sense, in terms of the theory of narcissism, of the observation Freud made in "Female Sexuality" about how
often women continue in the medium of their marriages the story of
their relationships with their mothers, and of his comment that second
marriages are often happier for not falling so directly heir to that conflicted mother-daughter story.)

At any rate, looked at from the vantage point of his later theory, the
remarks that Freud made in 1914 about females—about their self-love
and their difficulties in attaining object love—make sense for only a very
particular type of female. (And even for her Freud did not take into
account how compromised her self-love would be—according to his own
theory—by feelings of inadequacy stemming from her "narcissistic
wound.") For most people, female and male, it makes more sense to
think of the search for a caretaker as the chief narcissistic modality. And
it is easy to imagine why Anna Freud thought that the "Is everyone
taking care of me?" attitude was often preserved in the more acceptable
form of taking care of others, that is, by the mechanism she called "altruistic surrender"[5] A girl makes over her "masculine" ambitious (or self-
promoting) wishes to the men in her life, and her "feminine" wishes for
a child (her father's) to the women, and she enjoys the satisfaction of
her wishes vicariously, without immediate danger, in a condition that
might be called extended-psychic-family narcissism.

If there is a form of anaclitic relatedness that is served especially
well for women by the mechanism of projecting wishes onto others, as
I am suggesting, it might very well sustain a kind of creativity not tra-

▼ ▼ ▼ ▼ ▼

ditionally recognized as creativity—the people-serving sort of creativity so well suited to the running of households and, in more liberated times, the running of organizations. The possibility of a complementarity arising between this kind of creativity and "fealty in the service of a moral ideal," which I described earlier in association with a strong female superego, seems obvious.

The point of this theory-analysis exercise—if I may belabor it further for a moment in conclusion—is to show that reading Freud's view of female psychology from last to first, traveling back through the course of its development, discloses many of its problems and points toward ways of thinking about them. Most of the criticism of Freud's view that has been formulated since the 1920s is based on assumptions he did not share— specifically, assumptions about primary femininity and about the derivative nature of penis envy. The consequence has been that internal inconsistencies that would have shown up had Freud made a retrospective review of his earlier formulations (and perhaps of his cases as well) did not appear. I have tried to let some of those inconsistencies appear and to use them to indicate areas where, it seems to me, new work needs to be done. In general, with regard to female psychology, I hope for a resurgence of plurals: not further effort to compass *the* single story of female development, but interest in plural stories of (to recap the areas explored here) types of masochism, types of superego formation, types of narcissism, types of creativity. I have tried to argue that these plurals were latent in Freud's view of female psychology and need only interpretation to reveal themselves.

▼   After being delivered in several versions as a lecture, this essay was published in *Psychoanalytic Inquiry,* 11 (1991): 427–440, the issue devoted to "Contemporary Issues in Female Psychology."

▼ ▼ ▼ ▼

11

On Psychoanalysis
and Feminism

Within the last several years, articles, books, and essay anthologies with "psychoanalysis and feminism" in their titles have come pouring off presses in this country, in England, and in France.[1] The moment is dense with reassessments of the relations that have existed between feminism and psychoanalysis and of possibilities for the future. To understand the moment's meaning—for feminism, for psychoanalysis, and for the purposes past and present that have linked the two—we would like to offer a brief historical survey and a commentary. A much fuller history needs to be written, particularly one able to cross national boundaries and appreciate differences in types of cultural discourse, but what we can do here is to indicate what questions such a history would have to articulate.

To begin with, we can say that this moment of reassessment signals a transition toward a fourth paradigm—one might almost say an emergent fourth generation—of relations between feminism and psychoanalysis. The three preceding paradigms that have, we think, come and to varying extents gone—though none has gone completely—could be called, from the point of view of feminism, Dissent, Rejection, and Appropriation. For the fourth we will use Critique, as a political term. These relations of feminism and psychoanalysis, we will argue, need to be understood both historically and geographically or in relation to national cultures; so our survey will weave American, British, and French strands through the four frames.[2]

Dissent and Rejection

Aside from some skirmishes between first-generation Freudians and European feminists of the First World War period, the first type of sustained relation between feminism and psychoanalysis—Dissent—came about from within psychoanalysis.[3] Beginning in the 1920s, Freud's evolving view of female psychology was questioned by analysts, most of whom were women, located in Berlin—Karen Horney chief among them—and London and, later, New York. These questioners were basically modifiers, and the main focus of their modifying critique was the Freudian notion that penis envy plays a key role in determining whether a girl will persist in a "masculinity complex" as she grows up, or mature into a woman with "a normal female attitude," or develop as an ascetic—the three possibilities summarily evoked by Freud in his 1931 essay "Female Sexuality." Horney originally considered penis envy a secondary formation, a reaction girls have to disappointments in their Oedipal loves of their fathers. Melanie Klein, by contrast, assigned penis envy to the pre-Oedipal period and saw it arising in the infant's oral relationship with her mother. Both Horney and Klein asserted that girls are aware of their own genitals and vaginal sensations before they become aware of the male genitals and their own difference. Later Clara Thompson and Karen Horney in her New York years interpreted penis envy sociologically as envy of male prerogatives and status—as envy of the phallus symbolic, not the penis anatomical. Horney and Thompson thus became feminists without the name as they generated discussions and debates, supplying the first generation of nonanalyst feminist critics with a wedge: Psychoanalysis is not, their work said, a monolith; it has dissenting schools, and it has internal dissent over the nature of female psychology.

The second period of relations between feminism and psychoanalysis extends from immediately after the Second World War, with Simone de Beauvoir's anti-Freudian *Second Sex* (1949) and Viola Klein's *Feminine Character* (1946), through the early 1970s; and it is in this period that national differences became very important. In the United States, the rejectionist style of the period was augmented by Betty Friedan's *Feminine Mystique* (1963), and that style rose to a crescendo in the early 1970s, when Kate Millett's *Sexual Politics* (1970) was decisively influential.[4] In this American mode, rejection of psychoanalysis featured a Freud who was not just phallocentric (Ernest Jones's term from the 1920s) but misogynist; who was not just wrong about women because of male bias but wrong because of his own fundamental sexism. His work was said to be simplistically biologistic—his famous use of the phrase "anatomy is destiny" was the proof—and simplistically prescriptive about what should constitute feminine normalcy in everything from type

▼ ▼ ▼ ▼ ▼

of orgasm to type of "normal female attitude." Thus it seemed that the feminists were debunking psychoanalysis, and titles like "The Myth of the Vaginal Orgasm" (Ann Koedt) abounded. The distinction between sex and gender, biology and social experience, that was forged in this period meant "anatomy is *not* destiny." Or, as Simone de Beauvoir famously put it, woman is not born but made.

It is very interesting to note, however, that these early 1970s American rejecters of psychoanalysis were, at the same time, appropriating psychoanalytic insights for their understandings of male psychology and of sexism. Kate Millett, while she was rejecting Freud's views on women so vehemently, offered Freudian-style readings of texts by Norman Mailer, Henry Miller, and D. H. Lawrence to explore the modalities of sexism. For example, she supported the very Freudian idea that men who degrade or abuse women are fighting their own homosexuality. This (usually unstated) acceptance of psychoanalysis for the purpose of analyzing male sexism provided one of the venues, later, for the mid-1970s American reappropriation of psychoanalysis, which took it for granted that one of the key things to understand about women is what male expectations have meant for them. Thus later appropriators focused on what Millett had always referred to vaguely as "socialization." When Millett and others accepted Freud's psychology of masculinity, they also used it to support the idea that pathology in women should be viewed as caused by social factors, not intrapsychic ones, and regarded as a sign of protest, as a weapon in the battle against the male pathology built into social institutions. This stance helped make heroines out of hysterics, and it rendered the whole topic of female pathology extremely difficult for later theoreticians.

In Britain, by contrast, the feminist rejection of Freud was not so sweeping. Freudian biologism was certainly jettisoned, but Freud's cultural theories were appropriated for understanding the history of sexual inequality. Freud himself, then, could be read—as Juliet Mitchell read him—as an analyst of patriarchal society, not a patriarchal society planner. Freud came into 1960s British feminism, which was much more Marxist and alert to the Third World issues created by receding European imperialism than American feminism, in the medium of the study of socialization "as a process which is constitutive of any society" (as Mitchell noted). American use of the term "socialization" was vague, almost incantatory, but the British were systematic analysts, strong critics of state-sponsored sociology, attentive and careful materialists, and also creative adapters of the work of Louis Althusser. The British New Left

▼ ▼ ▼ ▼ ▼

renounced sheerly economistic Marxist understandings of society and of sexual inequality—including visions of how sexual inequality would disappear with the coming of a socialist revolution—in favor of a focus on ideology, which Althusser had defined as "the way we live ourselves in the world" or "the Imaginary relationship of individuals to their real conditions of existence." The British New Left feminists dedicated themselves to finding and cataloging in every material realm evidence of how the ideological category "woman" is created, especially by states. Whereas many Americans focused on private emotions and worked in the medium of literary analysis, especially of novels, as Kate Millett had in *Sexual Politics,* the British, by contrast, made their most remarkable contributions in the late 1960s and early 1970s to social science and social history.

At the same time, in France, the watershed year of 1968 brought with it the women's group Psychoanalyse et Politique. The very existence of such a group, with such a name, signals that psychoanalysis was crucially, if in complicated ways, allied with the radical, antibourgeois, antihumanist Marxism of the generation of 1968. But this was not Freudian psychoanalysis, it was Lacanian, or it was Freudian psychoanalysis as interpreted and propounded by Jacques Lacan. It was dissident psychoanalysis, alluring in its outlaw status with respect to official Freudianism in France and throughout the world. Lacan's Freud gave French feminists what Althusser's Marxism gave the British, a way to understand women's oppression as structured into the language, by which the French feminists meant the whole of life, conscious and unconscious. When the unconscious, "structured like a language" in Lacan's famous phrase, is revealed, it shows oppression, or patriarchal construction of femininity, as clearly as any of the materializations of ideology collected by the British. All sign systems articulate "the Law of the Father." But the French specialized in studying—one might even say allegorizing—language itself, texts, writing, the "logocentric" (as Jacques Derrida put it) philosophical tradition of the patriarchal West, and they found in certain ostensibly close-to-the-unconscious iconic texts models for the inversions and subversions of sexual role playing that became *de rigueur* for sexual-cultural revolution. Hélène Cixous, for example, included in her program of revolutionarily "feminine" French texts those of Colette, Marguerite Duras, and . . . Jean Genet.[5] On the French scene, homosexuality assumed the function of *épater les textes bourgeois,* even though there was very little in Lacanian psychoanalysis itself to challenge the pathologization of homosexuality that was typical of the American and

▼▼▼▼▼

British psychoanalytic establishments. Indeed, there was very little in Lacanian psychoanalysis to challenge any existing definitions of feminine or masculine normality or spheres of life—even though there was a challenge to understand how such definitions come about.

In distinct discourses that nonetheless trafficked with each other, then, feminists in America, Britain, and (much more equivocally) France propounded the idea that there neither is nor should be any recourse to a concept of feminine "normality." Despite their differences, it is no exaggeration to say that all versions of this idea had in common rejection of Freud's instinctual drive theory—his most biological postulation. The drive theory never again after this period escaped anathema in any of feminism's relations with psychoanalysis. And, on the psychoanalytic side of the pair "psychoanalysis and feminism," some psychoanalysts took notice of the rejection of instinctual drive theory. American analysts were alerted to the feminist consensus by the heated debate, prompted by gay and lesbian activism, that led to the American Psychiatric Association's decision in 1973 to stop classifying homosexuality as a pathological deviation from "normality."

The number of articles in American psychoanalytic professional journals devoted to female psychology increased dramatically in the late 1970s, and the debates of the 1920s began to be reviewed with interest. Research projects developed, many of them focused on the feminist distinction between sex and gender and filled with questions about whether and how the anatomical distinction between the sexes has psychical consequences. And, slowly, female practitioners who were not of the second generation, the generation trained by Freud and his followers, began to arrive in print and in positions of influence in institutions. In America, Jean Baker Miller edited a volume called *Psychoanalysis and Women* in 1973, and a collection of analytic papers from the mid-1970s was published in 1977 under the title *Female Psychology: Contemporary Psychoanalytic Views*. The first volume shows how some psychoanalysts opened themselves and their theorizing to American feminism and entertained the arguments of the rejectionist mode. The second volume shows how others (a much larger group) continued the older Horney-Klein-Thompson tradition of dissent and modification.

Among the mid-1970s revitalizers of this older dissenting tradition, the most commonly embraced revision of Freud was the one first advanced in the 1920s: the idea that there is a "primary femininity," a biological and psychic bent in women toward femininity, which nor-

▼ ▼ ▼ ▼ ▼

matively entails heterosexuality and motherhood.[6] This revisionist tendency, obviously, was a mixed blessing for feminism. It countered the Freudian theoretical phallocentrism by giving women an identity of their "own," not one organized in relation to viewing the male's anatomy. But it also countered the idea that gender is totally socially constructed and independent from sex or biology.[7] And, ironically, although the "primary femininity" formulation was meant as a revision, it posed no challenge to the conservatism of the medically trained majority of Freudian analysts, many of whom went right on trying to cure women of any deviations from "normality." The official depathologizing of homosexuality was, then, both a sign of liberalization and a sign that "normality" could be reasserted in new biologically based theoretical terms, more Freudian, as it were, than Freud's.

Among both feminists and psychoanalytic revisionists in the United States, a great deal of confusion was generated on the "sex versus gender" front in the 1970s due to the widely held assumption that it was the conservative wing of analysis that was being most true to Freud's theoretical and therapeutic intentions. Revisionists within the house of psychoanalysis were aiming at the notion that every little girl passes through a stage on her developmental road of being "a little man" (the so-called negative Oedipus Complex) and only gradually achieves "normal femininity," in the sense of an alignment, as it were, between female anatomical characteristics, feminine sexual attitude, and predominantly heterosexual object choice. The feminist rejectionists, by contrast, were attacking the idea that there is a "normal" developmental road at all. What Freud himself seems to have had in mind is not, however, accurately portrayed in either the modification or the rejection. He thought that both females and males are innately bisexual. They then become predominantly feminine or predominantly masculine, depending upon their constitutions, the environmental (especially family) factors that shape them, and their psychic representations or fantasies. Or, rarely, they maintain their bisexual equipoise. Among the ingredients of their sex-gender identities—anatomical, mental, object preference, aim preference—there are no necessary or biologically predetermined relations. Freud certainly did speak teleologically of "normal femininity," and he certainly did designate the genital pleasures and reproductive functions of females and males as "mature sexuality," but when he spoke in these ways he obscured the radicality of his own fully articulated theory of sexuality, to which we will return below.

▼ ▼ ▼ ▼ ▼

Appropriation

By the mid-1970s, American feminism's period of rejecting psychoanalysis had begun to wane and a third paradigm was emerging. Three feminists were particularly influential in bringing about the change: the English writer Juliet Mitchell, whose *Psychoanalysis and Feminism* was published in the United States in 1974, Gayle Rubin, an anthropologist whose essay "The Traffic in Women" came out in 1975, and Nancy Chodorow, a sociologist who published *The Reproduction of Mothering* in 1978. But it was Chodorow's work, along with that of others known collectively as object relations theorists, that came to dominate the American scene.[8] And they continued to dominate for a decade, even thought by the late 1970s the French writers who were reappropriating Freud in the medium of Jacques Lacan's work began to have some influence on several American academic feminists.

In Britain, by contrast, the French Lacanian influence was very strong (even though the British were quite skeptical about French feminist appropriations of Lacan because these seemed so uncritical of institutions and so willing to redefine "the feminine" rather than to criticize definitional processes). It was to Lacan rather than to any British psychoanalysts that British feminists turned—and there was no clinically inspired volume like Jean Baker Miller's *Psychoanalysis and Women* to build a bridge between feminists and analysts. Juliet Mitchell recognized in the Lacanian influence a continuation of the emphasis she and others on the British New Left had been establishing through Althusser. Comparing two of her essays, "Women: The Longest Revolution" (1966) and "Freud and Lacan" (1982), Mitchell noted that in the first "women were nothing other than the different social and economic structures in which they were created: there was no essential category: 'women.' Lacan's work sets up that realization at the very heart of the question of the construction of femininity."[9] The difference between the American turn toward object relations and the prevailing British feminist interest in ideological constructions of femininity is a continuation of the earlier difference between American and British conceptions of "socialization." To Americans it seemed very commonsensical to say that a child's "objects" (the people caring for her, loving her, and being loved by her) constitute a relational matrix in which her identity is shaped; and it also seemed commonsensical to think that a relational matrix could be adjusted, fixed, repaired—and a child's identity thus shaped differently. From the perspective of Lacanian theory, such a reformist program aimed

▼ ▼ ▼ ▼ ▼

at the family configuration seemed quintessentially American and naive, for Lacanian theory held that the unconscious is where "socialization" takes place, and the unconscious is not amenable to social manipulation.

But on both sides of the Atlantic it was nevertheless agreed, in spite of this dramatic difference, that "the very heart of the question of the construction of femininity" lies in the pre-Oedipal period—no matter how differently this period itself was constructed by different theorists, in different national contexts. The most diverse late 1970s appropriators of Freud thus had in common—we think—that they adopted Freud's late emphasis on the importance of the pre-Oedipal period for girls (and boys), and they then followed the turn in psychoanalysis itself (in America, Britain, and France) toward stress on the importance of the pre-Oedipal, sometimes nearly to the exclusion of later development. Feminists appropriated Margaret Mahler's pre-Oedipal emphasis on separation and individuation, Heinz Kohut's "self-psychology" on the early development of self-esteem, Kleinian work on the "schizoid" and "depressive" positions of children before the age of two, and so forth, eclectically. And, generally, psychoanalytic feminists found in the pre-Oedipal period the possibility of a feminist redemptive vision. To put this complex matter very summarily: They constructed the pre-Oedipal period as the period before gender roles get solidified, the period before a girl must suppress her primal tie with another woman—her mother; the period before she enters into what the Lacanians came to call "the Symbolic." The pre-Oedipal girl is, as it were, prepatriarchal.

Correlatively, to one extent or another, and in one way or another, many feminists used the new emphasis on the pre-Oedipal to link this first era in an individual's life with a prepatriarchal period in the life of the species, a matriarchal period.[10] These matriarchalist theorists did not, however, return to the redemptive vision of 1920s psychoanalytic versions of the matriarchy idea, like Wilhelm Reich's, or 1960s versions, like Herbert Marcuse's, in which prepatriarchal society had been associated with lack of sexual repression. The new matriarchies were envisioned with an emphasis on female bonding, not sexual experimentation.

The lack of emphasis on sexual experimentation is not coincidental. As we noted before, the earlier period of feminist rejection of psychoanalysis had been nearly fatal for Freud's biologically based drive theory, which was almost completely ignored by feminists. The generation of appropriators did not speak of three libidinal phases—oral, anal, phallic-genital—nor did they see two "upsurges" of libidinal energy, one in childhood and one in puberty; they did not accept the idea that there is any

▼ ▼ ▼ ▼ ▼

"erotogenic masochism" (or death drive unexpressed as aggression) giving rise to "feminine masochism"—indeed, the very words "feminine masochism" were not to be spoken. Thus, in the United States, the main form in which emphasis on the pre-Oedipal period had come into prominence—the so-called object relations psychoanalysis mentioned before—rejected any talk about biologically based libido and aggression. Development was discussed in terms of objects—incorporated part objects and the maternal object in the pre-Oedipal period, the paternal object later—but these objects were not envisioned as connected to libidinal or aggressive phases.[11] Autoerotism was not a topic; "masturbation," for example, was not even an entry in the index to Chodorow's *Reproduction of Mothering.*

The situation was rather different in France, however, where there was, among the French feminists influenced by Lacan, a drive theory, but not Freud's drive theory. The French Lacanian feminists spoke of feminine *jouissance* (roughly, desire); but this comes in two forms only: unalienated desire, which is what infants have in the pre-Oedipal period, in "the Imaginary" (to use Lacan's term), and alienated desire, which is desire under the influence of "the Symbolic," desire which can never find its object, desire distorted by partriarchy or the Law of the Father.

The absence of a Freudianly constructed drive theory is, we think, the main theoretical reason why the feminists of this period of appropriation never connected their work with earlier efforts to appropriate Freud for social criticism, especially not with Herbert Marcuse's *Eros and Civilization,* or with Angela Davis's 1971 application of Marcuse's work to feminist theory. Marcuse, of course, had found in the pre-Oedipal period—which he, like the later American and French feminists, associated with the feminine and the prepatriarchal—the "polymorphous" sexuality that he thought would, if recovered and liberated, check the death-driven, suicidal impulses of patriarchal civilization, of masculine fascism in all its forms. The pleasure principle was, for Marcuse, the feminine-erotic, while the reality principle, distorted under the "surplus repression" of late capitalism into the performance principle, was the masculine. Like Wilhelm Reich, Marcuse saw sexual liberation as the model for all liberation.

Such a vision of redemptive polymorphic sexuality, redemptive eroticism, was not echoed in the United States in the late 1970s, although in Britain Juliet Mitchell was interested in Wilhelm Reich, and there were whispers of redemptive eroticism in the French feminist invocations of bisexuality—an invocation made dazzlingly in Hélène Cixous's famous

▼ ▼ ▼ ▼ ▼

lyrical essay "The Laugh of the Medusa"—because there was, as noted, a kind of a drive theory to create a receptivity in the French tradition. Many of the French also spoke of a drive to language, which is an idea derived from Freud's notion of a component instinct called curiosity or the drive for knowledge. But, in general, in the period of feminist appropriation of psychoanalysis, any kind of speculation about "the feminine" was deemed to be biologizing and thus "essentialist." Those theories of this period that did speak of "the feminine," and were thus to some extent essentializing, were studiously nonbiological. With or without the help of psychoanalysis, they emphasized feminine intuition, feminine moral vision, women's ways of knowing, *écriture féminine*—they were part of what became known as "cultural feminism," which is, as the title conveys, focused on gender, not sex, and is concerned with the social construction of gender.

At issue in the quarrel over essentialism are claims and counterclaims about the universality and fixity of socially constructed gender, not any biological substratum of gender. The great popularity in America of cultural feminism's case for essentialism rests on the fact that "the feminine" is always construed positively and that even family structures said to reproduce conventional mothering are viewed positively. Nurturing and caregiving as virtues are stressed, and this is, of course, an anti-Freudian turn in the sense that Freud felt that all people come to altruism by default, their childhood egotism having beached on the shores of the reality principle or their having to get attention by the second-best route—by being good.

But there are also other and less directly theoretical reasons, it seems to us, why the American scene in the late 1970s did not reinvent a Reichian or Marcusian appropriation of psychoanalysis. Many American feminists had come to feel that the sexual politics of the 1960s was ill conceived, unliberating. And one of the key goals of 1960s feminism, summarized in the phrase "abolition of the family," had also receded, carrying many idealizations about sexual liberation with it. The hostility toward psychoanalysis that was summarized and extended so angrily by Kate Millett was deeply informed by Marxism, and deeply dedicated to the Marxist goal of abolition of the family, even though there was less socialism among American feminists than there was in Britain. Millet read Freud as the theorist who most powerfully rationalized the nuclear family and the subservient place of mothers and daughters in that family. She saw Freud and particularly Freudianism as the leading force in a huge conservative backlash against early-twentieth-century progressive

▼ ▼ ▼ ▼ ▼

attempts to institute more communal forms of living—against, for example, the early experiments with communal living made by the Bolsheviks in the Soviet Union. Simone de Beauvoir, the role-model theoretician of this period, had made it very clear that she considered marriage the antithesis of liberation and thought that no married woman, much less a mother, could ever fulfill the liberationist program articulated in the last chapter of *The Second Sex*. Women, de Beauvoir often said, need to be liberated from children.[12] Millett and many early 1970s feminists followed this line, and added to it many reflections on motherhood and reproductive technologies that might eventually free women of motherhood without bringing the species to a halt. Others combined calls for abolition of the family with calls for separatism and dedication to "women's culture"—a new matriarchy. The most widely discussed text of this sort was Jill Johnston's unrelenting *Lesbian Nation* (1973), although discussion of lesbianism itself was fraught with ambivalence in this period—it was feared and glamorized, politicized and marginalized.

But this huge upheaval over "the family" (which became more and more hypostatized) had a distressing dimension: the rebels found it much easier to imagine the rebellion than to live it. Patriarchal constructions of femininity had not yielded in a day, and slowly the idea grew that psychoanalysis, with its emphasis on the psychic factors in identity formation, might be of more help than Marxism or any theory of mere "socialization" for understanding how deeply and recalcitrantly gender had been constructed. Furthermore, many of the women who, in the rebellious period of feminism, had attacked Freud in the context of their revolution against "the family" found themselves suffering agonizing personal dilemmas over whether to have families, how to have families, how not to have families. It was the wrestling of women in the women's movement with decisions about families and familial identities that exposed them to minority, lesbian, and lower-class women who were interested in feminism but skeptical about the women's movement: The rebels stood out as white middle-class women who could afford—in every sense of the word—an identity crisis. At the time, prominent African American feminists were, to note a particularly striking contrast, engaged in a debate with male black militants about whether birth control was part of a genocidal plot by whites and thus something to be forgone while a new generation of revolutionary children was conceived.[13]

The American appropriation of psychoanalysis in the late 1970s, which was non-Marxist or at least very much less Marxist than the 1960s rejection, had as its practical agenda reform of the family. It was designed to explore how feminists could forgo abolition of the family or separatism and make families in which mothers were not oppressed and daughters were not born into oppression.[14] The psychodynamics of family oppression was the key topic as many feminists focused more on personal than on political or legal reform. From the object relations oriented appropriators like Dorothy Dinnerstein, Nancy Chodorow, and Jessica Benjamin came the idea known as "shared parenting." In a shared-parenting family, a girl will be able to maintain her bond with her mother—not sacrifice her first love or her foundation for future female friendships—while she achieves the autonomy and separation previously known only to boys (under conditions of disidentification with the mother). Juliet Mitchell and Gayle Rubin, who both stressed that economic barter or traffic in women was the foundation of culture, also argued that abolition of the family could not in itself bring cultural revolution. To them cultural revolution had to mean revolution in the unconscious—as it were, consciously pursued reform of the unconscious—where ownership and control over women have their roots.

Critique

The fourth and latest paradigm of relations between feminism and psychoanalysis is part of the current theoretical reorientation within feminism that is signaled by the trinity Gender, Race, Class. In the early 1970s, while the majority of feminists were rejecting psychoanalysis as part of their rejection of "the family," there had been, as we indicated before, protests from minority, lesbian, and lower-class women that the assault on the family was a white, heterosexual, and middle-class affair—as was the idea that psychoanalysis was a major source of oppression. Psychoanalysis, from these other viewpoints, was not so much oppressive as irrelevant. It was, after all, of, by, and for white, heterosexual, and middle-class people and had nothing to say to people of other backgrounds except to provide yet another outline of their inadequacies or abnormalities. Currently, these protests, with some very important differences, are alive again, particularly in Britain and the United States, where, respectively, waves of Third World immigration and the force of African American protest have shaken white feminism. French feminism, by contrast, has been relatively impervious to the paradigm we are going to call Critique.

We think it is becoming more and more widely recognized that the

▼ ▼ ▼ ▼ ▼

appropriation of psychoanalysis that focused on pre-Oedipal object relations or on the pre-Oedipal "Imaginary" (in Lacanian terms) focused on the areas of human development that are not only the most difficult to reconstruct (and thus the most open to the fantasies of theoreticians), but from a sociocultural point of view, the least reflective of sociocultural differences or specificities. The late 1970s appropriators assumed that because the pre-Oedipal period is crucial to many if not all therapies and perhaps even crucial to psychoanalytic developmental theory, it is also key to psychoanalytically informed social theory. Similarly, the feminist appropriators of psychoanalysis assumed that what is primary in development is also maximally determinative—and this is an assumption, a "genetic fallacy," that cannot be justified by appeal to Freud.

In Freud's view, events that occur after the pre-Oedipal period, in the many later stages of an individual's development—tracked by Anna Freud along "developmental lines"—can reorganize or disrupt habits and structures established early on. Unexpected traumas, for example, as he argued in *Inhibitions, Symptoms, and Anxiety,* the text in which he revised his original theory of anxiety, can harm the ego, virtually demolish it, no matter what the previous course of its development has been. (The same could be said for what is known as a cumulative trauma.) Or, to take another example, people who early acquire an unconscious sense of guilt and then find themselves later in an external situation in which they suffer constantly, or (as they may interpret their lot) are punished constantly, are frequently relieved of their neuroses—the context allows a "flight into health." Or, to take a different sort of example, people who develop adequate defenses in their early childhoods against forbidden desires may find that the upsurge of the instinctual drive (or, to speak in modern terms, the hormones) in puberty, or a particular type of temptation or trauma in adolescence, renders those defenses inadequate; so mild hysteria may grow debilitating, functional obsessional ceremonies may give way, a breakdown may ensue. Dora, for instance, to cite Freud's well-known case, was precipitated into her teenage illness by a seduction and betrayals, and Freud's Wolf Man, who had a breakdown when at the age of eighteen a gonorrhea infection profoundly wounded his narcissism, later had a period of good functioning during the First World War, when he was buffeted by external events that were, so to speak, much sicker than he was.

To put this matter of causality or determination in philosophical terms: there is a difference between proximate and ultimate causes. (Freud's terms were "precipitating causes" and "underlying disposi-

▼ ▼ ▼ ▼

tions.") Although ultimate causes prepare the ground in a person's psyche, proximate causes may be the most important for the final outcome of development. And social conditions very frequently operate as proximate causes in this sense. For example, Frantz Fanon, when he was writing as a clinician in *Black Skin, White Masks,* noted that many Martinician children were decisively shaped by the contrast between their early childhood home lives, among blacks, in quite matrifocal, extended families, and the society they entered when they went to school—they were, shaped by the moment when racism was made concrete for them, and was traumatizing. Comparable kinds of events (some psychoanalysts use the term organizing traumata) shape the lives of people who have been well loved and praised for their goodness at home until the moment that they announce their homosexuality and become objects of disgust, or people who have been insulated from much class prejudice until they journey from the country to the city, or from their ghetto or barrio to the precincts of the middle class, and so forth.

Our examples concentrate on children of oppressed groups who discover their oppression, because these kinds of examples can be simply presented—with the aid of a simplifying image of a moment, a revelation—whereas more commonly there is a series of experiences, which may be telescoped in retrospect or organized by a screen memory. But what we want to suggest with these examples is that, for people who understand their experiences both psychologically and sociologically, by virtue of the fact that they know themselves to be members of oppressed groups, the dimensions of psychoanalysis that may be most important or most revealing or most helpful (including clinically, therapeutically) are precisely not the dimensions—the pre-Oedipal period, particularly—focused upon by feminist appropriators in the late 1970s and 1980s.[15]

We would also like to make the same point from another angle. Those feminists whose work can be described in shorthand as Race, Class, and Gender are concerned with types of oppressors as well as types of victims. What psychoanalysis can show about the motivations and mechanisms of racism, classism, and sexism, feminists of this orientation discover, is not derived primarily from analysis of the pre-Oedipal. Children, as all psychoanalytic and empirical psychological research has shown repeatedly since the publication of Mary Ellen Goodman's *Race Awareness in Children* (1952), do not acquire racial (or, more generally, social) prejudices in the pre-Oedipal period; they do not acquire them until about the age of three (more or less, depending on

▼ ▼ ▼ ▼

how prejudice is defined and how the observations are made). Learning prejudice, of course, presupposes the learner's social formation or underlying disposition, but what a child's first experiences with prejudices mean is also deeply influenced by later reinforcing or unreinforcing events and contexts. Finally, the feminist focus on the pre-Oedipal period or on the oral stage (to use libidinal terms) occludes any discussion of anal sadism and aggressivity, and thus dangerously distorts—one might say pacifies—discussion of human social life. Aggressivity in women, for example, became virtually a forbidden topic in feminism—at least until black feminists forced white feminists to acknowledge the degree of racial aggressivity in the feminist heritage.[16]

Whether for thinking about modalities of oppression or modalites of being oppressed, it is quite possible that in the coming period of relations between feminism and psychoanalysis, feminists may begin at last to read the psychoanalytic literature on adolescence, starting with Freud's "Transformations of Puberty" in *Three Essays on the Theory of Sexuality* (1905). The effort could then go on to the early socialist psychoanalysts who worked with adolescents, August Aichhorn and Siegfried Bernfeld, and then to their heirs—Anna Freud, in *The Ego and the Mechanisms of Defense* (1936), as well as in her two later essays specifically on adolescence; Erik Erikson, whose fine work on identity, adolescence, and the life cycle feminists in America have largely ignored because of an "essentialist" essay he wrote on the pre-Oedipal period, Peter Blos; and Edith Jacobson and her younger colleagues at the Yale Child Study Center, like Samuel Ritvo.[17] Psychoanalysts may, in turn, become more inclined to supply work on adolescent experiences of sexism (including violent sexism in the form of seduction, abuse, and rape), racism, classism, and so forth. Good dialogue might go a long way to end what Michèle Barrett has rightly called a "feminist critical avoidance of contamination by 'the clinical' " or by concern with either the practice of psychoanalysis or the domain of pathology.[18]

The inclusion of a broader range of developmental topics within feminism—resulting from a diminution of feminism's white, middle-class preoccupations and, more important, from the slow broadening of the range of women involved in the feminist movement—is, we are suggesting, broadening the conception of psychoanalysis. Both the object relations narrative and the Lacanian one are before-and-after stories. Development, in these stories, has a single and decisive point of no return—in relation to the law of motherhood and reproduction or in relation to the Law of the Father—and feminism's strategy has been to

▼ ▼ ▼ ▼ ▼

attack at these points by changing the family structure or by supporting an unstructured "free" unconscious as a source of cultural renewal. The unstated assumption of both types of theorizing is that, in order to effect patriarchy, feminism must be grounded in nonpatriarchy or prepatriarchy. The image is Archimedean: with a place to stand, one can move patriarchy. But this image is too simple to account for all the influences— of race, class, and so forth—that are not located at a single point of no return. As far as we know, there has not yet been any critique of the before-and-after narrative as a kind of organizing myth—a version of the story of the Fall in which women are doomed to subservience to the Patriarchal Family or Patriarchy's Law—but it is clear that in the emergent paradigm of relations between feminism and psychoanalysis, human development is being understood as a more complex business, with many crucial junctures. Not revolution as a single-site reform, but subversion across the whole terrain is the new strategy.

Female Sexuality

This process might bring in its train a further development that we think is key. As we have been noting throughout this brief history and commentary, feminism has in its phases of dissent, rejection, and appropriation assumed that Freud's instinctual drive theory (often misrepresented) was the enemy, or the central command for all other enemy forces. To us, this seems a great misunderstanding with many unfortunate consequences. What has happened, to state the matter very summarily, is that feminist appropriators of psychoanalysis have thrown the drive theory out with the idea of "normality." They have jettisoned the instinct theory's most illuminating dimensions—the theory of bisexuality, the notion of erotogenic zones, the emphasis on biphasic instinctual upsurges, the theory of aggression, the radical idea that the objects and aims of the libido are variable and not tied in a necessary or predetermined relation to each other. Because Freud called the libido masculine and presented the phallic-genital stage as a universal experience in which girls and boys develop the idea that being female is being inferior—and because these views, rigidly interpreted, were central to much of conservative psychoanalytic practice—the rest of the drive theory was laid aside.

One of the consequences of this situation, we think, is that there has been very little psychoanalytically informed feminist discussion of female sexuality. Even when "sexual liberation" remained a stated goal

▼ ▼ ▼ ▼

of feminism, sexuality—standing, so to speak, at the border of the biological and the social—was problematic or made problematic by the "sex versus gender" distinction. Similarly, of the three dimensions of sexuality that Freud set out to study in his *Three Essays on the Theory of Sexuality*—libido or instinct, sexual objects, and sexual aims (which included types of sexual practices)—only objects and object relations have been at the center of American feminist attention, while libido and types of sexual practices have been largely ignored. In the early 1970s, celebrations of masturbation and of so-called open marriages or free sex were common, but these were not psychoanalytically oriented. Similarly, within lesbian communities, where sadomasochistic practices were, particularly in the early 1980s, a focus of violent debate, both sides of the debate were antipsychoanalytic. With the notable exceptions of the two essay volumes *Powers of Desire* and *Pleasure and Danger,* there has been little feminist discussion of sexual practices that was framed psychoanalytically.[19]

However, it is very interesting in this regard to note signs of change like the essay by the British feminist Parveen Adams in the collection *Between Feminism and Psychoanalysis* (1989), in which she tries to construe lesbian sadomasochism as a type of liberation practice or, as she puts it, a "trangressive sexuality," a "perverse intensification of pleasure," in which the lesbian has "refused to operate within the space of masculine and feminine choices."[20] The closeness of this view—despite intervening Lacanianism—to Marcuse's celebration of polymorphous perversity seems obvious, and it is also very close to Kate Millett's use of Freud to explore *male* sadomasochistic homosexuality, via the literary world of Jean Genet, as an example of sexual liberation.

But still no instinctual drive theory emerges along with the return of the repressed biological or anatomical distinction between the sexes in Adams's discussion. Further, Adams's lack of examination of Freud's instinctual drive theory makes it necessary for her to redeem and justify lesbian sadomasochism in a way Marcuse never felt constrained to do for polymorphous perversity. That is, Adams assumes that Freud thought of perverse practices as necessarily pathological, whereas, in fact, Freud argued again and again that a perverse object choice or aim choice acted out is the opposite of a perverse choice repressed—the former may or may not be combined with psychopathology, but the latter, presupposing repression, is psychopathological by definition. To cite the phrase Freud uses repeatedly in *Three Essays on the Theory of Sexuality,* the perversions are "the negative of the neuroses," which means, to cite Freud's 1920 exemplary case, that a homosexual eighteen-year-old woman can be described as "in no way ill."

Parveen Adams's redemption of lesbian sadomasochistic practices from the domain of pathology is, in fact, quite Freudian. Freud held sadomasochistic or any other kind of noninjurious perverse practices to be psychopathological only if they were indulged exclusively, either in the sense of "to the exclusion of any other kind of practice" or in the sense of "invariably preventing other practices, as foreplay becomes end-game."[21] A neurotic's symptoms become his or her sexual life, they take it over, substitute for it; a perverse person is neurotic if his or her practices do the same thing, with the same kind of formulaic rigidity (which implies inability to respond to another person). In other words, a person who merely mingles some perversity in his or her sexual practice—and in Freud's understanding, this is Everyperson—is normal. (We should note, lest what we have said be misconstrued, that if being transgressive is pleasurable in and of itself, not because of the pleasurable sensations involved in the practice, a different register of analysis is called for—this is not transgressive sexuality, but sexuality undertaken to be transgressive. Similarly, practices involving another person and questions of consent or physical harm may well call for moral consideration, not just considerations of mental health.)[22]

Freud really did not think that there is some fated or biologically predetermined conjunction between anatomical sex and gender (which he called "mental sexual characteristics")—much as some of his teleological statements sound as though he did. His key summary passage on this topic comes at the end of the case study of the eighteen-year-old homosexual woman, and it is worth quoting in full:

> The literature on homosexuality usually fails to distinguish clearly enough between the questions of choice of object on the one hand, and of the sexual characteristics [i.e., sex] and sexual attitude [i.e., gender] of the subject on the other, as though the answer to the former necessarily involved the answers to the latter ... It is instead a question of three sets of characteristics, namely—
>   Physical sexual characteristics
>   (physical hermaphroditism)
>   Mental sexual characteristics
>   (masculine or feminine attitude)
>   Kind of object choice
> which, up to a certain point, vary independently of one an-

other, and are met with in different individuals in manifold permutations.[23]

And this list of variables does not even include "kind of sexual practice or kind of pleasure aim," the fourth of Freud's quartet of sexual ingredients, and the one most clearly consolidated not in childhood but in puberty, or when mature genital sexuality becomes a possibility.

What Freud's way of thinking in this passage implies is that the sexuality which is most free is the sexuality in which there is least coercion from one's own superego, from other people, or from conventional notions or mores or laws operating in each of these domains and prescribing how these four domains are or ought to be related. Freedom is not just freedom from an oversevere superego, from coercion, or from conventionality on the topic of sex, nor is it just freedom on the topic of gender, or on the topic of object choice, or on the topic of sexual practice—it is all of the above. The form such freedom will take, then, will be different for each individual. For example, a prescription about which practices are transgressive or free of conventional masculinity and femininity (the domain of mental sexual characteristics) is just as prescriptive as (if more unusual than) a prescription that deals with "normality." Lesbian sadomasochism is not liberating for lesbians who can take no pleasure in it or do not wish to take pleasure in it—including those who object to it as a prescribed practice in their community, involving rules about the correct mental sexual characteristics for practitioners. Any prescription is potentially confining for people who are not at the time psychically organized to want or to fill the prescription or who have no desire to be thus organized.

Discussion of sexual practices in psychoanalytic terms is one sign of the emergent fourth paradigm we have been describing, and we would like to note another in closing. By the mid-1970s, the double importation into Britain that we noted, of Althusser's work on "the imaginary relationship of individuals to their real conditions of existence" and Lacan's emphasis on "the Imaginary" as the arena in which images of the self and of the other adhere, had led to an entirely new use of psychoanalysis among feminists. This was, specifically, film theory, but more generally theory positing the centrality of images to cultural production and reproduction, theory focused on what Jacqueline Rose called "the field of vision." Rozsika Parker and Griselda Pollock, two of British feminism's

▼ ▼ ▼ ▼ ▼

most distinguished art historians, described the cultural-political context:

> The feminist challenge to accepted ideas of what constitutes great art and great artists was part of a broad attack on the art establishment. The 1970's saw the birth of cultural studies in universities and polytechnics, the boom in community art projects and the beginning of radical artists groups, for example the Artists' Union and Artists for Democracy . . . economic and ideological transformations in the sphere of artistic production as well as larger social fields facilitated a coalescing of radical developments in cultural politics with vital forces for social change within the Women's Movement.[24]

The feminist visual theory, suffused with psychoanalytic notions, can be summed up very crudely as follows. If fantasy is where ideology is incubated, and if the imaginary is constructed by identification with images—with the same precision as if images really constituted a language—then it is clear that visual representations of all sorts are critical sites for feminism. Laura Mulvey, a film theorist, brilliantly conceptualized the "male gaze" as a quasi-material structure that follows the path a film camera takes and can, therefore, be made visible by noting the traces in celluloid of its gazing. This formulation relied heavily on Freud's instinctual drive theory, specifically on the concept of a scopic drive, an instinctual drive woven with sadistic and masochistic components, and it turned to Lacan for presenting the identificatory mechanisms—the imaginary—set up between the film screen and the spectator. For Mulvey and the other critics who wrote for the journal *Screen*, the filmic apparatus virtually was the apparatus of the unconscious as they saw it revealed by the psychoanalytic method. For example, mainstream Hollywood films could be criticized for at worst debasing and at best ignoring the conscious and unconscious pleasure of the female spectator by pandering to the male, presenting the "male gaze." Debate arose over how best to represent female pleasure, or even whether to represent it, or women, at all.

Visual representations have been understood in the new British theory as, at once, a privileged contemporary avenue for delivery of oppressive ideology and a privileged weapon of resistance. And feminists associated with the journal *m/f* have launched into this context a psychoanalytically informed critique of essentialism which insists that

▼▼▼▼▼

"woman" cannot be known apart from the cultural (including visual) forms and interests that represent her. While many other feminists in the period of emphasis in Race, Class and Gender in Britain and America have been turning to pluralism (some say muiticulturalism) as a way of conceptualizing "differences" between women and men and among women, the writers of *m/f* have insisted upon the strong presence of "division" by race and class among women, and even of division within the self. For a social theory that focuses on conflict, psychoanalysis understood as a theory of conflict is key.[25]

One further remark in closing: If it is the case, as the two examples we have noted imply, that "feminism and psychoanalysis" is moving into a period of greater range and richness, particularly as regards the experiences of people who oppress and are oppressed in the mediums of race and class as well as gender, and particularly as regards the topic of sexuality, then it will be very important to think about the relations that can and might exist among these areas. How, for example, can the goal of eliminating prejudices—sexism, racism, classism, and others—be conceived in relation to the goal of sexual liberation? There is, of course, a tradition of thinking about what connects sexism and racism[26]—but these are only two of the many forms of prejudice, and the two are not necessarily yet understood in and through the many phases of the life cycle, the many types of human individuals and social characters that exist, the many forms of life that flow from the many permutations of our psychic ingredients, and so forth. Viewed against the panorama of these questions, "feminism and psychoanalysis," although it is four generations old, is very young.

▼   This essay began as talk for a panel discussion at the Graduate Faculty of the New School for Social Research. My friend Laura Wexler, of Yale University's Women's Studies Program, who came to hear the talk, made so many important suggestions for its revision that I invited her to co-author the essay version. It appeared under both our names in *Social Research,* 59 (1992): 453–483, and I thank my co-author for allowing me to reprint it here.

12

What Happened to
"Anorexie Hystérique"?

Over the course of the last few decades, a clinical judgment about anorexia nervosa has become a commonplace: the disease is very different from hysteria. The commonplace has now been officially registered and certified by the third edition of the American Psychiatric Association's *Diagnostic and Statistical Manual of Mental Disorders*, which has two completely unrelated categories, "Eating Disorders" and "Somatoform Disorders, Conversion Type," into which anorexia and hysteria fit. The syndrome known by Jean Charcot and Pierre-Marie-Félix Janet as "anorexie hysterique," thus, no longer exists—in name anyway. And recently sociocultural historians and historians of psychiatry have ratified the clinical judgment by claiming that anorexia is to the late twentieth century what hysteria was to the late nineteenth—both diseases are "exaggerated stereotypes of their times"—and since the two fins des siècles are so different, the diseases are, of course, different as well.

We would like to question the commonplace argument about hysteria and anorexia on theoretical grounds and in terms of sociocultural history. That is, we want to question how the separation of anorexia from hysteria came about and which assumptions from sociocultural history have recently reflected and reinforced that separation. We are not clinicians, and we are not making any argument about treatment modalities, but we do think that anorexia nervosa presents an intriguing example of how clinical, theoretical, and historical assessments intermix—and specifically of how psychoanalysts have tried to put the past of their science behind them while cultural historians have both followed suit and reinforced the psychoanalytic judgment.

▼ ▼ ▼ ▼ ▼

When we look over the history of psychiatric and psychoanalytic work on anorexia nervosa, one thing is immediately obvious: whoever stresses the medical nature or somatic origins of the disease also stresses its distinction from hysteria.

The English physician William Gull, who is credited with discovering the disease, invented the term anorexia nervosa to replace his own earlier designations, "hysteric apepsia" and "anorexia hysterica" (a translation of the French "anorexie hysterique"), precisely in order to distinguish the disease from hysteria. Gull wanted to give his disease a name that would do for males as well as for females—because he subscribed to the mistaken but common assumption that hysteria existed only in females. But more important, he wanted to separate anorexia nervosa from hysteria in order to focus on the medical, not the mental, aspects of the disease.[1] In the early psychoanalytic tradition, by contrast, both anorexia nervosa and the more general condition of self-starvation called anorexia (without an adjective) were explored as hysterias. Freud did not, however, focus specifically on anorexia nervosa, and neither did his early followers.

During the First World War, the disease seemed temporarily to fall outside the orbit of psychology, just as Sir William Gull had wished. Between 1914 and about 1930, it was widely thought to be caused by pituitary failure, and "Simmond's cachexia" all but replaced anorexia nervosa in the medical literature. But when pituitary treatments proved largely unsuccessful, psychological discussions of anorexia started again, and by the late 1930s debates about anorexia nervosa revolved, instead, around nosological questions. Some clinicians thought the disease was a type of obsessional neurosis, others a type of psychosis, and still others that it was a distinct psychoneurotic syndrome distinguishable from all others. These questions are still much discussed in the literature.

When psychoanalysts began to consider anorexia again, after the Second World War, they did so largely on the basis of psychoanalytically oriented psychosomatic medicine, which tended, like earlier medical approaches, to separate anorexia from hysteria. Analysts of this sort sought correlations between psychic conditions and physical conditions, and, in this case, they agreed that the key correlation is between fear of pregnancy and refusal of food and consequent emaciation. Edward Lehman, in a general review of "Feeding Problems of Psychogenic Origin" (1949), could say confidently: "the psychosexual significance of eating is clearly expressed in anorexia nervosa, in which refusal of food and consequent emaciation may be so extreme that life is endangered.

▼ ▼ ▼ ▼ ▼

In this disorder, a number of different investigators have all reported approximately the same psychic mechanism. There is not only a marked repression of sex drives but also an inhibition of eating because the individuals unconsciously feel that eating is a sexual act. They have a disgust for food, which therefore is rejected, because eating is equated with intercourse, gratification and impregnation."[2] Within the psychosomatic tradition, it became more and more common to argue that those earlier psychoanalysts who had considered anorexia a form of hysteria had been observing only atypical cases of conversion hysteria. Analysts of the psychosomatic persuasion did, however, appropriate the emphasis on disturbed psychosexual development that had been central to earlier psychoanalytic approaches to hysteria. "There is always a much greater suppression of psychosexual development in these cases [of anorexia] than in conversion hysteria and this has occurred at all stages of development," one analyst noted in 1944.[3]

In general, there was little psychoanalytic work on anorexia nervosa between 1945 and the late 1950s except among those affiliated with schools of psychosomatic medicine. But the association between anorexia and hysteria was nonetheless loosened from the hysteria side. A debate arose about whether the designation "hysteria" should include severely impulsive (even psychotic-like) and addictive traits and symptoms, or whether the relative ego strength and maturity of hysterics precluded such traits and symptoms. This topic was related to a debate of long standing about whether the oral symptoms so typical of hysteria—of which food refusal was one—were clues to the pre-Oedipal origins of the hysteria or whether the oral symptoms were secondary to, or derivative from, or regressions from, Oedipal and genital conflicts. As this debate unfolded, anorexia nervosa, viewed as the most elaborate oral symptom complex, became a key issue on which an older generation of Freudians, accustomed to seeing the Oedipus Complex as the nucleus of the neuroses, was locked in controversy with a younger generation, drawn by both their scientific curiosity and their rebellion against their elders toward the pre-Oedipal period. In general, the greater the emphasis given to pre-Oedipal object relations and separation-individuation issues, the stronger the repudiation of any connection between anorexia nervosa and hysteria.

But the old association of anorexia and hysteria also became problematic for a quite nontheoretical reason while anorexia was being given renewed attention. Practitioners of all theoretical persuasions noted the mysterious diminution in the patient population—and, seemingly, in the

▾▾▾▾▾

populations from which patients came—of the *petite* and particularly the *grand hystérie* symptoms that had been central to Charcot's observations: the motor disruptions, involuntary actions, epileptiform seizures, trances, and hallucinations. While questions about how to understand the oral symptoms in hysteria grew, the range of gross motor symptoms—paraplegias, paralyses, anesthesias of limbs, and so forth—contracted. Otto Fenichel, who wrote a thorough and thoroughly Freudian description and analysis of hysteria in 1945, had noted as much as a decade earlier that analysts were seeing very few hysterics, and he had speculated that this showed the historical dynamic of the neuroses—that hysteria belonged to an earlier period of repressive social morality.[4]

At any rate, for psychoanalysts anorexia began to live a life of its own, independent of hysteria, both because the debates about oral symptoms challenged the old understandings of hysteria and because hysteria itself receded. This twofold tendency was reinforced, in turn, by two developments. On the side of theoretical inquiry, there was the pioneering but decidedly unpsychoanalytic, behaviorally and cognitively oriented work of Hilde Bruch, who stressed the pre-Oedipal origins of anorexic symptomology but rejected psychoanalytic therapy for or inquiry into the disease. Bruch and others gave tremendous impetus to approaches that minimized attention to drives, unconscious fantasies, or pathological developments of aggression and sexuality.[5] Like earlier medical writers, Bruch, by medicalizing anorexia, pulled it away from hysteria nosologically.

Second, on the side of "historical dynamics" in the neuroses, there was the beginning of a tremendous and relatively swift increase in the patient population of anorexics, an increase that by the late 1970s was being called an epidemic. This development reinforced a tendency among neo-Freudians or cultural Freudians, followers of Karen Horney, Eric Fromm, and others, to locate the primary cause of anorexia in social conditions, and particularly in the prescriptive behavioral imperatives of middle-class households in advanced capitalist economies, and in the imperatives of cultures enamored of dieting and thinness. This social etiology, in turn, appealed to a generation of feminist writers and therapists, who elaborated the idea that anorexia is a cultural disease, and not at all the same disease as hysteria because not at all a function of imperatives like those of the Victorian fin de siècle. As one writer in this vein said summarily: "eating disorders are not simply a modern version of hysteria; they stem from a very different set of issues to [sic] those that confronted women in the nineteenth century."[6]

▼ ▼ ▼ ▼ ▼

In sketching this general history, we noted in passing that Freud did not give anorexia nervosa his attention, even though each of his case studies of hysterics involves some kind of eating disturbance, which he designated anorexia (without the specific adjective "nervosa"). This silence in Freud's work has always complicated the approach to anorexia of the Freudians, but we think it even more significant that Freud's own theoretical work on the psychoneuroses in general was left unfinished. In the decade after he summarized his views on hysteria in the *Introductory Lectures* (1916–17), Freud of course made enormous revisions in the foundational concepts of psychoanalysis—advancing the "structural theory," the "dual instinct theory," the second theory of anxiety—but he also tried to formulate a general theory of the psychoneuroses, an effort which he then carried into his major essays on female psychology. The questions he was raising, it seems to us, are precisely the ones that have made psychoanalytic inquiry into anorexia nervosa such a complex and controversial business.

During the period of his inquiry that culminated with the major clinical review essay *Inhibitions, Symptoms, and Anxiety* (1926), Freud's systematizing attention centered on several questions. Are the psychoneuroses sequential—that is, does the sequence hysteria, phobia, obsessional neurosis that was so obvious in the Wolf Man's case (1918) occur generally? Is a childhood sequence recapitulated in adulthood—is this the way that infantile and adult neuroses are related? Are such layerings of psychoneuroses correlated to the sequence of libidinal phases—oral, anal, phallic-genital—and is there a corresponding sequence of aggression phases? Is there a correlated sequence of mechanisms of defense? Does the sequence of the psychoneuroses generally play itself out differently in men and women, or in those whose bisexuality is weighted toward masculinity and those whose bisexuality is weighted toward femininity?

The Wolf Man's case, so rich, so elusive, suggested or reactivated all of these theoretical questions, and it is also obvious in a passing remark made about anorexia nervosa in this case study that Freud understood anorexia nervosa as a disease in which comparable complexity could be found. "It is well known that there is a neurosis in girls which occurs at a much later age, at the time of puberty or soon after, and which expresses aversion to sexuality by means of anorexia. This neurosis will have to be brought into relation with the oral stage of sexual life."[7] Indeed, Freud seems to have been gesturing toward the idea that anorexia nervosa is the pathology in women that is most like the Wolf

Man's pathology, so multilayered and complexly referenced to the oral, anal, and phallic-genital stages, which Freud held to be more likely in males. This suggests that the key areas of inquiry pursued in the Wolf Man case and flowing into Freud's subsequent work could be fruitfully traversed with regard to anorexia nervosa, which is the path we would like to take in what follows. But we want, first, to set Freud's gesture in its immediate context with a quick and partial review of the Wolf Man's case.

In the chronology of the Wolf Man's symptoms, what is now called an eating disorder came first—the child would eat sweets and only sweets, refusing all other food. When Freud discussed "the very first of the patient's neurotic illnesses," he indicated both that it involved a regression to orality from a later stage and that it was connected to the patient's fear of being eaten by a wolf. The fear of being eaten Freud, in turn, connected to the Wolf Man's fear of being copulated with anally by his father. As the child developed, his sexual life became organized sadomasochistically and focused on intense fear of passivity. He manifested what Freud calls "a true hysteria" in which his bowel behaved "like a hysterically affected organ" (17:113). His bowel was, to use Wilhelm Reich's later term, "genitalized" in his fantasy of copulation.

It was while Freud was sketching this clinical picture that he made the brief remark about anorexia nervosa cited above. But rather than stopping to pursue the systematic question implied by the comparison of the Wolf Man's pathology and anorexia, he went on to sketch the key part of the Wolf Man's history, which was the boy's transition from the domain of hysteria and phobia to obsessional neurosis. The shift began at about the age of four and a half, when he was introduced by his mother to Christian religious doctrines: "The transformation did not occur spontaneously, through internal development, but through an outside influence. Its visible effect was that the patient's relation to his father, which stood in the foreground, and which had so far found expression in the wolf phobia, was now manifested in obsessional piety . . . The sadomasochistic sexual organization came slowly to an end, the wolf phobia quickly vanished, and, instead of sexuality being repudiated with anxiety, a higher method of suppressing it made its appearance" (17:114). The Wolf Man was then able in his adolescence to turn to female sexual objects, as a continuation of his obsessionally controlled fear of passivity and his repudiation of his homosexual desire related to his father: "There had been a violent revulsion in the direction of women, and he had thus

▼ ▼ ▼ ▼ ▼

won his way to complete masculinity," Freud remarked, a little ironically (17:117).

It was not until he looked back on the Wolf Man case in *Inhibitions, Symptoms, and Anxiety* that Freud drew a general conclusion about how obsessional neurosis relates to hysteria: "Obsessional neurosis originates, no doubt, in the same situation as hysteria, namely the necessity of fending off the libidinal demands of the Oedipus complex. Indeed, every obsessional neurosis seems to have a substratum of hysterical symptoms that have been formed at a very early stage" (17:113). Freud was also imagining a juncture in which males go on to an obsessional neurosis more frequently than females—"there is no doubt that hysteria has a strong affinity with femininity, just as obsessional neurosis does with masculinity"—because of the importance to males of castration anxiety and to females of anxiety over loss of love (20:143).

When the Wolf Man moved on from his hysterical symptoms, including his first one, the eating disturbance, toward obsessional symptoms, he was operating, as Freud stressed again and again, under his fear of castration. His homosexual longing for his father (his so-called negative Oedipus Complex) would, if satisfied, mean that he was a woman like his mother, a castrated man; and his longing for his mother, if satisfied, would bring him into rivalry with his father (the positive Oedipus Complex) and thus to the threat of castration. He was caught in an object relations impasse.

But, at the same time, the Wolf Man had a fantasy in the enjoyment of which he felt cured, free of his castration anxiety—that is, he felt his impasse to be safe. This was a fantasy in which he entered his mother's womb and was copulated with there by the father. In this complete (positive and negative) fantasy Oedipal fulfillment, he, as Freud put it, used "his genital organ to represent him . . . replacing that organ regressively by his whole person" (17:102).[8] This fantasy had a sustaining role in the Wolf Man's psychic life until his breakdown in early adulthood under the renewed castration anxiety represented by a gonorrhea infection; at that point, in his breakdown, his obsessionality ceased to fulfill its warding off function and he was cast back into his fear of being gobbled up—particularly in his therapy with Freud.

On the theoretical level, the Wolf Man case suggests three areas of focus for Freud's ongoing effort to formulate a general theory of the psychoneuroses, and we will take these up in relation to the current and historical literature on anorexia nervosa.

▼ ▼ ▼ ▼

The Psychoneuroses in a Series

First, it seems very obvious that Freud was working toward a theory of the psychoneuroses as a series or as a sequence of illness tributaries, branching off at key junctures from a complex developmental stream, not as a group of three distinct entities, hysteria, phobia, and obsessional neurosis. In fact, he uses this metaphor in *Inhibitions, Symptoms, and Anxiety*, where he speaks of the "current of the neurosis" and its tributaries. Or, to put the matter differently, he was returning to an idea he had expressed in his 1896 paper entitled "Heredity and the Aetiology of the Neuroses," where he had noted that among obsessionals, "the framework of the symptoms is [regularly complicated] by a certain number of symptoms which are simply hysterical" (3:156). It seems that Freud was working with the idea that before the end of adolescence, when a character is (usually) consolidated and the plasticity of the psyche diminishes, people can slip back and forth among the psychoneuroses under the impact of external and internal events. Phobia can serve them in either a hysterical mode or an obsessional mode (as an anxiety hysteria or as obsessional phobia).

This conception is particularly illuminating for syndromes—and anorexia is one—in which there is much disagreement among clinicians and theorists about nosology because symptoms common to all three of the psychoneuroses are apparent. These symptom complexes would tend to arise, Freud's argument implies, most typically in people, like the Wolf Man, whose bisexuality was most heightened, who are in what might be called a bisexual paralysis. They are stuck rigidly like Buridan's ass between two bales of hay, rather than being able to alternate between different types of object choices or types of sexual activities in the more "polymorphously perverse" or labilely "trickster" ways of relatively unneurotic bisexuals. These symptom complexes would also mark people who, also like the Wolf Man, are sustained by a bisexual fantasy comparable to his fantasy of himself as a phallus. The fantasy allows both returning to the mother and being a part of the father.[9]

Freud's incipient formulation about the psychoneuroses has another possible application to anorexia. Anorexics are, as all clinicians note, obsessional. They pursue thinness with calorie counting, charts and measurements, exercise regimes, and the kind of ferocious discipline observable in religious ascetics (as Rudolph Bell noted in detail in his historical study of medieval ascetics, *Holy Anorexia*). They may also employ obsessionally the binge-purge behavior known as bulimia.

▼ ▼ ▼ ▼ ▼

Indeed, as we noted, some clinicians are so impressed by this obsession-ality that they wish to see anorexia classified as a form of obsessional neurosis.[10] But it is also possible to view anorexia as a juncture psycho-neurosis. The anorexic somatizes or develops conversion symptoms in the manner of a hysteric, using her mouth as a means to shape her whole body, rather than isolating her fantasies from consciousness in the Wolf Man's manner. But she then uses the defenses typical of obsessional neurosis, particularly intellectualization, to protect and rationalize her behavior.

Freud's conception of the psychoneuroses as layered was also designed to identify different strategies for fending off the temptation to masturbate, which, he reiterated in *Inhibitions, Symptoms, and Anxiety,* seemed to him "the chief task during the latency period" (20:16). Hys-terical symptoms, phobias, and obsessional ceremonials can all fulfill this task. But Freud was emphasizing, as he worked toward a general theory of the psychoneuroses, that fantasies such as the fantasy of the whole body as a phallus fulfill the function of fending off masturbation for both hysterics and obsessionals. Freud had noted in 1919, in an essay called "A Child Is Being Beaten," and partly with reference to the Wolf Man's case, that the masochistic fantasy of being beaten on the penis (or the buttocks as a displacement for the penis) can substitute for masturba-tion. He also noted that the female cases discussed in that essay, one a hysteric and the others to differing degrees obsessional, tended to fan-tasize themselves as boys to circumvent their incestuous desires for their fathers (at that time Freud was not thinking of girls and their mothers at all). They renounced sexuality in this way, at the price of masochism as well as asceticism, and became spectators at the scene—the beating fantasy—that substituted for their sexual lives.

Along these same lines, it is important to note a feature common to almost all anorexics: they are exhibitionists of their thin bodies; they take enormous narcissistic pleasure in being marveled over for their thin-ness, the small size of the clothes they wear, their discipline and success as dieters, and so forth. They are competitive in the medium of thinness. Their bodies, in this sense, represent them as do the penises of exhibi-tionistic boys and men (although a much closer comparison might be with transvestite males who fantasize themselves and exhibit themselves as girl phalluses).[11] But this dimension of the anorexic's syndrome could also be viewed as a way of bringing along other spectators to join her at the scene of a beating fantasy slightly altered into the mode of a maso-chistic body-shaping fantasy. She is a "hunger artist."[12]

▼ ▼ ▼ ▼ ▼

The Bisexuality of Symptoms and Fantasies

The second theoretical conclusion that was emerging from Freud's innovatory and retrospective work in the mid-1920s was that there is a complex intertwining of libidinal developmental stages and fantasies specific to them, which will usually have both active and passive dimensions (even if these are hard to discover because one predominates over the other). In the phallic-genital stage, for example, children are at a pitch of sexual curiosity and generate theories about sexual difference and the origin of babies. But their theories draw on earlier experiences—they imagine oral impregnation, anal birth. When a neurotic regresses, he or she may reactivate or fall under the influence of a fantasy as well as regressing to the eroticism of the stage, or these two types of regression may be distinct.[13]

One of the key reasons why the preponderance of anorexics are female is that their adolescent physical changes and their surrounding society's expectations for their eventual motherhood give direct grounds for the resuscitation of long-buried impregnation fantasies, whether these be oral or anal or genital. The boy's development and social context exert other pressures on him. But the anorexic girl cannot let herself be sexual or be womanly in any way that implies pregnancy, as almost all psychoanalytic clinicians note. Amenorrhea is a symptom that makes her feel protected—it is like fantasy birth control. But it is important to stress that desexualization also means she must find a way to break whatever identificatory bond she has with her mother. If she fantasizes herself a boy or a phallus, to use the example noted before, she is disidentified with her mother, but still in a form, as it were, to love her, to return to her. The pursuit of thinness is (among other things) a way to displace her active desires onto her own body—as little girls displace them onto dolls and stuffed animals.

One reason why anorexia has been so problematic among psychoanalysts is that most analysts persist in seeing the anorexic's symptoms only in their oral dimensions, which has meant (among psychosomatic writers) emphasizing fears of oral impregnation or (among object relations and self-psychology writers) stressing pre-Oedipal issues of separation and individuation or self-concept.[14] Freud's emphasis on bisexualism in fantasies and behaviors suggests that the feature of anorexia that has rightly become central in psychoanalytic theorizing—the anorexic girl's enmeshment (the current term) with her mother—should be viewed as both active and passive. Stressing passive enmeshment, ana-

▼ ▼ ▼ ▼ ▼

lysts note that the anorexic cannot get away from her suckling role, her dependency, so she revolts in the oral medium, she refuses her mother's nurture. But the negative Oedipus Complex, the active love of the mother, is less seldom noticed—and it is difficult to judge whether this is because it is less often present or because the negative Oedipus Complex has been rejected theoretically, along with the instinctual drive theory and the notion of penis envy. Hilde Bruch, who was trained in psychoanalysis, put more emphasis than any other clinician specializing in eating disorders on the bisexuality of anorexics, but she did not discuss this in terms of penis envy. She spoke in "neo-Freudian" (Karen Horneyian) terms of envy of boys' prerogatives and privileges, and in later feminist terms of gender identity confusion. By contrast, the clinicians who tended to stress the girl's active (negative Oedipal) desire for her mother in the manner of Freud's 1930s essay on female psychology—these were, chiefly, Helene Deutsch, Marie Bonaparte, and Jeanne Lampl-de Groot, then the group around Sandor Rado in New York and finally the psychosomatic medicine group around Franz Alexander in Chicago—often went to the other extreme and underestimated the oral-impregnation fear while they found "latent homosexuality" and "the masculinity complex" everywhere.

The Double Function of Defenses: Against Libido and against Aggression

In *Inhibitions, Symptoms, and Anxiety,* Freud was also moving toward a more systematic conception of the defense mechanisms. He reflected on repression as the defense most central to hysteria, but he also emphasized that repression is one among the many defenses. The question tacit in his review is whether specific defense mechanisms originate in specific libidinal or developmental stages, but he was also faced with the question, having formulated the so-called dual instinct theory and brought aggression much more prominently into the foreground of psychoanalytic observation, of whether there are developmental stages of aggression, either related to or different from the libidinal stages. Freud's expansion and systematization of his theory of defenses was, in a preliminary way, an effort to encompass defenses against both libidinal strivings and aggression.[15]

The way this effort was taking shape in Freud's thought is clear in his 1931 essay "Female Sexuality," in which he discusses the passive and

▼ ▼ ▼ ▼ ▼

active trends in female sexuality and the corresponding (by stage) trends of aggression, particularly in relation to the mother. For example, he discusses passive oral and anal impulses being converted into active ones as a child is weaned and trained, and then notes: "We find the little girl's aggressive oral and sadistic wishes in a form forced on them by early repression, as a fear of being killed by her mother."[16] Similarly, he discusses passive and active impulses in the phallic phase, stressing how often the mother, as she washes and toilet trains her daughter, initiates the girl's passive pleasures by stimulating her genitals, and how often girls actively engage in masturbation and also desire to have a baby with their mothers. The girl's aggression against her mother in the phallic stage is, Freud held, crucial for her development, for it is aggression against the mother that brings about her shift toward her father. She protests prohibitions on her masturbation, registers anger at her mother for having brought her into the world a female or for having undernourished her or produced rival siblings, but she maintains her love of her mother nonetheless. This ambivalence is common, but outstanding in obsessional neurotics, whose love relationships feature hate and love in a kind of equipoise.

In this context, again, the juncture between hysteria and obsessional neurosis and the reliance of both neuroses on phobias is very instructive. Hysterics, Freud had always noted, cling to their symptoms and wage war via the symptoms with those around them. But the anorexic's starvation, so suicidal in the view of those around her, is particularly disruptive to family life and frightening to physicians and therapists. The anorexic compels attention and love and rejects it in the same instant, often employing phobias to defend against both the loving and the aggressive side of her ambivalence.

The food refusal and body-shaping symptoms are also made up of a mix of libidinal and aggressive elements. Those few clinicians who have focused their attention on anorexics' fantasies of being a phallus note that vomiting can be equated with ejaculation, which can be both libidinal and aggressive. Similarly, diarrhea, hysterical or induced with laxatives, can signify "elimination" of an incorporated penis—an aggressive act against the father as well as a means to love the mother. Aggression turned on the self is obvious in all of the facets of the starving and body shaping, but it is important to note how libidinally exciting this masochism is, for this excitement seems to be (as we indicated before) one of the chief reasons why the anorexic cannot realistically see her body becoming emaciated: she loves herself—her genitalized self—with

▼ ▼ ▼ ▼ ▼

the unrealism or the idealizing typical of those who have (as Annie Reich once described it) a "pathological increase of primitive narcissism."[17]

Most clinicians note that anorexics characteristically view themselves as always capitulating to the wishes of others and thus desperately in need of control and autonomy; they are willful and independent on the surface, and underneath they are accommodators, particular to the demands for proper behavior and achievement that their typically very strict, cold, and sometimes ambitious parents make on them. They give the impression of being early and disappointingly weaned into a condition of what might be called false independence and precocity, which teaches them to win praise—their substitute for nursing—by being good at something the parents (particularly the mother) designate as important. They very often take over the mothering functions in a family. The aggressive dimensions of the anorexic's struggle for control and autonomy are usually appreciated clinically—even celebrated by some feminist commentators, like Susie Orbach, who refer to anorexia as hunger striking and see it as a form of struggle for liberation.[18] But the libidinal content of control, particularly when it is active in relation to the mother, when it is a form of mother love or return to the mother, is not so often noted.

When Freud made a tour in *Inhibitions, Symptoms, and Anxiety* of the types of psychoneurotic symptoms, he was impressed anew with how diverse and protean the symptoms of hysteria are: "The picture presented is so manifold that it is difficult to discover the factor which permits all these variations and yet allows a uniform explanation of them" (20:112). But the various theoretical developments that we have been tracking— in combination, no one being adequate alone—gave Freud at least a tentative map of the factors (not a single factor) that permitted hysteria's variations and its explanation. The symptoms were protean, in sum, because they were peculiarly fed by both genital and oral streams, the oral stream being made up of both fixation and regression; because they were active and passive, or bisexual; and because they were laced with both libidinal and aggressive elements. With each of these ranges involving many variations, the variations of their combinations could be multitudinous, and even more numerous to the extent that phobic and obsessional elements were interwoven (or that specific traumas might come into consideration—a topic that would require a separate discussion).

But this summary leaves out any familial and social conditions

▼ ▼ ▼ ▼ ▼

viewed as such, not as reflected in object relations or the psychodynamics of desires and identifications. It leaves out the kinds of factors that Freud discussed in " 'Civilized Morality' and Modern Nervous Illness," his 1908 catalog of the discontents produced by patriarchal sexual puritanism (with its double standard for women) and monogamous marriage. It leaves out, in other words, the field of sociocultural inquiry in which the separation of hysteria and anorexia has recently been emphasized, as we noted at the beginning of this essay.

Generally, when sociocultural historians consider anorexia nervosa during its recent period of increased incidence, that is, when they look at anorexia since 1965 or so, they conclude that it is a disease that reflects conditions of sexual liberation for women—with all of the anxieties and challenges that assuming once all-male responsibilities implies for women. They suggest, further, that it is a disease of affluence or of a kind of middle-class overfeeding. Similarities between anorexia now and hysteria at the turn of the century are noted, but these similarities are said to be of no significance in comparison to the differences. Richard Gordon, for example, referring to anorexia with George Devereux's term "ethnic disease," begins by cataloging the psycho-sociological similarities: both diseases had abrupt and dramatic increases in incidence; both had predominantly female disease populations; both reflected nuclear family dynamics and had dramatic, disruptive effects on the family; both showed signs of contagion or spread by imitation and suggestion; so that there has been an eating disorders analog to earlier mass hysteria.[19] But Gordon also assumed that the diseases are different because anorexia has waxed under conditions of sexual liberation and conspicuous consumption, while hysteria flourished under conditions of sexual repression and a relative scarcity of food. Similarly, Hannah Decker, in *Freud, Dora, and Vienna, 1900,* remarks confidently, "Anorexia is not hysteria in modern dress," even though in both diseases "the culture reinforces the familial pathology that fosters the condition."[20]

Curiously, this argument passes over the fact that eating disorders, and anorexia nervosa particularly, were common at the turn of the last century, and that "anorexie hysterique" was much studied by Lasegue, Charcot, and Janet, as well as by its namer, Sir William Gull. It also ignores the extent to which hysteria at the turn of the century involved reactions against sexualization of milieus, not repressiveness—as was the case, certainly, with Freud's Dora, who was surrounded with sexual activity and seduction. What has changed over the course of the twentieth century is the incidence: Anorexia nervosa is *more* common now, and

▼ ▼ ▼ ▼ ▼

the "classic" hysterias are *less* common. And to understand this shift it seems to us better to begin with a hypothesis opposite to the prevailing one—that is, to say that anorexia *is* the most common modern dress of hysteria—and then to ask: Why this dress rather than another? Why have the motor disruption symptoms and paresthesias of hysteria at the turn of the last century declined and the specific ones of food refusal and disturbance of body image (we would say, in the service of body shaping) increased?

What we have been suggesting with our review of the literature on anorexia nervosa in light of Freud's inquiries is that anorexia is (1) a form of hysteria very intensely interwoven with phobic and obsessional features; (2) a form of hysteria that, in women, involves bisexualism in which the masculine features are often prominent; and (3) a form of hysteria that involves a mixture of libidinal and aggressive features in which the aggressive features are often prominent (as aggression against others and against self). The implication is that, for women particularly, modern familial and social conditions promote obsessionality and allow room for the masculine and aggressive features of anorexia. Or, to put it another way, anorexia nervosa is a form of hysteria quite suitable for contemporary conditions of less rigidly separate "spheres" of family and social life, while the "classic" hysterias, which were not so interwoven with obsessional features, and in which the masculine and aggressive dimensions were more muted, were more suitable to turn-of-the-last-century conditions that promoted only "femininity."

Viewed in this way, modern sexual liberation and the general sexualization of mass culture appear as what they are to most anorexics—something intensely frightening, requiring defenses much more complex than repression, the speciality of the "classic" hysteric. The liberty an anorexic is given to be sexual, to be a woman as a very young woman, is not a liberty she wants. As the Wolf Man turned to religious practices for his help, the anorexic turns to dieting and exercising practices—the cult of beauty and fitness in our culture, a cult that can be, by a determined person, made just as asceticizing as Christian piety. And it may also do well in combination with Christian piety, particularly when that piety is represented in the contemporary culture by new forms of puritanism.

For the modern anorexic hysteric, to put this matter the other way around, to put the stress on the masculine sides of the anorexic hysteric's fantasies, the possibilities our society presents for being able to do things that were once the prerogative of men is terrifying—even while it is

▼▼▼▼▼

alluring. Society does not put its repressive stamp so securely on her active fantasies, so she must do so herself—not with simple repression, but with more complex modes of defense. She may chose a traditionally masculine activity now permitted to women—like athletics—and confine her fantasy life to it, exercising it frantically, so to speak, rather than giving it any range in the fields of heterosexual or homosexual sexuality.

These general remarks about the dangers—from the anorexic's point of view, we should stress—of sexual liberation and sexualization of the mass culture can be illustrated with the particular instance of changing attitudes toward masturbation. When masturbation, which could be an outlet for genital and Oedipal desires and fantasies, was strictly forbidden and punished, social repression was added, as it were, to repression combined with guilt for the incestuous desires and fantasies. Conversion symptoms arose when this double weight of repression was insufficient, and these were largely symptoms of motor disruption, "masturbatory tics," or paralysis and anesthesia of limbs—the "classic" hysteria. But, it seems to us, when masturbation is much less strenuously, and sometimes not at all, forbidden, the weight of repression is less, and the more likely outcome of the instinctual drives' battle against this "unaided" intrapsychic repression is not the motor conversion symptoms but substitutes for masturbation. Shifting masturbation to the oral zone is such a manner of substitution—so that starvation, but also other symptoms such as mutism, stammering, and compulsive eating or talking, may result. Body shaping is also such a substitute, for which starvation can be the means. Exercising can thus be masturbatory, particularly if it involves excitement cycles of a "high," climax, and relaxation, but so can activities in which guilt is much more pronounced and masochistic, like undergoing body-changing surgery, perhaps very literally at the hands of a male figure of power, whose power can be borrowed or submitted to or both.[21]

Viewing anorexia nervosa as a form of hysteria, as chiefly a means of avoiding sexuality or transferring sexual fantasies into other modes, also suggests a way of understanding why, in the last decade, many more cases of anorexia and bulimia in combination have been reported. Anorexia is—culturally speaking—an antiliberation mode, a type of conservatism, a personal puritanism. (We do not agree with the most prevalent feminist interpretation of it as primarily or even exclusively a liberationist protest against the culture's rampant sexual objectification of women and distorting ideals of thinness.) The generation in which bulimia is rampant came into adolescence in the 1980s, which was no

▼ ▼ ▼ ▼ ▼

longer a time for celebrating sexual freedom. It was at once—particularly for the middle class—a period of conspicuous material consumption, binge consumerism, and of backlash against sexual liberation and all of the frightening sexual freedom of the 1960s, a new puritanism. That is, American middle-class society was in a mode of consumption followed by punishment—and that is what bulimia is as well. The bulimic does not have to rebel against sexual liberation on her own; she can find help in the society's undercurrent of puritanism. And such bulimic symptomology is, so to speak, just what an anorexic needs: it is obsessional, it can involve repudiation of femininity (and pregnancy) specifically as well as sexuality in general, and it is tremendously aggressive.

Generally, it seems to us, the effort cultural historians have made to distinguish the turn of the last century from the turn of this one—to contrast a period of sexual restriction with a period of sexual liberation— misrepresents the "fit" between psychoneuroses and social conditions while it refuses to see how sexual liberation can itself be hysteria-promoting. The effort promotes a view of social conditions as monolithic—all repressive or all liberationist—when it is obvious in the way that psychoneurotics both find in social conditions what they need and feel overwhelming pressures from those conditions, that social conditions are made up of cross-currents, some stronger, some weaker at any given time and place. Anorexia nervosa has existed under conditions predominantly restrictive (but with a strong undertow of sexualization) and under conditions of liberation (but with a strong undertow of puritanism)—it just becomes more common in proportion to the degree of liberation (and perhaps also, less obviously, to the type of contradictions between restriction and liberation). Or, at least, this is our hypothesis— and, unfortunately, the backlash now occurring against feminism and sexual liberation in general offers an opportunity to see in the laboratory of our society whether the incidence of anorexia nervosa declines with declining freedom and increasing antifeminism.

▼   This essay was co-authored with Sarah Cummins Townsend, one of my undergraduate students at Wesleyan University. Sarah wrote a very fine senior thesis on hysteria under my supervision, and we decided to develop our discussions of her work into an essay. After we presented our joint product at the Chicago Institute for Psychoanalysis, for a conference on the history of psychoanalysis, in March 1992, it was published in the *Annual of Psychoanalysis*, 21 (1993): 179–199. Sarah Cummins Townsend is now a psychotherapist practiciing in Seattle, Washington.

13

Feminism, Psychoanalysis,
and Anorexia Nervosa

In the last two decades, a kind of rapprochement between psychoanalysis and feminism has been developing. But the discourse is not easy to understand, either for onlookers or for participants—indeed, two different languages are constantly being spoken. There is a language of psychoanalytic feminism, which many psychoanalysts find not very psychoanalytic, and there is a language of feminist psychoanalysis, which many feminists find not very feminist. I offer here an example of a topic—anorexia nervosa, a disorder that reached epidemic proportions just as the rapprochement between feminism and psychoanalysis began—over which the confusion of tongues was particularly great, and also, I think, particularly instructive. My purpose is not, however, to offer a translator's guide, but to suggest the kinds of theoretical questions that needed asking in the 1970s and still need asking.[1]

Psychoanalytic Femnisms

Angry rejection of psychoanalysis was very common in American feminism from the late 1960s through the mid-1970s, and the hostility continues unabated to this day among many feminists and within the feminist therapy movement, which explicitly attacked psychoanalytic theory and all the—so the charges went—patriarchal, authoritarian, and dehumanizing regulations of medicalized psychoanalytic therapy.

But after antipsychoanalysis had its heyday, in the mid-1970s, a number of feminist writers turned their attention to creating a psychoanalytic feminism. The effort has many forms, but all have as their centerpiece, it seems to me, exploration of what came to be known as "the social construction of gender," or "gender identity" for short. In terms of the basic feminist distinction between sex and gender, the exploration stayed with gender. The American feminist focus has been primarily on family relations (referred to very loosely with the psychoanalytic term "object relations"), especially on mother-daughter relations in the pre-Oedipal period, and on how women are prepared for social roles by their object relations, which are, in turn, created in the nexus of their parents' social roles.

In most psychoanalytic feminists' appropriations of the term "object relations," it has little to do with psychic representations or unconscious processes, and much to do with conscious relations to actually existing persons and with what is known outside of psychoanalysis as role modeling or imitation.

British object relations theorists from Melanie Klein and Ronald Fairbairn through Harry Guntrip and D. W. Winnicott are claimed as the sources for the American feminist theory, either directly or through the works of their American feminist interpreters, such as Dorothy Dinnerstein, Nancy Chodorow, and Jessica Benjamin. But the appropriation of these sources in psychoanalytic feminism constitutes one of the main language problems between feminists and psychoanalysts. For example, Luise Eichenbaum and Susie Orbach, in their 1983 volume *Understanding Women: A Feminist Psychoanalytic Approach,* called themselves object relations therapists, but they emphasized that a developing child's mother should be thought of as a social and psychological *person,* not an object. Children, they said, internalize many different aspects of their mothers—and they meant features of her personality, not what psychoanalysts mean when they speak of internalizations, introjections, or identifications. Even though psychoanalysts are not always precise in their use of these terms, they do always refer to modes of psychic representation, and they are clear that a child's image of her mother is colored by the child's unconscious processes and fantasies. But Eichenbaum and Orbach claimed that "what the object relations theorists have failed to take into account is the psychology of the mother and the effect of the social position of women on the mother's psychology."[2]

The emphasis that Eichenbaum and Orbach put on real mother-daughter relations is not uncontested among psychoanalytic feminists. Advocates of a more "family systems" approach (such as Harriet Lerner of the Menninger Foundation) are critical of this emphasis because they think it obscures the multiplicity of relations that make up the family

▼ ▼ ▼ ▼ ▼

and extended family life. Others (such as the group associated with Jean Baker Miller at the Stone Center in Wellesley, Massachusetts) find the object relations emphasis on the struggle a daughter must conduct to separate from her mother too one-sided. They counter with the idea that girls and women have a special strength—a kind of built-in communitarianism—because of their connection to their mother, because of their empathy with her and through their relations with her. From a different stance, and with a sophisticated appreciation for the intrapsychic focus of psychoanalysis that is lacking in many versions of psychoanalytic feminism, Jessica Benjamin (1988) argued for what she calls "the intersubjective viewpoint": As she noted clearly, "The idea of intersubjectivity reorients the conception of the psychic world from a subject's relation to its object toward a subject meeting another subject . . . The crucial area we uncover with interpsychic [psychoanalytic] theory is the unconscious; the crucial element we explore with intersubjective theory is the representation of self and other as distinct but interrelated beings."[3] From most psychoanalytic points of view, all of these varieties of psychoanalytic feminism look like object relations minus the idea of unconscious psychic representation—that is, they look hardly like object relations at all.

Further, from a Freudian point of view, these various psychoanalytic feminisms have dropped not only the unconscious, but the theory of instinctual drives and the economic framework, the concern with quantities of libido and aggression. In the context of the structural theory, there is no id in these theories, and the superego, which Freud held to be derived from the id, has been replaced by actual parental presences and very forceful social conventions or cultural imperatives that shape both parents and then, via the parents, children. This means that the psychopathologies that Freud analyzed as having repression of the id's forces at their center as well as those he analyzed as having harsh, punitive superego commands at their center—in short, types of hysteria and obsessional neurosis—are not part of psychoanalytic feminism's picture. Generally, the omnibus description now used among psychoanalytic feminists for psychoneuroses is "low self-esteem," and this is meant as a—so to speak—psychosocial designation.

To what extent the Freudian tenets are held among psychoanalysts who are feminists is another matter, and not an easy one to assess. There is, as is well known, considerable disagreement about the Freudian instinctual drive theory, and some psychoanalysts do their best to live without it or to minimize its role in their thought and therapy. Those

▼ ▼ ▼ ▼ ▼

writing specifically about female psychology seldom engage the instinct theory on the metapsychological level, where questions have been raised, for example, about whether "the death instinct" is a therapeutically necessary or theoretically reasonable hypothesis. But there is—and has been for seventy years—enormous contention about specific tenets of the drive theory concerning the importance of penis envy in female development, the existence of feminine masochism, the "natural" narcissism in women, the unformed quality of the female superego, and so forth. Many questions about whether or to what extent there is such a thing as "normal" female development swirl in the literature written by psychoanalysts who are feminists, and there is a growing debate about the idea that people have a "core gender identity." Interestingly, much of the recent revisionary work by psychoanalysts focuses not on manifestations of libido and aggression, but specifically on genital awareness and perceptions of anatomical sexual difference—on when and how and with what effects children experience or learn about their own sexual organs and sexual difference. Sexuality often appears as perception-of-sex, without much reference to biological maturation and what would now be called hormonal levels, or to the energy, the dynamism that is implied by the word *Trieb*, which Freud referred to as a "constant force," a pressure, an activity.[4]

However, about two broad claims, which are also made by nonanalytic and even antianalytic feminists, there is no controversy. All feminist analysts agree that Freud's theories were (to adopt the shorthand terms of their critique) to a greater or lesser extent "phallocentric" and "patriarchal." "Phallocentric" is used to summarize the problem of bias (or the problem of false claims to objectivity) built into all the specific tenets of Freudian psychology of female development, and "patriarchal" summarizes the feminist cultural critique.

So, there is common critical ground between feminist analysts and psychoanalytic feminists, despite the differences on psychoanalytic tenets. But even this common ground looks rather small when it is viewed from the perspective of psychoanalytic psychopathology. In the mid-1970s, when feminist theorists and therapists began to turn their attention to psychopathology, focusing on what might be called "the social construction of mental illness," the hostility toward psychoanalysis that was characteristic of the 1969–1975 period remained firmly in place. Phyllis Chesler's *Women and Madness* (1972) remained the touchstone text, and it still plays that role, particularly when the patriarchal nature of psychoanalytic therapeutic techniques and medical practices is in

▼▼▼▼▼

question.[5] This dimension of hostility stays strong, it seems to me, because it was almost universally concluded in feminist circles that psychoanalysis completely lacks any notion that psychopathology can be socially caused (not just socially influenced). There really is no such thing as a psychoanalytic feminist psychopathology. And among academic feminists, as opposed to therapists, there is a tendency to stay away from any discussion of psychopathology—or to consider it only in fictions or in other eras (especially the fin de siècle, the period of Freud's initial discoveries).[6]

Nowhere was this feminist hostility toward psychoanalytic psychopathology more evident than in the enormous feminist literature on eating disorders that surged forth just as the partial rapprochement between feminism and the psychoanalytic theory of "normal" (under patriarchy) development was being negotiated. In the five years between 1978 and 1983, half a dozen influential feminist books and a stream of articles on obesity, anorexia, and bulimia—on "eating disorders" generally—were published, and these set the terms for the ongoing feminist project of exploring the sociocultural causes of mental illnesses.[7] These books powerfully and importantly established Orbach's (1978) memorable claim that "fat is a feminist issue" but they also established the ways in which the "sex versus gender" distinction was read across the whole field of pathology and across the whole topic of mental illnesses with a high gender-specificity. Hostility toward psychoanalytic theory and practice has remained marked in this feminist literature, and the literature has also decidedly rejected the context in which psychoanalysts first studied eating disorders: the eating disorders have been disconnected nosologically from hysteria. The main theoretical reason for this, it seems to me, is a specific instance of the general tendency I noted before: Freud's view of hysteria rested firmly upon his libido theory, and the libido theory is not to be found in the feminist literature on eating disorders.

On the other hand, it is very interesting to note that in recent years, as the (loosely termed) object relations type of feminist analysis, particularly as articulated in theoretical (not clinical) works like Nancy Chodorow's (1978) *Reproduction of Mothering* (1978), has become more and more influential, it has been adopted by many feminist therapists writing about eating disorders. The very broad claim that eating disorders are socially caused has more and more often been amended to a claim that in the eating disorders social causes and a particular configuration of object relations combine. Let me sketch briefly how this developed.

▼▼▼▼▼

On Eating Disorders

Eating disorders became the main field for the feminist project of articulating sociocultural etiologies for mental illnesses for basically three reasons: (1) the patient population suffering from eating disorders was (and is) overwhelmingly female; (2) the disorders achieved (and still maintain) epidemic proportions in a specific historical moment (and some would also say in specific socioeconomic milieus); and, most important, (3) the sociocultural etiological factor in eating disorders seemed completely obvious. That factor was, to adopt Kim Chernin's (1981) phrase, the "tyranny of slenderness," the draconian sociocultural imperative that women must be very thin (and later also physically fit) to be considered beautiful, desirable, and worthy of male esteem.[8]

At the heart of the late 1970s feminist approach to eating disorders as socially induced diseases was the question: How does this imperative to be thin operate? How and why do women respond to it? The only concept available from feminist literature of the 1969–1975 period for approaching this question was "socialization," and the early feminist therapeutic work on anorexia was full of images of the tyranny of thinness being imprinted on passive subjects. The terminology was close to that of behaviorism.

But this approach eventually seemed too simple. As Orbach noted in her second book, *Hunger Strike:* "The fact that women come to take up the call of manufacturers and the allied forces arrayed against them in the form of the advertisers, the beauty editors, the exercise teachers, the fashion industry, and so on, addresses a more fundamental question in women's psychology. For in order that women should be receptive to the dismembering [sic] of their bodies there must be a preexisting state of discomfort with and within their bodies, a profound alienation."[9] The route to exploring this "preexisting state of discomfort" was analysis of the family dynamics of women with eating disorders. And the conclusion, generally shared although articulated differently by different writers, was that body insecurity is the result of "current child-rearing practices and the psychology of femininity that mothers are vested with passing on to their daughters."[10] The reproduction-of-mothering object relations version of psychoanalytic feminism, as this assessment indicates, has captured the discussion of the social etiology of eating disorders.

Orbach's best-selling books are widely known among feminists, but virtually ignored among psychoanalysts, even among psychoanalysts

▼ ▼ ▼ ▼

who want a feminist psychoanalysis and who find the work of theoreticians like Chodorow and Benjamin stimulating. This is so because, from the psychoanalysts' point of view, Orbach's work has no psychodynamic or intrapsychic dimension. It depends upon a "mother" (very implausibly, she is of the same type for all anorexics) who is a restricter of her daughter's possibilities and who is also an agent—the key agent—of society's restrictions. There is really no distinction between the mother-as-person and the mother-as-cultural-imperative, between the mother's psychology and her social role.

A theory that equates the mother-as-person and cultural imperatives cannot take an intrapsychic mother, a mother of a patient's fantasy, into account, but it also cannot question how cultural imperatives affect patients—it can only say they operate through the mother. But this means, of course, that it is impossible to explain why one young woman develops an eating disorder and another only conforms to her mother and her culture by dieting, or why one develops anorexia and another compulsive eating or another bulimia. It is also impossible to consider whether it is correct to view the eating disorders as expressing basically the same dynamics rather than as quite different symptom complexes that have been given the common name "eating disorders." (Of course, one should note in fairness that this common name "eating disorders" is sanctioned by the 1980 edition of the American Psychiatric Association's *Diagnostic and Statistical Manual of Mental Disorders,* where it is offered as a catch-all without the slightest questioning.)

Similarly, questions of degree or specificities of symptom formation cannot, by definition, be approached as a matter of psychodynamics or—to use the Freudian structural terminology—a matter of conflict among id, ego, and superego. This is so not just because the feminist literature does not deal with biology—not even with the specific matters of medical preconditions,[11] the physiology of hunger, or the hormonal and metabolic conditions of weight. More important, it is so because the literature does not deal with sexuality or with the libido or, generally, with the id. For example, all feminist therapists note that anorexics are ascetic, at least in terms of heterosexual intercourse, and all emphasize the anorexic's search for self-control and fear of being out of control, but none comments on the sexual activities or fantasies of anorexics. To be more specific, there is no discussion of autoerotism in any form, none of masturbation, in the major feminist works on eating disorders. Orbach claimed that for the anorexic "fat has come to stand for need, greed, indulgence, wantonness, unruliness, a loss of control, an unstoppability,"

▼ ▼ ▼ ▼ ▼

but these vague words give no indication of what kinds of needs, greeds, indulgences, and so forth are being feared and warded off.[12] When they do speak of sexuality, the feminist authors speak not of libido or desires, not of fantasies or practices, but only of sexual roles. Anorexics do not reject sexuality in these books, they reject only cultural prescriptions for femininity.[13]

To illustrate this distinction between consideration of sexuality and consideration of sexual roles as cultural imperatives, let me note that Orbach (1986) said that all anorexics suffer from "ambivalence about femininity." But she then explained that they are making a "rebellion against feminization" that reflects their ambivalence, in the sense that the rebellion represents "both a rejection of and an exaggeration of the image" of feminization current in the culture.[14] As this passage indicates, the notion of ambivalence being employed here is specific—it is ambivalence in relation to feminization, a process, an image, an ideal. That is, this is not Freudian ambivalence, which always concerned sexual aims and love objects; and this is not Freudian bisexuality, which always had three spheres of reference—a postulated biological dimension, a dimension called mental sexual attitude (there being two extremes of attitudes, femininity and masculinity, and a range between), and a dimension related to choices of sexual aim and object. The anorexic's feeling for her sociocultural situation and its expectations overrules all else in Orbach's conception: The anorexic does not bring ambivalences to her situation; she becomes ambivalent in it. The idea that symptoms are multivalent, that symptoms are the product of overdetermination, is not entertained. And the further Freudian claim that symptoms are bisexual in meaning, so that symptoms, like fantasies, will have elements that present feminine desires and attitudes and elements that present masculine ones, is not considered at all.

There is, however, a very curious layer of thought behind the feminist stress on object relations and social roles. Again and again in the feminist literature, vaguely described needs and appetites are mentioned and eating disorder symptomatology is said to negate them. But even though the needs and appetites are left unspecified, they are just what the therapist is supposed to reach and release from their bondage. Orbach thinks that each anorexic has a "nascent psychosomatic self," a self that can truly live in the body, be embodied, as opposed to the socially conditioned self that is only hostile toward the body. This "undeveloped embryonic self which has remained strangled behind a defense structure" is what the therapist should reach out to. Borrowing D. W.

▼▼▼▼▼

Winnicott's true/false self terms, Orbach writes: "The 'false self' of ordinary social intercourse is not the point of contact in the therapy relationship. Instead it is the task of the therapist to make a relationship with the vulnerable undeveloped self so that it can continue through its developmental paces."[15] There is a hidden self in the anorexic—as in every woman—that is the locus of appetites. This child within is, so to speak, the natural self, the presocial self.

This image, which has come forth strongly within the evolving tradition of feminist work on eating disorders, has also become the basis for a premise articulated more generally by many feminist therapists who continue the tendency of complete hostility toward psychoanalysis and particularly toward psychoanalytic psychopathology. Let me note this by turning to Harriet Lerman's 1985 presidential address to the American Psychological Association's Division of the Psychology of Women: "If we care to emulate Freud to the extent of wishing to suggest a single psychic root cause of emotional dysfunction, the most appropriate one that I can suggest is the conflict between basic human strivings (which no one has yet fully described) and the prohibitions imposed by a particular cultural milieu."[16]

A Rapprochement

I am suggesting that vague notions like "basic human strivings" are coming up more and more frequently in feminist therapy's theory because the absence of any kind of drive theory is being felt, if not acknowledged. It will be interesting to see, should this tendency continue, whether it eventually permits the assumed basic conflict between strivings and cultural prohibitions (mediated by the mother) to be reconsidered as well—whether, in effect, it restores the intrapsychic meaning of object relations to the currently exclusive focus on persons. If it does, then it would be a happy event for the rapprochement between feminism and psychoanalysis if feminism were met halfway by a shift within psychoanalysis toward closer consideration of the question so crucial to feminism—the question of cultural influence. To indicate what I mean, let me return to the example of eating disorders as they are currently conceived.

I want to suggest that there are both more and more complex cultural imperatives involved in the eating disorders epidemic of the period from 1965 or so to the present than have been accounted for by either feminist theory or psychoanalytic theory. Theorists coming, as it were, from both directions, should be able to account in psychodynamic terms

▼ ▼ ▼ ▼ ▼

for how—precisely, concretely—cultural imperatives are built into ill-nesses. Obeying an imperative, obeying an imperative to a pathological degree (one might say overobeying it or obeying it masochistically), rejecting an imperative, and rejecting it to a pathological degree are all quite different processes. Building an imperative into a hysteria, using it phobically, adopting its strictures as part and parcel of obsessional ideas and practices—these, too, are quite different processes. And, very impor-tant, different consequences follow if a girl imagines that her mother is the agent of the "tyranny of slenderness," or if she feels her mother is an overfeeder in a dieting culture, or if she gets completely mixed mes-sages from one day to the next from her mother's own eating pathology as she experiences it, as she relates to her images of it. And these possible types of relations between mothers and cultural imperatives—offered as indications, not as a complete list—look very different in contexts where the father or other figures in a girl's family are constructed in her inner drama as supporting players, opponents of the mother, rivals, and so forth.

The existence of cultural imperatives is obvious, as is the fact that our culture has been marked during this period with an imperative to achieve thinness—excellent social-historical work, most of it by femi-nists, has documented (independently of therapeutic contexts) a shift away from fuller-figured ideals of female beauty that was noticeable by the early 1960s. But it is important to note that this thinness imperative has more than one meaning. At the least, it can mean "be thin in order to be more sexual or more sexy," while it can also mean "be thin in order to be less sexual or to be inaccessible by means of aesthetic (or athletic) perfection." Similarly, it can be interpreted by girls in *either* of these ways, or in *both* of these ways at once. It can be interpreted in both ways, for example, if a girl sets out consciously to be thinly beautiful and sexy at the same time that she is setting out unconsciously to take herself out of the domain of sexuality, to make herself asexual; or it can be inter-preted in both ways at once if being thin serves her masculine strivings and being asexual serves to block her feminine ones, or vice versa.

If an adolescent is trying to escape her new, nearly adult sexuality (an upsurge of libido in drive theory terms), she may also be responding to another cultural imperative, one that is not considered in the feminist literature, which is, after all, a literature that supports sexual liberation. This second imperative might be called "the tyranny of youthful sexual experimentation" or, to use the ethnopsychoanalyst George Devereux's phrase, "compulsory promiscuousness."[17] It is very difficult to admit that

▼▼▼▼▼

the laudable feminist goal of sexual liberation—liberation from oppression in sexual relationships as well as liberation for sexual activity, for feeling and being sexual—filtered down to many pubescent and adolescent girls of the early 1970s and later as pressure to be sexually active. That is, it was another type of social or peer pressure, but also sometimes pressure from the mother (and/or father) as well, particularly if the parents were consciously or unconsciously reponding to the movement for sexual liberation and to their own needs in the medium of their children's sexual activity. When this imperative did come from parental figures, it could be, of course, not only disturbingly seductive, but antagonistic to the possibility of adolescent rebellion through sexual activity (since a rebellion cannot be staged via activities a society promotes or sanctions). Those who find this imperative to be sexual terrifying often find some kind of regimentation to escape it—the regimentation of a cult or fundamentalist church or physical training routine, for example, or the regimentation of anorexia nervosa. Others may find it terrifying but respond with a kind of conformity, engaging in pleasureless, mechanical sexual activity, even to the point of pregnancy to end sexuality—which is starvation of another sort. Asexuality and hypersexuality can have much in common in terms of avoidance of mature, pleasurable sexuality, even though they may reflect differently the imperatives "Be thin!" and "Be sexual!"—especially as these are combined (variously) with parental evaluative imperatives like "You are perfect!" and "You are worthless!"

All feminists, including Orbach, note that anorexics are puritans, but they do not see them as puritans revolting against an imperative to be sexually active. In *Hunger Strike* Orbach presented these puritans as critics of a culture in which women are objectified, treated as sexual objects, in which women experience their bodies as commodities. They are comparable to political hunger strikers—to suffragettes—in her mind. But she does not see them retreating from a (to them) frighteningly sexualized culture. A similar kind of bias is built into feminist discussions of fin de siècle hysteria, which is read as a revolt or protest against repressive social conditions that denied female desire and strictly defined femininity. Sometimes, hysteria does seem to reflect such conditions, but just as often it reflects conditions of sexualization. Freud's Dora, whose sphere for desire and action was very restricted, was also, after all, escaping into illness from an atmosphere which the adults around her had charged with their passions for each other and for her. Hysteria can be a mode of "flight into illness."[18]

▼ ▼ ▼ ▼ ▼

For the rapprochement between feminism and psychoanalysis that started in the mid-1970s to move beyond its current condition, which I suggested is like a conversation in two languages, it seems to me that there will have to be admissions from both camps. From the feminist camp, there is need for admission that it is not possible to ignore Freud's drive theory (though not all its tenets are needed) without producing, as it were, a psychology without dynamics, a vision of people moved by social pressures but without their own motion, their own needs; and admission that intrapsychic objects cannot be ignored while attention is focused on to object relations conceived of as relations between persons and reflections of cultural relations. From the psychoanalytic side, there is need for attention to cultural imperatives—to the plurality of them, to the plural meanings of each of them, to the dissonances among them, to the relations between them and their psychic representations, which may, under varying conditions, mesh with or contradict intrapsychic objects. Many psychoanalysts have taken feminist political and cultural criticism seriously, and worked to determine how this criticism bears on Freudian theory. But the type of psychoanalytic work that, in the 1950s, used to be called "personality and culture" or sometimes "ethnopsychoanalysis" has not been revived by psychoanalysis for this era of second wave feminism.

I have focused on anorexia nervosa because it was the chief social-context disease at the beginning of the era of rapprochement between feminism and psychoanalysis. It stands as a kind of paradigmatic case for showing where feminism and psychoanalysis did, and mostly did not, meet. I think it is important to consider this moment historically, but I also think it is important to learn from it so that we can cope better with the culturally dominant social-context epidemic of today and therapeutic endeavors to relieve it. The difficulties of that earlier era of rapprochement are being replayed now, in a different and much more strenuous key, but with the same basic theoretical questions at issue.

What I have in mind is the present epidemic of sexual abuse and domestic violence in which women and children, especially girls, are the main victims. As this epidemic has developed, antipsychoanalytic feminist therapists and many feminists associated with groups that work against abuse, violence, and pornography have directed a new stream of criticism at Freud. According to many feminists, Freud abandoned the so-called seduction theory—his hypothesis that behind every hysteria he had seen in analysis, there was an episode of childhood seduction, often of a girl by her own father—because he could not face the reality of widespread abuse. He was unable and unwilling to see around him a traumatizing culture of violence against women, and psychoanalysis has fallen heir to this blindness. Even psychoanalysts who are feminists have adopted this critical line, for example, the San Francisco–based analyst Charlotte Prozan in *Feminist Psychoanalytic Psychotherapy.*[19] Freud's effort to argue for the universality of childhood fantasies of love and rivalry toward parental figures meant distinguishing fantasies from realities because seduction, though it is common, and sometimes very common, is not universal, as Oedipal fantasies are. That effort has been quite misunderstood, I think, precisely because it runs into the confusion in feminist circles over object relations and the lack in feminist circles of any drive theory. That is, when there is no distinction between intrapsychic objects and persons in the world, there is not likely to be one between fantasies or wishes and events; and when there is no notion of how libido and aggression become represented in fantasies, there is not likely to be much sense for how a victim's wishes and fantasies can be bound up in, tragically locked into, either a seductive milieu or any sexual acts and violence to which she is subjected.

Anorexia nervosa was very widely understood in feminist therapeutic and social critical literature as the disease of a sick culture that was inflicted upon women. Mothers were the social agents of transmission and daughters were the victims. The sickness of our culture now is violence and abuse. Fathers and other familiar or familial males in the culture of violence, in a society where images of violence tyrannize, are the agents of transmission—from one generation to the next, as abused turn into abusers. This is certainly, and horribly, so. But it is also very difficult in the present moment to go beyond this picture of the culture of violence and examine more thoroughly its multifarious dimensions, and its multifarious relations to women's psyches and lives, without being charged with "blaming the victim."

The rapprochement between feminism and psychoanalysis was a complex affair when it began in the mid-1970s, and now it is more, not less complex. But it does now have a history to draw on—and perhaps to be moved by.

▼   This essay was presented to Division 39 of the American Psychological Association, at the April 1992 meeting in Philadelphia, and then published in *Psychoanalytic Psychology,* 10 (1993): 317–330.

▼ ▼ ▼ ▼

14

Gender and Psychoanalysis

In the last few years the major American psychoanalytic journals have each published a full volume or a symposium entitled "Gender," or "Feminine and Masculine Gender Identities," or "Sexuality/Sexualities," or "Female Psychology" (the last also the title for the 1996 supplementary volume of the *Journal of the American Psychoanalytic Association*). The collections make it very clear that in the past two decades a great change has been coming over the theory and practice of psychoanalysis, a change in which old controversies about femaleness and maleness, and about femininity and masculinity—now called "gender"—have been reenvisioned and related to a world profoundly changed since the 1905 publication of Freud's *Three Essays on the Theory of Sexuality*.

The introductions to these journal volumes and symposia have necessarily been historical, as, of course, have the introductory paragraphs of the articles they contain and the first chapters of the shelves of recent books to which they allude. So, many dozens of brief histories focused on psychoanalysis since the early 1970s now exist, each one reflecting the theoretical and clinical allegiances of its author while surveying the more or less common territory. At the same time, from outside psychoanalysis, cultural historians, academics from women's studies and gay and lesbian studies, literary critics, philosophers, social scientists—among them specialists in a novelty, "gender theory"—have offered a profusion of other tours of the new psychoanalysis, some meant to track an expedition of interdisciplinary discovery and some meant to mark a spot for more and future controversy. When this kind of ferment in and redefining of a field are obvious, the moment is right for a meeting place, a forum, an ongoing symposium, a series of volumes; a place where new

▼ ▼ ▼ ▼ ▼

perspectives and types of inquiry can be gathered, any emergent consensus registered, and, at the same time, any new orthodoxies questioned, lest the psychoanalysis that has been deemed confining be replaced by something just as confining or lest a repetition be mistaken for an innovation. Hence the launching in 1996 of *Gender and Psychoanalysis: An Interdisciplinary Journal.*

Because psychoanalyst readers, readers from various disciplines, and general readers cannot be presumed to share a frame of reference for the term or the topic gender, I would like to begin with a lexical and conceptual guide. In the academic disciplines—at least in those receptive to feminism—gender has been a rich working term and an enormously fertile topic for several scholarly generations, but in psychoanalysis it is relatively new and—except among those analysts who have been influenced by feminism—its significance is unassessed.

"Gender" is not a term from the *Standard Edition* of Freud's works nor was it current in time to be examined in *Vocabulaire de la psychoanalyse* (1967), Jean Laplanche and J.-B. Pontalis's standard-setting conceptual lexicon.[1] Freud did, of course, speak of masculinity and femininity, *Mannlichkeit* and *Weiblichkeit,* and he was very well aware that these are complex, composite terms, with significance relating biologically to primary and secondary sexual characteristics, psychosexually to activity and passivity, as well as sociologically to the observable real and symbolic functions assigned to men and women in their various cultures. These three dimensions of significance, he understood, do not line up in any neat way: activity is not necessarily linked with biological masculinity nor passivity with femininity, and "in human beings pure masculinity or femininity is not to be found in either a psychological or a biological sense. Every individual on the contrary displays a mixture of character traits belonging to his own or to the opposite sex; and he shows a combination of activity and passivity whether or not the last characteristics tally with his biological ones."[2] In discussing human beings from the point of view of their characters, Freud also carefully distinguished physical sexual characters from mental sexual characters ("masculine and feminine attitude") and both of these from kind of object choice (sexual partner orientation) and also from choice of sexual aim or practice. He even—quite radically for his day and even for now—noted that there is no necessary or formulaic relationship among these four dimensions. But, nonetheless, his early theorizing was definitely oriented toward exploring "the psychical consequences of the anatomical dis-

▼ ▼ ▼ ▼ ▼

tinction between the sexes."[3] Specifically, he emphasized the psychical consequences for both males and females of having or not having the penis, of discovering—and being made anxious by—the penis or its absence. Before making their discoveries of sexual difference, girls and boys, Freud held, have developed without distinction into feminine and masculine characters or attitudes.

Freud's attention was directed at developed mental sexual characters and not at gender as a psychosocial construct, a way of being categorized and categorizing oneself. Mental sexual character was for him, in other words, a key dimension of overall character, a feature to be compassed in individual characterology and in theories of familial and ethnic or national character. However, there are certainly threads in Freud's work, especially in his late work on splitting of the ego which make it very clear that he also thought of the anatomical distinction between the sexes as taking on its meaning or being constructed along psychic or ego developmental lines formed independently of the anatomical distinction.[4] That is, he tried thinking in terms of what consequences the acquired psychical distinctions between the sexes have for people's experiences of their anatomies. But it is not this unfinished and little-known Freudian thread that gave rise to the current interest in gender; instead, it is only the curent interest that is slowly bringing this late Freudian venture into view. The topic of Gender first arose within psychoanalysis in the late 1960s, and it represented a move away from the early Freudian theoretical emphasis on "psychical consequences" toward a focus on constructing and categorizing, a move away from characterology to identity study.

The rising star of "gender" had two quite different sources. The concept, if not the specific term, had been given to feminism in 1949 by Simone de Beauvoir, whose guiding maxim in *Le deuxieme sexe*—"a woman is not born but made"—was built upon her very qualified acceptance of the psychoanalytic point of view, which she described thus:

> The tremendous advance accomplished by psychoanalysis over pychophysiology lies in the view that no factor becomes involved in the psychic life without having taken on human significance; it is not the body-object described by biologists that actually exists, but the body as lived in by the subject [in society]. Woman is female to the extent that she feels herself as such. There are biologically essential features that are not part of her real, experienced situation; thus the structure of an egg is not reflected in it, but on the contrary an organ of no great biological importance, like the

▼ ▼ ▼ ▼ ▼

clitoris, plays in it a part of the first rank. It is not nature that defines woman; it is she who defines herself by dealing with nature on her own account in her emotional life.[5]

De Beauvoir's trenchant criticism of Freud's female psychology, that it was based "upon a masculine model," reverberated along with this sex/ gender distinction into such later classics of second wave feminism as Kate Millett's *Sexual Politics* (1971).[6] De Beauvoir's distinction was meant to say, as forcefully as possible, that "anatomy is not destiny," and Millett's echo was an excited vision of the gender-androgynous future, the "bisex revolution."

This "anatomy is not destiny" negation was meant to fight psychoanalysis (of women) with psychoanalytic weapons, which meant that while Freud was being faulted by most feminists for his sexism, his theories about male development—"upon a masculine model"—were being appropriated. Millett's psychological analysis of "the patriarchy" and of sexism and of Freud himself is Freudian. Similarly, feminist anthropologists and sociologists of the early 1970s used Freud's work, along with that of thinkers influenced by Freud, like Claude Lévi-Strauss, to articulate the framework that governed the feminist revolutions in these fields.[7] "The sex/gender system" presupposed distinctions between "sex" and "gender roles" (socioculturally created behaviors and attitudes assigned differentially to women and men), and set up study of how sex and gender roles intertwine. No society is without its "sex/ gender system"; there are no ungendered destinies.

As theory influenced by Freudian thinking advanced the critical work of feminism, the way was paved during the late 1970s for hostility to psychoanalysis to yield among many American feminists to an even more appropriative stance: Using a version of British object relations theory that emphasized the pre-Oedipal mother-infant dyad and repudiated Freud's instinctual drive theory—a version in which instinctual drives are not destiny—a diverse group of feminists created a psychoanalytic feminism focused on gender differences and containing a vision of social reform. They did not invoke a "bisex revolution," but imagined gender differences being ameliorated over time by changes in the way in which parenting has been culturally assigned to mothers. For the current generation of feminists using psychoanalysis, works like Dorothy Dinnerstein's *Mermaid and the Minotaur* (1976) and Nancy Chodorow's *Reproduction of Mothering* (1978) have been signposts, as have the slightly later efforts by feminist psychoanalysts such as Ethel Person,

▼▼▼▼▼

Irene Fast, and Jessica Benjamin to reconceptualize and culturally contextualize female development.[8]

Within psychoanalysis itelf, which was almost impervious to feminism in the 1970s, a changing of the generational guard and the entry of many more women and nonmedical psychologists into practice have finally given this feminist tradition a hearing and allowed it to influence clinical practice. Among analysts, the feminist tradition has met with a more easily acknowledged strain of clinical revision originating in Paris and collected as *Recherches pychoanalytiques nouvelles sur la sexualité feminine* (1964), translated into English in 1970 as *Female Sexuality,* in which Janine Chassequet-Smirgel, Maria Torok, Joyce McDougall, and others worked with British object relations theory but placed less emphasis on rejecting Freud's drive theory. At the same time, the feminist tradition has allowed analysts to look back on the history of debates about female psychology within psychoanalysis, and to appreciate—to recover the lost legacy of—the contributions of Freud's critics in the 1920s, especially Karen Horney, Melanie Klein, and Ernest Jones.

Both the hostile feminists like Kate Millett and the later feminist appropriators of psychoanalysis adopted the actual term "gender" from a second source: the late 1960s work of the Los Angeles psychoanalyst Robert Stoller, who was then, and for some still is, the touchstone psychoanalytic theorist of gender. Stoller drew heavily on empirical work done by John Money and his associates at Johns Hopkins, who had studied hermaphroditic children assigned at birth by their doctors and parents to a boy or girl "gender role" (a term these researchers innovated for empirical psychology) into which the children then developed. Living out their gender roles, the children assumed a gender identity, understood as their subjective sense of maleness or femaleness, which was claimed by the researchers to be a matter largely of assignment, not of biological sex. This unexpected result precipitated a new, and still evolving, contested conceptual language. Many theoreticians and researchers now use two terms: "gender role," the equivalent of the anthropological and sociological term compassing observable traits, attitudes, and behaviors that are culturally associated with masculinity and femininity (that is, that are conventional in a given culture); and "gender identity." Others theorists, including John Money himself, object to such a distinction because it seems to disconnect internal experience from external behavior.[9] Money insisted on a dialectic: "Gender identity is a private experience of gender role, and gender role is the public expression of gender identity."[10] A third term, coined by Stoller, "core gender identity" des-

▼ ▼ ▼ ▼ ▼

ignates a more specific subjective sense that each child and then person has of being one sex or the other, of being the right sex or of being somehow not the right sex ("I am a girl," or "I am a boy but I want to be a girl"). With respect to the Freudian view of mental sexual characteristics, the key element of Stoller's theory is its claim that "core gender identity" arises before the Oedipal period. Not in the resolution (or alleged relative lack of resolution in females) of the Oedipus Complex, nor in the "transformations of puberty," but in the stage known from the work of Margaret Mahler and others as "separation-individuation" (from the mother) are the ingredients of core gender identity established.

Robert Stoller's approach to the question of whether "anatomy is destiny" was rooted in a reversal; like many revolutions, the one he hoped to bring about in psychoanalysis demanded, he argued, a turning upside-down, an overthrow. Freud had initially posited a predisposition to masculinity—both the little boy and the little girl start out as little men, with a libido Freud called (without an argument for doing so) masculine. In the first generation of critics, which included Karen Horney, Melanie Klein, and Ernest Jones, femininity was posited as an inborn predisposition in females and heterosexuality was posited as the natural outcome of this femininity. But for Robert Stoller "protofemininity" is the predisposition of both females and males—the reverse of Freud's early formulation for both sexes—and it has an innate or constitutional component. In his words:

> The concept of the core gender identity, however, modifies Freud's theory as follows. Though it is true that the boy's first love is heterosexual, and though fathers are too-powerful rivals, there is an earlier stage in gender identity development wherein the boy is *merged with mother.* Only after months does she gradually become a clearly separate object. Sensing oneself a part of mother— a primeval and thus profound part of character structure (core gender identity)—lays the groundwork for an infant's sense of femininity. This sets the girl firmly on the path to femininity in adulthood but puts the boy in danger of building into his core gender identity a sense of oneness with mother (a sense of female-ness). Depending on how and at what pace a mother allows her son to separate, this phase of merging with her will leave residual effects that may be expressed as disturbances of masculinity.[11]

From Money's empirical research and Stoller's clinical work and theorizing about core gender identity has come a stream of investigations of sex differences and of typical and atypical gender developments. By

▼ ▼ ▼ ▼ ▼

around 1980, when the American Psychoanalytic Association gave its imprimatur to "gender" by convening a panel, chaired by Robert Stoller, on "Gender and Gender Role," it was widely accepted in the field that to the catalog of developmental lines, worked out in greatest detail by Anna Freud and her colleagues and Margaret Mahler and hers, should be added a developmental line for gender.[12] Through most of the 1980s psychoanalytic gender research, so excitingly informed by new and methodologically very sophisticated child observational studies and child analytic cases, focused on working out the stations on such a developmental line. Many efforts have been made in this direction since, some—like the rich clinical studies offered by Doris Bernstein—even once again making creative synthetic use of revised versions of Freud's libido theory.[13] This work continues to be very vibrant, but the developmental approach has also begun to be challenged.

Commonly, contemporaries begin their work on "gender" with assessments of what two decades of empirical research on inborn psychobiological sex differences has so far yielded. There are only a very few widely accepted results about infants (for example: boys, at birth somewhat less physically mature than girls, are generally more difficult to soothe and are more reactive, especially to maternal depression), toddlers (for example: in terms of observable gender role behavior, toddler girls are usually less aggressive and active in exploring their environments than boys), and older children (among whom, for example, spatial-visual tests reveal differences).[14] Considering these modest results has led to the idea that the two population groups, males and females, overlap so much that the degree of variance within them is about the same as or greater than the mean difference between them—a situation that would be comparable to that which long ago rendered the notion of inborn psychobiological "race" differences completely suspect to scientific researchers. Similarly, taken-for-granted ideas about the relationship between atypical gender developments—in recent diagnostic manuals designated with categories like "gender identity disorder" (GID)— and such biological factors as hormone differences have been deconstructed: no hormone differences among male children with GID have been found.[15] Further, taken-for-granted links between childhood GID and later homosexuality have come into question: homosexuality and heterosexuality are not automatically correlated with atypical and typical gender developments, respectively, and both have come to be viewed much more frequently as continua (in Freud's manner, if not in his universal bisexuality terms). Stoller's emphasis on mother-merger has been countered by other efforts to track the development of male homosexuality, including some reversals, throwbacks to reductive monocausal theories, which place the emphasis on father love.[16] Such controversies have become so complex that many analysts now admit either that the routes to homosexual object choices for men and for women are many and diverse or that the causality of homosexuality should just be declared *terra incognita*. The mystery that Freud identified as "the mystery of homosexuality" has returned.[17] And it has brought with it the realization or rerealization that heterosexuality, too, is mysterious, as Nancy Chodorow, among others, has indicated in both clinical and theoretical detail.[18]

As this sketch of recent research indicates, the focus on Gender also marks a shift in psychoanalysis away from a situation in which the topic of female psychology was the chief source of controversy and upheaval and the Freudian image of "the castrated woman" was the chief shibboleth. Masculinity is understood to be no less in need of rethinking and reexploring. Like Stoller, many feminists and feminist psychoanalysts have stressed that boys, conceptualized as needing to disidentify with their mothers, to establish a gender identity through disidentification as well as through identification with the father and other males, follow a more complex developmental line than girls.[19] "Gender identity" is a comparative concept, and those inheritors of the feminist critique who now focus on it focus on both females and males. They also bring into greater research and theorizing prominence familial *dramatis personae* who had tended to drop out of sight when the mother-daughter dyad and early female object relations took center stage: the pre-Oedipal father, the Oedipal parents, siblings, extended familial figures and imagoes, peers as intimates. A few theorists also recognize that so much emphasis was given during the emergence of gender as a key area of investigation to pre-Oedipal phenomena, including early-manifesting gender disorders such as transsexualism, that "the transformations of puberty" or the processes called "second individuation" by Peter Blos and others have been relatively neglected. And, in yet another thread of work, sexuality—in light of revised Freudian drive theories or of Lacanian notions about the ambiguity of sexual desire—is being reconsidered, and the original feminist "sex/gender" distinction is being reevaluated both clinically and as part of the emergent discipline of the history of sexuality. Interest in anatomical hermaphrodites and in transsexuals is now often focused on seeing the very notion of "sexuality" as more complicated and socioculturally constructed than it was in the early 1970s.

▼ ▼ ▼ ▼ ▼

But the comparative concept "gender" has also, in recent years, been influenced by the turbulent deconstructive theoretical discourse known vaguely in the academic disciplines by a designation that used to refer only to the work of the Freudian-Marxian Frankfurt School, "critical theory." The idea that there are two—and only two—genders has been called in question.[20] Bringing the binary division of gender into view is key to many current reflections and to many reformist efforts by feminists, especially those associated with cultural studies and the newly emergent "queer studies." The reformist focus here is not so much on shared parenting or on reshaping families as on culture critique: the concept of "gender" itself, once the liberating concept, begins to look like a trap, a determination—"gender binarism is destiny"—in need of deconstruction. From the extremes of this perspective, Robert Stoller's "core gender identity" looks like a psychoanalytic artifact: females and males may have a "core gender identity," but it will have no meaning to them or to their analysts outside of the histories of their infinitely complicated lives and loves; the histories of their delimitations (perhaps one might say their resignations); the power politics of "gender hierarchy"; as well as whatever discoveries they made as two-year-olds.[21]

As gender itself has come more and more into question theoretically, and the meaning of concepts such as "gender identity" and "core gender identity" has shifted, psychoanalytic clinical practice has also become, generally, more tentative and questioning about the whole subject of sexualities and genders. The developments are, of course, interrrelated. Gender came into reflections on clinical practice in the the form of critiques of analytic practice as patriarachal and authoritarianly prescriptive—especially prescriptive about sex and gender normality—and then in the form of inquiries about the roles in transference and countertransference of the analyst's gender and of the analyst's theories about gender. But now the terrain of critique and inquiry is much wider, and gender provides a point of access, an entryway for reexamining the dynamics of the analytic situation and the interplay in it of the analytic process and the analyst's theorizing and retheorizing.

It is not surprising that a term and topic like "gender," which for a quarter of a century did such ubiquitous service in the feminist-sexual-cultural revolution as well as in the process of psychoanalytic revisionism, should have come to be a whirling maelstrom of meanings and debates. This development may well signal that the contrast "sex/gender" is ready for rethinking, and that sexuality, now in theoretical neglect, will return for inquiry, too.

▼ ▼ ▼ ▼ ▼

▼ This essay was prepared to introduce the inaugural issue in January 1996 of *Gender and Psychoanalysis: An Interdisciplinary Journal,* published by International Universities Press. Members of the Editorial Board responded to it in that issue. Now the Editorial Board has moved to a journal named *Studies in Gender and Sexuality,* due to appear in January 2000 from Analytic Press.

▼ ▼ ▼ ▼ ▼

15

What Theories Women Want

The Shift in Psychoanalytic Theory

In the last twenty years, a paradigm shift has been occuring in Anglo-American psychoanalytic theory and practice. This shift is still occurring and its outcome is uncertain, for, while it is being promoted and celebrated, it is also being criticized and rejected within the worldwide guild of psychoanalysts. Further, the history, causes, implications, and meanings of the shift have only begun to be studied, and it has not generated a critique in its own terms—a psychoanalytic critique. That is, it has not gotten to the point of being depoliticized. Polemic is still its mode, and it is marked—pro and con—by vying for leadership, for influence, for historical place, and for succession, which might mean, in the paradigm shifters' camp, triumph over Freud or, at least, the capacity to go on without looking constantly backward to the founder.

Two elements of this shift are, however, completed and no longer have an atmosphere of battle about them. First, there is general agreement that psychoanalysis needs to be—and to an extent has been—purged of its period-piece scientific assumptions; that is, purged of its nineteenth-century mechanistic concepts, its Helmholtzian hydraulic metaphors, its Darwinian teleological supports for prescriptive notions of normality, its reductive biologism, and its consistently dualistic *esprit de système*. Second, there is general agreement that Freud's views of female psychology were (in Ernest Jones's term) "phallocentric" and need revision. Of the plethora of revisions that have been offered, it seems to me that two have passed into common Anglo-American acceptance. Little girls, one new clinical consensus states, have genital sensations and are aware of their genitals earlier than Freud thought and probably before they become conscious of sexual difference. A related consensus stipulates that female penis envy is neither so undifferentiated nor so determinative as Freud thought. Penis envy is very obvious in many clinical contexts, but it need not constitute for women generally an identity-determining factor and it should not be considered as arising in a particular developmental moment. Penis envy does not begin with a single flash of unhappy visual recognition, but assumes different forms in different developmental stages. Both of these claims imply that female development has a course of its own—or, more likely, courses (in the plural)—and is understandable neither from reference to female children's recognition of male children nor by extrapolation from male development.

Beyond these areas of consensus, however, the topic of female development opens out on the wider arena of the psychoanalytic shift and is part of the embattled state of psychoanalysis. To see why this is so, and to begin to describe the shift, let me name it with reference to its *ancien régime*—it is "anti-Oedipus." The paradigm shifters say, most fundamentally, the Oedipus Complex is not, as Freud constantly and consistently argued, the nucleus of the neuroses. The nucleus of the neuroses as well as the crux of development is the period called pre-Oedipal. Almost all psychoanalysts would agree that the pre-Oedipal period needed the closer attention that Freud began to give it late in his life, but not all would agree that it is *the* pathogenic arena or *the* crux of development. But this controversy really centers on the critical claim that the pre-Oedipal is not to be understood as "the pregenital," to use Freud's synonym; that is, it is not to be understood in terms of Freud's instinctual drive theory as the period in which the libido is expressed primarily in and through the oral and anal erotogenic zones and in which aggression takes primarily the forms of oral sadism and anal sadism. Neither anatomy nor the instinctual drives are in any way destiny, and the erotogenic zones do not, in their erotogenicity, reflect any inborn program of biological maturation.[1]

Within the camp of the new psychoanalysis, there are many contingents. Some, under the influence of Melanie Klein, do have a drive theory, one focused on the death instinct and aggression as much or more than on sexuality. But, generally, it is Klein's object relations narrative that has been appropriated, and her drive theory left behind, as her work has been read together with that of other British analysts— Harry Guntrip, Ronald Fairbairn, and D. W. Winnicott in Klein's gen-

▼ ▼ ▼ ▼ ▼

eration—by those who make up a broad contingent advocating "object relations." This group is much more concerned with intrapsychic object relations—introjections, identifications, and projective identifications— than is the American contingent, influenced by Harry Stack Sullivan, by Karen Horney and the "cultural Freudians," and by empirical social psychology, who stress intersubjective or interpersonal relations. Among those of a third contingent, whose primary influences are theorists of narcissism like Heinz Kohut, pre-Oedipally constructed "self objects" are the focus of attention.

But, although the object relations schools and the interpersonalists and the self psychologists are separated by many theoretical differences, they do share the conviction that developing children and adults should be conceptualized as beings who have a basic need and capacity for relationships. Humans should not be conceptualized as moved by their desire for erotic (in the broadest sense) pleasure and as pursuing their goal aggressively. Development is not a story of drives necessarily—even tragically—in conflict with "the reality principle" and with familial and societal regulations, with civilization. Stephen Mitchell puts the contrast this way: "Mind has been redefined from a set of predetermined structures emerging from inside an individual organism to transactional patterns and internal structures derived from an interactive, interpersonal field."[2] And it is very clear that this contrast supports a basically optimistic vision of humans having the capacity to develop as unconflicted, harmonious beings capable of harmoniously living together.

From this fundamental anti-Oedipus, anti-instinctual drive theory position, many auxiliary theoretical claims follow. First, since the maternal dyad, not the triad of father-mother-child, is the crux of development, "good enough mothering," to use Winnicott's phrase, is the key to the envisioned mental health and harmony. Many contemporary analysts will even go so far as to divide the world into those who have had good enough mothering and those who have not—the well and the ill— and argue, further, that all of the ill suffer from narcissistic disorders, disorders of self-esteem, or relational disorders. This for example, is Donald Rinsley of the Menninger Clinic speaking in the graceless jargon of today:

> [While] oedipal-type conflicts and rivalries certainly appear during the latter part of a child's pre-school years, the healthy child, possessed of a sound, nascent self-identity resulting from an optimal balance of interdigitated growth and dependency needs,

▼ ▼ ▼ ▼

proceeds to deal with these conflicts and rivalries with little or no personal and interpersonal perturbation. Of course, such balance is achieved as a result of the child's mutual attunement with an empathic, good enough mother and a healthy father who both nurtures the mother and provides for the child's ongoing separation-individuation . . . The same may be said of the period of adolescence, the regressive-recapitulative features of which were classically cited to support the long since discredited view of the adolescent as a turmoil-ridden, even normally psychotic victim of untrammeled instinctual drives unleashed by surging and shifting hormones and the psychological effects of frightening bodily changes.[3]

As this passage indicates, another feature of the new psychoanalysis is its focus on issues of separation and individuation from the mother, from the mother-child dyad, but with a slant in favor of normal dependency, not the achievement of autonomy. The child does not begin in a symbiosis with the mother, but in a relation with her, and then the child grows into a more mature relation with her that is modeled on the original one. Individuation does not mean autonomy; it means connectedness, relatedness. There is, correlatively, much less stress on adolescence as the period in which a "second individuation" brings about autonomy or independence from the family and from intrapsychic dominance by paternal imagoes. Indeed, adolescence almost falls out of the picture in the new psychoanalysis, for a healthy childhood simply leads to an unproblematic adolescence, as this quotation from Rinsley says explicitly, without qualification.

There are, as I indicated, differences in the new psychoanalytic camp, but more often than not the mother who is central to the new psychoanalysis is the child's real mother; she is not a mixture of a real person and the child's fantasy, not a mixture of perception and imagination or representation. The emphasis is on intersubjectivity. And the mother's needs as well as her relational abilities are assessed theoretically while the child's needs and developing abilities are assessed—they are an interactive unit. Similarly, in terms of technique, the focus on the real mother and her empathic "good enough mothering"—and the lack of such in pathology, or *as* pathology—entails stress on relational reparations. Analytic therapy is to provide the missing mothering, to allow the patient to begin again. Where deprivation was, there empathic nourishing shall be—that is the therapeutic motto, not "where id was, there ego shall be."

▼ ▼ ▼ ▼ ▼

The mature individual envisioned in the new psychoanalysis is not someone who has negotiated what Freud called the "transformations of puberty"—who has achieved a satisfying genital sexuality and become capable of loving outside of the original family—but someone who has developed self-esteem and relational capabilities generally. From the ideal therapeutic mother, the ideal personhood can be learned—and that is a mothering personhood. It is significant—and certainly not accidental—that this person of relational abilities, this empathic person, fulfills precisely the ideal of so-called cultural feminism. She is cultural feminism's image of a woman who is destined for relationality, either essentially or by deep forces of social conditioning. In her, maternal relationality has been reproduced as a matter of upbringing; she has intuitive understanding—not masculine rationality and logicality—her moral compass holds no categorical imperatives; hers is " a different voice," which is valued by other women, even if not by patriarchal institutions. She is a woman who has the whole world—and the very possibility of future harmonious living together—in her hands.

It is not surprising, therefore, that feminist writers who have assessed the new psychoanalysis have assumed that it is just what feminism needs, that it is what women want, that it addresses the complaints women have had about psychoanalysis since the end of the First World War. In a description by Janet Sayers of the new psychoanalysis, you can hear the triumph of feminist vision come true: "Psychoanalysis has been turned upside down. Once patriarchal and phallocentric, it is now almost entirely mother-centered. Its focus has shifted from the past and individual issues concerning patriarchal power, repression, resistance, knowledge, sex and castration, to the present and interpersonal issues concerning maternal care and its vicissitudes—identification, idealization and envy, deprivation and loss, love and hate, introjection and projection."[4]

A similar passage from Nancy Chodorow, who is not just an assessor but a contributor to the new psychoanalysis, also sounds the theme of reversal:

> Thus the object relations perspective takes the construction of masculinity and femininity to be interconnected and constitutes a critique of masculinity as well as a reformulation of our understanding of the female self. It stands the traditional Freudian understanding on its head, as it to some extent revalorizes women's construction of self and makes normal masculinity extremely problematic. Feminist object-relations theorists have

▾▾▾▾▾

also argued strongly for theoretical and developmental treatment of the mother as a subject, against psychoanalytic (including object-relational) tendencies to treat her as an object whose role is evaluated in terms of the presumed needs and fantasies of the child alone. This leads to a reformulation of the psychoanalytic self as well, as it emphasizes not only that separateness, not connectedness, needs explaining, but that intersubjectivity and the mutual recognition of the other and the self are fundamental to satisfactory development.[5]

Feminist Theorizing and the New Psychoanalysis

Among psychoanalysts, as opposed to Anglo-American feminist appropriators of psychoanalysis, the ascendancy of pre-Oedipally focused relational theory is a source of great controversy, and of great opposition. Anglo-American opponents think that it implies complete repudiation of the dynamic unconscious and/or a dangerous underestimation of the importance in human life of sexuality and aggression. Another strong current of opposition has emanated from Jacques Lacan and his followers, who argue that focusing on the mother-child dyad, highlighting a child's experiences of frustration and efforts at individuation, completely obfuscates the key Freudian theory of the castration complex (the "Law of the Father") and its revelations about the indeterminacy of sexual identity for females and males. Efforts of many sorts to stop the paradigm shift with reassertions of Freudian orthodoxy, Lacanian claims about the "real" Freud, an eclectic blending of old and new, or some form of transcending synthetic vision have been offered.[6] This battle is of great interest—indeed, it seems currently to be defining the whole field of psychoanalysis—but it is not the battle itself that I want to discuss here. I want to focus, rather, on the opportunity that this battle offers for reflecting on how theories satisfy desires.

I am going to consider this controversy in psychoanalysis from two angles. First, I want to offer some reflections on what might be called the psychodynamics of theory making, or to engage in what might be called psychotheoretical criticism. Second, I want to try to put the controversy in a larger social and therapeutic context, to ask what it has meant for the therapeutic atmosphere in which we now live and work—not just in the field of psychoanalysis itself, but generally. Anyone who contemplates the history of psychotherapy in this country will notice immediately that there are junctures in it which are characterized by

▼ ▼ ▼ ▼

single-cause theories of pathology, moments in which, across very different types and modes of therapy, a single cause emerges as the one toward which a preponderance of therapeutic attention is directed. In the war years and through the 1950s, for example, the figure to whom Anna Freud gave the name "the rejecting mother" was at the center of attention as all manner of pathologies were attributed to an undifferentiated maternal rejection.[7] We are, it seems to me, currently in another such moment, and it is defined by the unrelational parent or parents, who, whether female or male, are masculine. They are not rejecting, but abusive; the theme of pathology is not abandonment, but exploitation. I want to suggest that the rejecting mother causal theory arose as the old phallocentric Freudian psychoanalysis was first being criticized, and that in the late 1980s and early 1990s the abusive masculinity theory is being sustained by the new pre-Oedipally focused psychoanalytic theory in its vulgar and caricatured forms.

To begin to explore the psychodynamics of theory making and to argue this social claim, let me make a few historical notes on how this new psychoanalysis developed, particularly in relation to the issues that are key to feminism. Its roots are in the 1920s debates between Vienna- and London-based analysts over female psychology.[8] Women, all agreed, following Freud's late statements, have more complex (and some said longer) pre-Oedipal periods than Freud had initially thought. For Freud and his followers, the complexity was due chiefly to the girl's "masculine" libido being invested first in her mother and then, by detours and indirections, tenuously, in her father. For the London group, depending upon Melanie Klein's clinical and Karen Horney's cultural writings, as marshaled for battle by Ernest Jones, the girl's complexity centers on how her femininity, which is her condition at birth, becomes shaped by an initial introjection of the paternal penis, which she fantasizes as inside the mother, that is, by a masculinization. Both of these positions were based on Freud's drive theory, but the drive theory became, as the positions were crafted and recrafted, a topic of increasing controversy because it had received two such different interpretations—one that called all libido masculine and one that saw libido as from birth dual, masculine and feminine.[9] (It did not occur to the contestants, apparently, to speak of libido as indeterminate until it becomes more or less determined as a child develops, and this unenvisioned third possibility shows, I will argue later, how narcissistically invested the two contesting theories were.)

▼ ▼ ▼ ▼

As the grounds for the new psychoanalysis developed after the Second World War, its tie to the debate about female psychology loosened. In the 1950s, emphasis on the pre-Oedipal was buttressed much more strongly by the extension of psychoanalytic therapy to the psychoses and by efforts to map the territory of the vaguely titled "borderline" and narcissistic disorders. Both of these endeavors had the effect of showing that the male's pre-Oedipal period is also more complex than the original Freudian formulations indicated. But they also had the consequence of bringing to the fore, especially in studies directed at boys, the image of the rejecting mother. Specifically, a new approach to male homosexuality emerged. A pre-Oedipally rejected boy will end up seeking love from his father—and thus be homosexual—while a pre-Oedipally rejected girl who seeks such love will, at least, find her heterosexual destination. In this period, although the pre-Oedipal was being stressed, the old psychoanalytic emphasis—more apparent in his followers than in Freud himself—on heterosexuality as normality and homosexuality as pathology was firmly stressed.

While the therapeutic scope of psychoanalysis was widening, the drive theory continued to be questioned, and then it became the focus of critique when female psychology once again took center stage, in the early 1970s, under the impact of second wave feminism. The most recent phase of the psychoanalytic revolution, its most politicized phase, has been defined by psychoanalysis's encounter with feminist critiques. And it is also important to acknowledge that within the many mansions of the larger therapeutic house, as Ilene Phillipson has shown in detail in her recent study *On the Shoulders of Women: The Feminization of Psychotherapy,* women have become the majority population, both as therapists and as clients, so that women are, thus, both the chief therapeutic focus of the new psychoanalysis and its chief practitioners. Although the major psychoanalytic theoreticians continue to be male, the new psychoanalysis is of women, for women, and—more and more—by women.

The women practitioners and theoreticians within psychoanalysis, however, are standing on the shoulders of women within feminism for whom the pre-Oedipally focused relational psychoanalysis was alluring for, basically, two reasons. The first was that the view of female psychology implied by the Oedipally focused and drive theory–based Freudian psychoanalysis was unacceptable to feminists—to feminists of the most diverse persuasions—because it was "phallocentric." This was female psychology viewed from a male angle, under the aegis of the male child and the male adult preoccupations with the phallus and with castration anxiety, in the sphere of paternal household rule. The Freudian view of women was, the critique went summarily, that they were failed men, inferior humans. Further, the viewpoint was sexist in the sense that it confused prejudices against women with scientific theories, conventional notions of femininity and feminine subservience and passivity in heterosexual relations with scientific discourse about normal femininity. Freud and his followers were self-conscious neither about their own theoretical and clinical vantage point nor about how influenced they were by their prerogatives and their milieu. They did not understand themselves, to say the same thing, relationally. They were also speaking for unproblematic scientific objectivity just as scientific objectivity was poised to undergo a thunderous transformation into problematization at the hands of, first, philosophers of science and then feminists.

The second reason why this new psychoanalysis was embraced in feminist theory circles is that it promised a women's liberation of quite a different sort than had emerged on the basis of the old psychoanalysis. The old psychoanalysis had been taken up (and usually vulgarized beyond recognition) for its liberationist potential by people of the left, mostly Marxists who wanted some kind of Marx-Freud synthesis. Beginning with Wilhelm Reich in the 1920s and continuing through the 1960s appropriations of his position by some affiliates of the Frankfurt School as well as by independents like Norman O. Brown, the liberationist theme was always the same: an inhumane and killing—some would say a fascistic—civilization has been built upon repressed instinctual drives, and freedom will come from unrepression.[10] Sexual freedom, which is to be won with an assault upon the patriarchal nuclear family, is both the source and the model of political freedom. To feminists in the late 1960s and 1970s who were arguing that "the personal is political," this liberationist vision was appealing, but it also clearly had its sexist elements. For example, the Freudian-Marxist view was, in most of its incarnations, aimed at abolishing not only constrainingly normative visions of "mature sexuality," and the constraining patriarchal nuclear family, but motherhood as it had become instituted. Either separation of sexuality from reproduction or actual liberation from having children was part of a program that could be called "rejecting of motherhood." And in a certain sense, this rejecting of motherhood was a reaction to the then widely disseminated image of the rejecting mother.

In the late 1960s, many feminists, calling Simone de Beauvoir to witness, did subscribe to the critical vision of motherhood as necessarily constraining female sexuality, but for many more it seemed a great

▼ ▼ ▼ ▼ ▼

error.[11] Those feminists who urged the women's liberation movement to accept psychoanalysis's view of women, arguing that it was not or did not need to be a mainstay of sexism, began their arguments with a critique of the Marxian left's liberationist appropriation of psychoanalysis. Juliet Mitchell started the trend by taking on Wilhelm Reich in *Psychoanalysis and Feminism*. Nancy Chodorow took aim at Herbert Marcuse and Norman O. Brown. In opposition to the Marx-Freudians, feminist theoreticians constructed an image of liberation not *from* the constraints of civilization—that is, patriarchy—but a liberation *for* relationality. Sexual liberation was not to be individualistic, not to be narcissistic. The ideal was not unrepression but mutuality, sharing.

The pre-Oedipally oriented relational psychoanalysis promised a female psychology that did not pathologize women, that emphasized the complexities of male identity—and specifically the complexities that support sexism, including the dimension of sexism that pathologizes women—and a liberating vision of human beings designed for relatedness, for connection. In this psychoanalysis, it was acknowledged clearly that motherhood is reproduced in daughters—and that this process exists cross-culturally, because mothers have primary responsibility for child-care under the most diverse social arrangements. But the stress was not on maternal constraint. Mothers who mother well—good enough mothers—give their daughters the gift of an identity more secure than that of sons, who achieve their identities by disidentification with their mothers. And they give them the maternal virtue—relationality. Trouble comes into this picture from patriarchal institutions that constrain the mother and thus her daughter. In very crude terms—or in very crude interpretations of the theory—trouble comes from masculinity.

Is This What Women Need? Critical Reflections

As these currents of feminist argument developed in the early 1980s, there grew with them a realization that all kinds of theorizing which are in the service of political visions bear the imprint of their purposefulness, or, to say the same thing, the theoretical is political just as much as the personal is. The realization grew that if Freudian psychoanalysis is phallocentric, any theory aimed at correcting for its bias runs the risk of bias in the opposite direction, compensatory bias.

This critical turn began as a cautionary streak within the emergent object relations camp. It was noted that embracing an ideal of femininity as an empathic, relational mothering could end up, practically, sanctioning relegation of women to the mommy track; that it could turn out to support or rationalize a new and more complexly psychologized doctrine of essentially separate feminine and masculine spheres. Further, an uncritical valorization of women's relationality could both blunt appreciation of what good can come from autonomy, aggression, and intellectual mastery—the "masculine" attributes—and obscure the many ways in which women want and try to achieve what these "masculine" attributes bring.

This important tempering of the theory by examining its consequences, by translating it from theory into practice and considering the consequences, is different, however from exploring the psychodynamics of theory making, and it is also different from exploring how theories can become vulgarized, how they have social theoretical consequences. But the psychotheoretical project has emerged, to a small degree. Feminists have reflected, for example, on how the focus on motherhood in the new psychoanalytic theorizing has attracted fantasies about motherhood, fantasies of good mothers, of bad mothers, of past mothers and future mothers, of male mothers and mothering without men.[12] At least in a preliminary way, processes of idealization in feminism have been studied—as they have been studied in the intellectual histories of other oppressed groups who use theory as a weapon of liberation. On a social level, theories that compensatorily valorize women share limitations with theories like those of negritude or black pride that take all of the charges against blacks made in the history of white racism and change their valences—so "Black is beautiful"—or those of gay pride that hold up homosexuality as the only truly wonderful and humane type of sexuality, the very opposite of a deviancy.[13]

But it seems to me that this study needs to go much further—not because I believe that there is some theoretical place to stand that is not involved or invested, a position of purity over theory making, but because I think that people suffer from their idealizing as well as from being the victims of other people's opposite idealizations. Using the terms of Freud's instinctual drive theory, we can say that group idealizations generally involve either displacements of aggression onto outgroups or projections of aggression onto a specific "other," and both the displacement and projection processes subtend—to put the matter bluntly—prejudices.

Now that we have had, historically, a phallocentric psychoanalysis and a psychoanalysis self-consciously constructed as not phallocentric, we are in a position to reflect generally on how the ingredients of psy-

▼ ▼ ▼ ▼ ▼

chosexual identity play into, are projected into, two ideal types. We are in a position to reflect psychoanalytically—taking into account the two modes—on a process of theory making. And the first reflection that the situation calls for, I think, is that emphasizing sex or gender differences seems to be a function of a disposition or a need to identify with a single sex or gender and usually to valorize it by asserting that the other sex or gender is lacking. Denial of femininity in men has its theoretical corollary in denigration of women; denial of masculinity in women has its theoretical corollary in denigration of men. And the same rule of thumb extends to cross-identifications. Women who are masculinely identified, who live and work and have their psychosexual pleasure in male company, are "sexist" and denigrate women in their theories and mythologies, just as men who are femininely identified denigrate men (even though they, unlike their female counterparts, are generally homosexual in object choice).[14]

These general psychotheoretical rules of thumb hold for the surface of theorizing, but below them there is the level of theoretical narcissism, where I think the story is more complex. Masculine narcissism, which denies the feminine, construing the feminine as the castrated, appears theoretically as a claim that "the woman is castrated." That is, the theoretical image of women is the displacement site for anxiety about castration. But the theory that "the woman is castrated" will go right along with a theoretical strand in which the phallic woman, the woman who is *not* castrated, the omnipotent pre-Oedipally fantasized mother, is retained. In Freudian theory, for example, the phallic woman appears as the woman who gets a penis by having a baby—she is the adoring, unrejecting mother with her son; she is the mother that a son most needs in his life and his theory. And she is, theoretically, the mother of the Oedipus Complex, impregnated by a penis that might well be his, or that might well be *him*.

On the other side of this dynamic, there is feminine narcissism creating the theory to satisfy feminine narcissism, which is not a narcissism primarily focused on the phallus, at least not on an unintrojected phallus. Female narcissism creates the image of a male who is lacking, and what he lacks is the mother-bond and mother identification—the experience of sameness with the mother—that the girl has and loves. He is not-*us* (in the plural, while male narcissism says how she is in relation to *me,* singular).[15] The image also captures a complaint: he does not know how to pay attention to women, not in a motherly way or an idealized (feminine, maternal) fatherly way—he is not nurturing and he cannot appreciate a woman as a woman and as women do. And along with this image goes a strand of theorizing about the perfect mother, the mother perfect in her containment of all things, and in her female body, including her genitals, who *should* as the good mother produce the perfect daughter. Her perfection is, however, complex, because her genitals are so largely hidden from her daughter's view. That is, the daughter may have a narcissistic attachment to the female genitals, referenced to her own sensations, but it will be less representable or externalizable than the boy's; and she may—if one credits Melanie Klein's clinical observations—have a narcissistic attachment to an introjected phallus that she has claimed *from her mother.*

What I have said so far about male and female narcissism is on a rather general level, not depending on a specific type of psychoanalytic theory. But if we want to go further and note that there is also great ambivalence about the mother in female theorizing, investigating will require stepping into the fray of psychoanalytic views—old and new— on female narcissism. In the literature on this topic, I find compelling some (not all) of Bela Grunberger's observations about why heterosexual women, whose narcissism very often takes the form of wanting to be loved, organizing psychically and behaviorally around love-solicitation or narcissistic confirmation, reject the pregenital drives, the component instincts, and the pleasures associated with them.[16] When heterosexual women, for whom the mother is, eventually, an unsatisfactory object, look to their fathers for love, they reject what they have experienced sexually in infant self-exploration and in relation to their mothers— pregenital eroticism, especially autoerotism. The love they seek is more in the domain of object relations, confirmation, than that of instinctual satisfaction. This bent is, then, I think, reflected in theory making that rejects the instinctual drive theory. It might follow from this observation that homosexual women, for whom the paternal object is not necessary in the same way, would be less inclined, in their lives and in their theories, to reject pregenital satisfactions or to reject the instinctual drive theory.[17]

I made a turn here, to keep focusing on female narcissism, into a type of Freudian theory that is still very much tied to the instinctual drive theory—a type well represented by the anthology *Female Sexuality* edited by Janine Chasseguet-Smirgel. This seemed necessary to me because the feminist object relations theory is very—of course, given its orientation—uninterested in female narcissism. There is no female (or male) narcissism in this theory; there is only failed female relationality.[18]

▼ ▼ ▼ ▼ ▼

Similarly, there is no female oral, anal, or phallic sadism or masochism, no scopophilia and exhibitionism, no masturbation or autoerotism in general. The theory seems to me as blind to these manifestations as most versions of the phallocentric theory are to male investment in the phallic mother as a figure of relational bliss rather than as a castrator—that is, to primary rather than secondary narcissism, to denial of sexual difference rather than to accentuation of it.[19]

Let me take up this problem of blindness to female desire from another angle. In the recent feminist theoretical literature on the new relational psychoanalysis, it is interesting to observe how prominent is the question—to put it very simply—why do women ever become heterosexual? If a woman's deepest and oldest bond is with her mother, what would move her to her father? It was Freud himself, of course, who first posed this question and noted, as he considered it, that bisexuality is more obvious in women than in men, and also that women with strong father ties have in their earlier histories equally strong or stronger mother ties.[20] In the recent literature, feminist theorists frequently make the related claim that women are less tied to or dependent emotionally (as opposed to materially) upon men than men are upon women. Women recover from heterosexual love losses, so this argument goes, with more resiliency than men because they have, as it were, only half an investment in the heterosexual sphere and they do not, in loss, lose their female bonding, while men lose both the female love object and the mother who stands behind her.[21]

Women, to translate this result into caricature, do not need men. Nothing psychological compels them toward men, although much in social and economic organization and convention may, as may—at least until recent technological developments complicated this matter—their desire for children (or their desire to be mothers). This is a story, of course, in which the reckoning is done exclusively in object relations terms. For the heterosexual turn to show up as predestined, a theory must posit either some form of primary femininity (an inborn biological program aimed at reproductive sexuality) or some form of instinctual drive theory, which, in a modification of the Freudian one, stresses a little girl's very early awareness (unconscious) of her genitals. Grunberger's theory, worked out in conjunction with Chasseguet-Smirgel, goes in this second direction. Grunberger attributes the girl's heterosexual turn to her need for narcissistic confirmation, which the father can give because he is the truly satisfying (genital) sexual object, the one who offers a prototype of the integration of sexual and narcissistic needs. The

▼ ▼ ▼ ▼ ▼

good enough father—the one who is the very opposite of an abusing father—is key to his daughter's heterosexuality because his confirmation of her allows her, as it were, to leave her mother without repressing her desires.

In complete contrast to most object relations feminists, Grunberger understands men to be more invested in their instinctual satisfactions than they are in narcissistic confirmation, so that they are less dependent upon their objects and more able to recover from a wound to their narcissism in a loss of love than women are. Correlatively, Grunberger's approach can also indicate why sexual liberation in the form of paeans to polymorphous perversity is typical of males in the Reich-to-Marcuse left-Freudian tradition and why many female theorists might be inclined, for psychological rather than political reasons, to find this tradition unsatisfactory. Because the male does not change his object, he does not reject the pleasures of his first love, and consequently he continues to take his pleasure in the component instincts (and is more frequently given to perversions than females) and would want to celebrate them theoretically.

I started this reflection on narcissistic positions projected into theory-making with the suggestion that identifications with one sex or gender sustain (if they do not actually produce) theories in which male-female difference is emphasized—either inborn sex difference (on the old model) or socially constructed gender difference (on the new model). On the basis of the sketch I made of the male and female narcissistic theorizing modes, I want to suggest now that such singular identifications and operations on a narcissistic basis also tend to sustain either/or thinking. That is, they tend to support the intellectual habit of saying things like "either the drive theory or the object relations theory." Theoretical positions get genderized—there are "masculine" and "feminine" theories—and are embraced or rejected as such. The level on which this happens, however, seems to me to be Oedipal. These are "either father or mother" theoretical moves.

Quite different in their mode of operation are people who have what Lawrence Kubie called "the drive to become both sexes" and who stress in their theories or their mythologies the similarities between the sexes.[22] They may be quite narcissistic, too, but their narcissism is not single-sex–linked—it is a narcissism keyed to omnipotent thinking, as all-embracing thinking. Such people, it seems to me, tend both to idealize androgyny and to find the differences among people in dimensions other

▼ ▼ ▼ ▼ ▼

than or in addition to those of biological or socially constructed sex. General differences of character impress them more, or, if they are psychologists, differences of pathology type strike them more than differences of sex. Freud himself, it seems to me, in his early theorizing, at the moment when he was adventurously exploring his own bisexuality in the letters to Wilhelm Fliess and the *Three Essays on the Theory of Sexuality*, was more interested in pathology types (or what he called "the choice of neurosis") and general characterology than he was later, when he became more rigidly masculine in his identifications and more inclined than ever to present women as failed men. His rigidification can be seen growing in the 1914 essay "On Narcissism," which is an example of psychotheoretical masculine narcissism. The good lovers in that essay are men who project their narcissism onto women, overvaluing them, and thus loving women—themselves in their women—with great self-enhancing intensity.[23]

There are also, it seems to me, people who desire to be neither sex—either in the sense that they are ascetics, or in the sense that they relish gender bending, identity shifting, masquerade, and imposture. Ascetics seem to me prone to cathect images of development rather than visions of masculinity or femininity. They valorize normality (and usually this translates into visions of heterosexual normality, but there are also those who envision homosexual normality). Socially, they tend, also, to be conservative, to make good proponents of orthodoxy, whether that be established orthodoxy (such as Freudian orthodoxy) or orthodoxy invented to make the new into the established. By contrast, those who are identity shifters generate anti-theories, theories that attack the terms of other developmental theories, that deconstruct, that celebrate transgressive (not polymorphous) sexual modes. These are unconfident but supercilious or superior sorts whose main division of the world is not into feminine and masculine but into free and enslaved, worthy and unworthy. Like most anarchists, they are ferocious Manicheans. In characterological terms, ascetics seem to me to be more obsessional, and gender shifters more hysterical—in contrast to the two sorts of narcissistic character-trait dominance that mark those who identify with one gender and those who desire to be both.

The kind of typology I am sketching—and just sketching—here can provide, I think, a kind of cautionary tale about psychoanalytic theorizing and the needs it can serve. But I also think it provides a foundation for a more social theoretical evaluation of theory. As I suggested before,

▼ ▼ ▼ ▼

theory-making involves not only processes of idealization and denigration, but processes that can be easily debased or vulgarized—that attract fantasizing which is psychotechnic. When theories can be construed as ideals—as portraying the ideal masculinity or the ideal femininity—they are picked up by those in need of ideals. But further, on a deeper level, theories that can be construed as Rousseauistically presenting human beings as born good and then corrupted by their environments offer restoration of an ego ideal focused on perfection and featuring "society" or "patriarchy" or some hypostatized out-there as the sole source of loss.[24] People whose own ego ideals have either dissolved or become hopelessly demanding under the impact of reality, rather than becoming tempered and realistic, are especially prone to use quick-fix versions of theoretical ideals to help themselves, to orient themselves, give themselves meaning and direction. And they do the same with negative ideals—which currently take the form of images of bad masculinity.

The new psychoanalysis that valorizes women has attracted a particular vulgarization in theory and practice—one its theoreticians certainly did not imagine, do not want, and are not responsible for—that suits our social moment. This vulgarization goes: When women are not empathic and relational, that is because they have been exploited or abused—not rejected so much as invaded—by bad masculinity. The way to get cured of this condition is through therapy, the locus of female empowerment, as consciousness-raising groups were in the late 1960s and early 1970s. And this now means feminist therapy, which used to be quite hostile to psychoanalysis—the old phallocentric psychoanalysis—but which is quite receptive to the new object relations psychoanalysis.

There is much that is salutary in this development, but also much that seems very dangerous. To my mind, the worst theoretical and therapeutic consequence of the theory-vulgarization process is the one that valorizes—rather than analyzes—female pathology, making women's illnesses into heroic endeavors to reject masculine impositions. This development echoes the beginning of the feminist therapy movement, in the early 1970s, when anorexics got conceptualized as hunger strikers, women who were making a protest against patriarchal culture and its (truly) insane standards of female beauty. This is happening again now as women with all sorts of different pathologies (including eating disorders) are being conceptualized as victims of abuse, as "survivors." "Abuse" is becoming just as all-encompassing a term as "rejection" was in the 1950s, so that verbal abuse, emotional abuse, physical abuse, sexual abuse, and so forth, no matter what the developmental stage at which they may have been experienced, are all undifferentiatedly "abuse" (or sometimes "trauma," to fit with the diagnostic category "post-traumatic stress disorder"). And the new psychoanalysis, which does not have an instinctual drive theory or any of the analysis of children's and adult's sexual fantasies that the instinctual drive theory supported, is much better suited to an image of females as purely passive victims of such abuse.[25]

At the mid-century, as average family size in America contracted and women moved into workplaces and public roles in unprecedented numbers, "the rejecting mother" appeared. Again, a real social phenomenon—the increase in abuse of children that has occurred with the breakdown of familial regulation and with the horrible consequences of "polymorphous perversity" embraced not as a mode of liberation but as a regressive escape from mature sexuality—has been accompanied by a simplifying theory. But this time, the burden of accusation has shifted from femininity to masculinity (whether in females or males, mothers or fathers). There is, as in the earlier era, a degree of insightfulness and appropriate social critique in the accusation, but also a great deal of pendulum-effect and psychotheoretical distortion, which will fall to future clinicians to assess and to correct.

▼   This essay was prepared for a conference on female psychology sponsored by the Western New England Institute of Psychoanalysis in April 1994, and I owe thanks to my fellow panelists Nancy Chodorow, Jane Flax, and Kirsten Dahl for their comments on it. The essay was later published by *American Imago*, 51 (1994): 373–396.

▼ ▼ ▼ ▼

Notes

2. Psychoanalytic Reflections on Creativity

1. Here and henceforth I refer to Freud's works by volume and page number of the *Standard Edition of the Complete Psychological Works of Sigmund Freud,* trans. James Strachey, 24 vols. (London: Hogarth, 1953–1974).

4. Looking for Anna Freud's Mother

1. References to Freud's works are to the *Standard Edition of the Complete Psychological Works of Sigmund Freud,* trans. James Strachey, 24 vols. (London: Hogarth, 1953–1974). I will give further references by volume and page number of this edition. *Three Essays on the Theory of Sexuality* appears in 7:125–243; "Female Sexuality" in 21:223–243; and "Femininity" in 22:112–135.

2. "Beating Fantasies and Daydreams" appears in *The Writings of Anna Freud,* 8 vols. (New York: International Universities Press, 1966–1981), 1:137–157.

3. Nancy Chodorow, *The Reproduction of Mothering* (Berkeley: University of California Press, 1978).

4. Karl Abraham, "Manifestations of the Female Castration Complex," in *Selected Papers on Psycho-Analysis* (London: Hogarth, 1949), pp. 338–369; and Karen Horney, "On the Genesis of the Castration Complex in Women," *International Journal of Psychoanalysis,* 5 (1924): 50–65.

5. Melanie Klein, *Contributions to Psycho-Analysis, 1921–1945* (London: Hogarth, 1948).

6. *The Ego and the Mechanisms of Defense,* in *The Writings of Anna Freud,* vol. 2.

7. Kerry Novick and Jack Novick, "The Essence of Masochism," *The Psychoanalytic Study of the Child,* 42 (1987): 355.

8. Ibid., p. 377.

5. Anna Freud as a Historian of Psychoanalysis

1. There have been books purporting to be *A History of Psychoanalysis,* the title of one by Reuben Fine (New York: Columbia University Press, 1979), which

is a bibliographic tour. Edith Kurzweil's *Freudians: A Comparative Perspective* (New Haven: Yale University Press, 1989) is a helpful survey, taking into account what has been written nation by nation historically. Nathan Hale's *Rise and Crisis of Psychoanalysis in the United States: Freud and the Americans, 1917–1985* (New York: Oxford University Press, 1995), the sequel to his *Freud and the Americans: The Beginnings of Psychoanalysis in the United States, 1896–1917,* is a good history of American psychoanalysis in its cultural setting, which contains in its notes a guide to recent historical writing.

2. In 1966, Anna Freud summarized this complex training issue, which has so much to do with why psychoanalysts do not write their own history well, as follows: "Thus candidates are guided how to extract the maximum of information from transference, resistance, dreams, other id derivatives, or ego mechanisms; how to time their interpretations; in short, how to cure their patients. They receive no guidance in such important matters as how to record their material, or sift and summarize it, or verify their findings, or pool them with others; how to trace the history of psychoanalytic concepts, to inquire into their definitions, and to clarify and unify their technical terms; how to select specific areas for their research interests or to become alerted to the gaps in our knowledge" (7:57). (In this note and others, as well as in the text, I refer to Anna Freud's writings by citing volume and page number of *The Writings of Anna Freud,* 8 vols. (New York: International Universities Press, 1966–1981).

3. Particularly important among these papers (in volumes 7 and 8 of her *Writings*) are: "A Short History of Child Analysis" (1966), "The Ideal Psychoanalytic Institute: A Utopia" (1966), "Difficulties in the Path of Psychoanalysis: A Confrontation of Past with Present Viewpoints" (1969), "Child Analysis as a Subspecialty of Psychoanalysis" (1970), "The Widening Scope of Psychoanalytic Child Psychology, Normal and Abnormal" (1972), "Beyond the Infantile Neurosis" (1974), "The Principal Task of Child Analysis" (1978), "Changes in Psychoanalytic Practice and Experience" (1976), and "A Study Guide to Freud's Writings" (1978).

4. See especially "Child Analysis as a Subspecialty of Psychoanalysis," prepared in 1970 (7:204–219).

5. In terms of the defense mechanisms that Anna Freud had explored so brilliantly earlier in her career, the one at work here was "altruistic surrender," her elaboration of the maneuver to which Freud himself had originally given the name "retiring in favor of another."

6. In the next year, 1976, Anna Freud attended a symposium entitled "The Identity of the Psychoanalyst," where she felt herself to be something of a token, a "representative of the past," and where she wanted to make it quite clear that she did not have a personal relation to the topic. Allowing a herself a little sarcasm, she said: "[About] the question of the identity of the analyst, I really have no justification to speak: I have never gone through a crisis of identity

▼ ▼ ▼ ▼

as an analyst. I can remember that during my analytic life I have met several crises, in the external world and in the internal world, but what I have missed out on evidently is that I felt my own identity shaken . . . With me [social identity, professional identity, and personal identity] fell together into one" (8:189–190).

7. At the end of this paragraph, Anna Freud was clearly responding to the then current charge (of which there are many echoes in the last few years) that the "orthodox" analytic stance was too authoritarian: she presents the founding generation as anti-authoritarian, particularly in comparison to the psychiatric attitude Freud battled. She knew very well that the ideal of analysis as a "shared endeavor" between analysts and patients had emerged as a consensus among her colleagues, especially under the challenge of Sándor Ferenczi and his "active technique." Only in the next generation, replete with medical people and men with military psychiatry experience, did school-bound authoritarianism flourish, particularly in hospital settings—producing, of course, a counter-trend among the more independent and innovative, like the best of the Middle Group in Britain or Hans Loewald in America.

8. See "Child Observation and Prediction of Development," 5:104.

9. "As in the field of adult analysis, the descriptive nature of many of the current diagnostic categories runs counter to the essence of psychoanalytic thinking, since it emphasizes the identity of or difference between manifest symptomology while neglecting those of the underlying pathogenic factors" (6:110).

10. Among Anna Freud's contemporaries, the one who was most in accord with her approach to metapsychology and its intricacy was Robert Waelder, particularly in his classic paper "The Principle of Multiple Function," collected in *Psychoanalysis: Observation, Theory, Application* (New York: International Universities Press, 1976), pp. 68–83.

11. For example, see Axel Hoffer, "Ferenczi's Relevance to Contemporary Psychoanalytic Technique," in Lewis Aron and Adrienne Harris, eds., *The Legacy of Sandor Ferenczi* (Hillsdale, N.J.: Analytic Press, 1993), pp. 75–80.

6. Profile of Anna Freud as a Latency Woman

1. For a more extensive discussion, see Essay 7 in this volume.

2. The optimal nursery unit, Anna Freud said in reflecting on her wartime nurseries, was a worker and five children—one less than the Freud sibling group. This was an empirical finding, but it is hard to imagine that it did not reverberate with her feeling, which I reported in my biography, that she was the unwanted youngest child, the sixth, one too many.

3. All quotations from Anna Freud will be indicated, as here, with volume and page number of *The Writings of Anna Freud*, 8 vols. (New York: International Universities Press, 1966–1981).

▼ ▼ ▼ ▼ ▼

7. A History of Freud Biographies

1. Perhaps a sign of historiography to come is given by John E. Toew's review essay "Historicizing Psychoanalysis: Freud in His Time and for Our Time," *Journal of Modern History*, 43 (September 1991): 504.

2. There is an extensive, helpful, and very opinionated review of the literature on Freud, including much but not all of the biographical literature, in Peter Gay's *Freud: A Life for Our Time* (New York: Norton, 1988).

3. Freud's *On the Psychoanalytic Movement* and *An Autobiographical Study* appear in the *Standard Edition of the Complete Works of Sigmund Freud*, trans. James Strachey, 24 vols. (London: Hogarth, 1953–1974), vols. 14 and 22, respectively. Ernest Jones's three-volume *Life and Work of Sigmund Freud* was published from 1953 to 1957 (New York, Basic Books).

4. Otto Fenichel, *The Psychoanalytic Theory of the Neuroses* (New York: Norton, 1945); Freida Fromm-Reichmann, *Principles of Intensive Psychotherapy* (London: Allen & Unwin, 1953); Herman Nunberg, *Principles of Psychoanalysis*, rev. ed. (New York: International Universities Press, 1955); and Robert Waelder, *Basic Theory of Psychoanalysis* (New York: International Universities Press, 1960).

5. Helen Walker Puner, *Freud: His Life and Mind* (New York: Howell, Soskin, 1947), and Emil Ludwig, *Doctor Freud: An Analysis and a Warning* (New York: Hellman, Williams, 1947).

6. Other examples of amateur psychoanalyzing are numerous: see, for one, Maurice Natenberg's *Case History of Sigmund Freud: A Psycho-Biography* (Chicago: Regent House, 1955), in which Freud appears as a severe neurotic with a fantastic delusional system.

7. Ernest Kris et al., eds., *The Origin of Psychoanalysis: Letters to Wilhelm Fliess, Drafts and Notes, 1887–1902, by Sigmund Freud* (New York: Basic Books, 1954).

8. Bernfeld's essays are listed in Gay's bibliography in *Freud*; Philip Utley is writing a biography of Bernfeld and has already published *Siegfried Bernfeld: Left Wing Youth Leader, Psychoanalyst, and Zionist, 1910–April 1918* (Ann Arbor, 1975).

9. Hanns Sachs, *Freud: Master and Friend* (Cambridge, Mass.: Harvard University Press, 1944), and Sachs, *Masks of Life and Love* (Cambridge, Mass.: Sci-Art Publishers, 1948).

10. These letters and a more extensive discussion of the history of the Jones biography can be found in my *Anna Freud: A Biography* (New York: Summit Books, 1988).

11. Martin Freud, *Sigmund Freud: Man and Father* (New York: Vanguard, 1958).

12. See Jones, *Life and Work of Sigmund Freud*, 2:409.

13. See *The Letters of Sigmund Freud*, selected and edited by Ernst Freud (London: Hogarth, 1961), and also Ernst Freud's collaborative work with his

wife, Lucie Freud, and Ilse Grubrich-Simitis, *Sigmund Freud: His Life in Pictures and Words* (London: Andre Deutsch, 1978), a superb volume.

14. See Max Schur, *Freud: Living and Dying* (New York: International Universities Press, 1972).

15. Lionel Trilling, *Freud and the Crisis of Our Culture* (Boston: Beacon Press, 1955); Erich Fromm, *Sigmund Freud's Mission: An Analysis of His Personality and Influence* (New York: Harper & Brothers, 1959); and Philip Rieff, *Freud: The Mind of a Moralist* (New York: Viking Press, 1959).

16. Herbert Marcuse, *Eros and Civilization* (Boston: Beacon Press, 1955).

17. Betty Friedan, *The Feminine Mystique* (New York: Norton, 1963).

18. For a superficial review see Justin Miller, "Interpretations of Freud's Jewishness, 1924–1974," *Journal of the History of the Behavioral Sciences*, 17 (1981): 357–374.

19. David Bakan, *Sigmund Freud and the Jewish Mystical Tradition* (Princeton: Van Nostrand, 1958), and D. B. Klein, *Jewish Origins of the Psychoanalytic Movement* (Chicago: University of Chicago Press, 1985).

20. See Peter Gay, *A Godless Jew: Freud, Atheism, and the Making of Psychoanalysis* (New Haven: Yale University Press, 1987); Emanuel Rice, *Freud and Moses: The Long Journey Home* (Albay: State University of New York Press, 1990); and Yosef Yerushalmi, *Freud's Moses* (New Haven: Yale University Press, 1991).

21. Didier Anzieu, *L'auto-analyse: son rôle dans la decouverte de la psychoanalyse par Freud* (Paris: Presses Universitaires de France, 1959); translated as *Freud's Self-Analysis* (New York: International Universities Press, 1986).

22. Henri Ellenberger, *The Discovery of the Unconscious* (New York: Basic Books, 1970).

23. Paul Roazen, *Brother Animal: The Story of Freud and Tausk* (New York: Knopf, 1969), and Roazen, *Freud and His Followers* (New York: Knopf, 1975).

24. Kurt R. Eissler, *Talent and Genius* (New York: Quadrangle Books, 1971). Eissler also produced *Viktor Tausk's Suicide* (New York: International Universities Press, 1982). There is much valuable biographical information in his *Sigmund Freud und die Wiener Universität* (1966), but I find his most interesting contribution to be a reflection on Freud's adolescence in *The Psychoanalytic Study of the Child*, 33 (1978).

25. Frank Sulloway, *Freud: Biologist of the Mind* (New York: Basic Books, 1979).

26. Kate Millett, *Sexual Politics* (New York: Doubleday, 1970); Simone de Beauvoir, *The Second Sex* (New York: Knopf, 1952); and Viola Klein, *The Feminine Character* (London: Routledge & Kegan Paul, 1946). For a brief history of relations between psychoanalysis and feminism, see Essay 11 in this volume.

27. Marthe Robert, *From Oedipus to Moses* (Garden City, N.Y.: Anchor Books, 1976); Marie Balmary, *Psychoanalyzing Psychoanalysis* (Baltimore: Johns Hop-

kins University Press, 1982; and Marianne Krüll, *Freud and His Father* (New York: Norton, 1986).

28. Peter Homans, *The Ability to Mourn: Disillusionment and the Social Origins of Psychoanalysis* (Chicago: University of Chicago Press, 1989), p. 17.

29. Heinz Kohut, "Creativeness, Charisma, and Group Psychology: Reflections on Freud's Self-Analysis," in John E. Gedo and George H. Pollock, eds., *Freud: Fusion of Science and Humanism* (New York: International Universities Press, 1976), pp. 379–425.

30. Richard Wollheim, *Sigmund Freud* (New York: Viking Press, 1971); Gay, *Freud*; and Octave Mannoni, *Freud* (New York: Random House, 1971).

31. Freud's October 3, 1897, letter in Jeffrey Masson, ed., *The Complete Letters of Sigmund Freud to Wilhelm Fliess, 1887–1904* (Cambridge, Mass.: Harvard University Press, 1985), p. 168.

32. See Walter Boehlick, ed., *The Letters of Sigmund Freud to Eduard Silberstein, 1871–1881* (Cambridge, Mass.: Harvard University Press, 1990).

33. Paul Ricoeur, *Freud and Philosophy* (New Haven: Yale University Press, 1971); Carl Schorske, *Fin de Siècle Vienna* (New York: Vintage Books, 1981); and William McGrath, *Freud's Discovery of Psychoanalysis: The Politics of Hysteria* (Ithaca: Cornell University Pess, 1986).

34. Ronald W. Clark, *Freud: The Man and His Cause* (New York: Random House, 1980); Gay, *Freud*; Janet Malcolm, *In the Freud Archives* (New York: Knopf, 1984); and Jeffrey Masson, *The Assault on Truth: Freud's Suppression of the Seduction Theory* (New York: Farrar, Straus, and Giroux, 1984).

35. See Peter Swales, "Freud, Minna Bernays, and the Conquest of Rome: New Light on the Origins of Psychoanalysis," *The New American Review,* Spring/Summer, 1982; and J. N. Isbister, *Freud: An Introduction to His Life and Work* (New York: Blackwell, 1985).

36. Gay, *Freud*, p. 89.

37. There are gestures in this direction in Homans, *The Ability to Mourn,* and in a not very good but suggestive British work: Barry Richards, *Images of Freud: Cultural Responses to Psychoanalysis* (New York: St. Martins Press, 1989).

8. Hannah Arendt among Feminists

1. Bonnie Honig, ed., *Feminist Interpretations of Hannah Arendt* (State Park, Penn.: Pennsylvania State University Press, 1995); and Lawrence May and Jerome Kohn, eds. *Hannah Arendt: Twenty Years Later* (Cambridge, Mass.: MIT Press, 1996).

2. See "On the Emancipation of Women" in *Arendt: Essays in Understanding, 1930–1954,* ed. J. Kohn (New York: Harcourt Brace Jovanovich, 1994).

3. An unilluminating example is Anne Norton's badly argued tract "Heart of Darkness: Africa and African Americans in the Writings of Hannah Arendt," in Honig, ed., *Feminist Interpretations of Hannah Arendt.*

▼ ▼ ▼ ▼

4. There are exceptions to this generalization. For example, Nancy Harstock in *Money, Sex, and Power* (New York: Longman, 1983), writing from a socialist point of view, calls Arendt a theorist writing out of female experience and articulating a concept of power as potentiality rather than as domination, the more masculine conceptualization.

5. Adrienne Rich, *On Lies, Secrets, and Silence: Selected Prose, 1966–1978* (New York: Norton, 1979), pp. 211–212; this passage was quoted again and again in feminist writings on Arendt.

6. See, for example, a reassessment from the late 1980s: Maria Markus, "The 'Anti-Feminism' of Hannah Arendt," in G. Kaplan and C. Kessler, eds., *Hannah Arendt: Thinking, Judging, Freedom* (Sydney: Allen & Unwin, 1989).

7. Mary Dietz, "Feminist Receptions of Hannah Arendt," in Honig, ed., *Feminist Interpretations of Hannah Arendt*.

8. As Arendt's biographer, in my *Hannah Arendt: For Love of the World*, I stressed Arendt's Jewishness and gave little attention to her life as a woman— as little as she gave it herself or as was reflected in her literary estate, as little as she gave to Rahel Varnhagen in her biography, which stressed Varnhagen's Jewishness, not her life as a woman. In keeping with the spirit prevailing in 1970s feminism, this approach was criticized by Elizabeth Minnich, "Friendship between Women: The Act of Feminist Biography," *Feminist Studies* 11/2 (Summer 1985): 287–305, although Minnich praised Arendt's own biographical method as relational and "feminist." I find Minnich's position narrow, almost sectarian, because to me it seems to prescribe that biographers should fit their subject's lives to a feminist agenda rather than respecting the way a woman lived her life and understood herself. In retrospect, however, I wish that I had devoted a longer passage to exploring why Arendt was not interested in feminism (in the Germany of her youth or later in America) and why she did not analyze— especially in the privacy of her correspondence—her own position as a woman. She reacted strongly when she thought she had been treated as an exception or as a token woman, on the model of "the exception Jew" she had often written about (see my biography, *Hannah Arendt* [New York: Summit Books, 1988], p. 272), but she ignored what might be called the ordinary sexism of everyday life. I think the key to this silence is her strict distinction between social anti-Semitism and the truly dangerous political anti-Semitism, and her assumption that social anti-Semitism can and ought to be ignored as inconsequential—personally hurtful, but politically inconsequential. The following statement, which she wrote shortly after the war, makes the point starkly, and it can be extrapolated to social sexism: "It should be borne in mind that whether a person does or does not like Jews is of little interest. If, however, somebody maintains 'we fought this war for the Jews,' then his statement assumes importance. The person who declares 'the Jews want to dominate the world' is clearly an antisemite; the same is not necessarily true for people who prefer not to share a hotel with Jews, or even declare that Jews are greedy." (See also note 11.)

▼▼▼▼▼

9. Carol Lee Bacchi, *Same Difference: Feminism and Sexual Difference* (Sydney: Allen & Unwin, 1990), p. ix.

10. I have set out a history of psychoanalytic chracterology and a rationale for this statement in my *Creative Characters* (New York: Routledge & Kegan Paul, 1991) and in *The Anatomy of Prejudices* (Cambridge, Mass.: Harvard University Press, 1996).

11. To continue the line of thought expressed in note 8, I would speculate that one of the key reasons why Hannah Arendt did not focus her attention on sexism is that she never had to confront personally the complexities of combining motherhood with an intellectual public life. She could also stress the private side of childrearing and insist on the prepolitical nature of education without having been challenged as a parent by the gray zone where private and public meet—the zone she encountered in the Little Rock dispute.

9. The Exemplary Independence of Hannah Arendt

1. After *Eichmann in Jerusalem,* Arendt used the now famous phrase "the banality of evil" to indicate the thoughtlessness rather than the psychopathology of the totalitarian perpetrators, but her description of the resulting evil—making humans superfluous as humans—remained the same.

2. *Hannah Arendt—Karl Jaspers—Correspondence 1926–1969,* ed. L. Kohler and H. Saner (New York: Harcourt Brace Jovanovich, 1992), p. 163 (January 7, 1951); her reply, p. 167 (March 4, 1951); Jaspers's continuation, p. 205 (December 29, 1952); Arendt's acquiescence, p. 216 (May 13, 1953). And cf. Heinrich Bluecher to Jaspers, p. 186, July 21, 1952: "He uses his insight and intelligence to satisfy his will for justice, a will that from the beginning was both a will to power and a desire for vengeance. Marx does not use his hate and his love as organs of cognizance and then put them on ice, turn away from them, play them off against each other in order to achieve through self-criticism a maximum of truth. Instead, he falls victim to his own hatred and follows it, in the name of justice, into an abominable vision . . . In any case, Marx is still a blameless human being, a 'respectable citizen,' compared to the literati, to whom Hannah does not deny her high regard and her human tolerance, a tolerance that I feel capable of only if I slip into the role of a psychiatrist." Page numbers for further quotes from this *Correspondence* will be given in the text and notes.

3. Hannah Arendt, "Civil Disobedience," in *Crises of the Republic* (New York: Penguin, 1975), p. 64.

4. Jaspers to Heinrich Bluecher, July 21, 1952 (p. 186): "Hannah has, it seems to me, undergone an evolution in recent years. Her great rage is almost gone. She is becoming more just, tolerant toward what is most alien to her. She shows greater detachment toward Germany. I haven't progressed so far, and so there is sometimes a desirable tension between us."

5. Arendt, "Civil Disobedience," p. 56.

▼ ▼ ▼ ▼

6. Ibid., p. 79.

7. Hannah Arendt, *Men in Dark Times* (New York: Penguin, 1973), p. 18.

8. Similarly, she understood the American race question in terms borrowed from "the Jewish Question," which produced the unusual attitude she took toward school integration. See her "Reflections on Little Rock," *Dissent*, 6 (1959): 45–56.

9. As far as I know, there does not exist a commentary on Hannah Arendt by a deconstructionist or an opponent of essentialist notions of identity. Bonnie Honig has edited a collection of feminist essays called *Feminist Interpretations of Hannah Arendt* (University Park, Penn.: Pennsylvania State University Press, 1996).

10. Arendt, *Men in Dark Times*, p. 6. Such vitality may exist in an unhealthy person or one who is mentally ill as long as those conditions of illness are not of the sort that induce or consist of withdrawal from the world.

11. On Arendt's fiftieth birthday in 1956, Jaspers wrote to her, "What a life you have led, a life given to you and earned by you with a steadfastness that has mastered that evil, the horror that has come from without and ground down so many others; also with a wonderful strength rooted in noble impulses, a strength that has transformed your vulnerable softness, your precarious vacillation, your tendency to let your passions run away with you, into the informing forces of your being . . . This strength stems in part from your physical vitality. Health is a wonderful thing, and beauty, the ability to delight others. But these are not the things that have truly carried you. They were put in your service" (pp. 300–301).

12. When Jaspers read the manuscript of Arendt's Varnhagen biography in 1952, he understood that her work on that book had played a role in allowing her to join Bluecher, a gentile, because it had been very focused on "the Jewish Question," which Arendt had had to work out for herself: "You wrote this book before Heinrich Blucher came into our life. Perhaps your work on Rahel made it possible for you to keep your heart and eye open for the new direction in your life, which in no way resembles Rahel's" (p. 195).

13. Arendt, *Men in Dark Times*, pp. 110, 109.

14. Hannah Arendt, *Essays in Understanding*, ed. Jerome Kohn (New York: Harcourt Brace Jovanovich, 1994), p. 17 (in an interview with Christian Gauss). Arendt sometimes spoke of the Jews of her mother's generation as "worldless," but this seems to be an inexact use of her own terminology: The Jews were outside of society, but not worldless in the sense of being without connection to natural and cultural things and to the interests connecting people. When Arendt developed her distinction between pariahs (whom she sometimes called worldless) and parvenus, she had not yet developed (in *The Human Condition*) distinctions between the private and the political and the hybrid social and had not articulated the situation categories plurality, natality, mortality, earth, and world.

▼ ▼ ▼ ▼ ▼

15. Voltaire, one of the theorists of power whom Arendt cited in *On Violence*, was characteristically personal in his notion that power is rule: "Power consists in making others act as I choose." Jaspers focused his attention on Voltaire during the controversy over Arendt's Eichmann book because he was thinking about the "literary life" and how corrupting it is: "Why am I spending my time with this? Because I think that among all the heterogeneous forces that marshaled themselves against you this literary element as such, without prior agreement, found itself by its very nature united against you" (p. 590).

16. Arendt, *Men in Dark Times*, p. 17.

10. Rereading Freud on Female Development

1. All of the Freud works referred to in this essay appear in the *Standard Edition of the Complete Psychological Works of Sigmund Freud*, trans. James Strachey, 24 vols. (London: Hogarth, 1953–1974). References in the text to volume and page number are to this edition.

2. Karen Horney, "On the Genesis of the Castration Complex in Women," *International Journal of Psychoanalysis*, 5 (1924): 50–65; and Melanie Klein, "The Oedipus Complex in Light of Early Anxieties," in her *Contributions to Psychoanalysis, 1921–1945* (New York: McGraw-Hill, 1964), pp. 339–390.

3. See Carol Gilligan, *In a Different Voice: Psychological Theory and Women's Development* (Cambridge, Mass.: Harvard University Press, 1982).

4. Ruth Mack Brunswick, "A Pre-Oedipal Phase of the Libido," in Robert Fliess, ed., *The Psychoanalytic Reader* (New York: International Universities Press, 1948), p. 276.

5. Anna Freud, *The Ego and the Mechanisms of Defense* (1936), in *The Writings of Anna Freud*, 8 vols. (New York: International Universities Press, 1966–1981), vol. 2.

11. On Psychoanalysis and Feminism

1. Two anthologies could be consulted for a sense of the literature: Richard Feldstein and Judith Roof, eds., *Feminism and Psychoanalysis* (Ithaca: Cornell University Press, 1989), and Teresa Brennan, ed., *Between Feminism and Psychoanalysis* (New York: Routledge & Kegan Paul, 1989). The Winter 1992 issue of *Signs* contains two long review essays on psychoanalysis and feminism by Judith Gardiner and Michele Barrett. A volume of interviews with analysts, Elaine Baruch and Lucienne Serrano, eds., *Women Analyze Women in France, England, and the United States* (New York: New York University Press, 1988), contains interesting reflections on psychoanalysis and feminism.

2. A fuller history would have to consider the contributions of German feminists, particularly in the late 1960s and early 1970s, and particularly in terms of their influence in Britain. In her *Sexual/Textual Politics* (New York:

Routledge & Kegan Paul, 1985), Toril Moi has offered a history of feminist literary theory that contains many gestures at a history of "psychoanalysis and feminism," but she has perpetuated the idea that "Anglo-American Feminist Criticism" and "French Feminist Theory" are the two forms in which theory comes, even though she notes (p. 93) that this conceptualization does not challenge either the dominance of the two types of theory she describes or the idea that there are only two.

3. Freud was well aware that his views would provoke feminists: "It is to he anticipated that men analysts with feminist views, as well as our women analysts, will disagree with what I have said here," he noted in "Female Sexuality," in the *Standard Edition of the Complete Psychological Works of Sigmund Freud,* trans. James Strachey, 24 vols. (London: Hogarth, 1953–1974), 21:230, n. 1. For a history of debates within psychoanalysis, see Z. O. Fliegel, "Women's Development in Analytic Theory: Six Decades of Controversy." in J. L. Alpert, ed., *Psychoanalysis and Women* (Hillsdale, N.J.: Analytic Press, 1986), pp. 3–32.

4. Other pertinent works of the period are Shulamith Firestone's *Dialectic of Sex* (1970), Eva Figes's *Patriarchal Attitudes* (1970), Germaine Greer's *Female Eunuch* (1971), Elizabeth Janeway's *Man's World, Woman's Place* (1971), and Phyllis Chesler's *Women and Madness* (1972).

5. Hélène Cixous, "The Laugh of the Medusa," in Elaine Marks and Isabelle de Courtivron, eds., *New French Feminisms* (New York: Schocken Books, 1981), p. 249.

6. See, for example, Robert Stoller, "Primary Femininity." in Harold Blum, ed., *Female Psychology: Contemporary Psychanalytic Views* (Hillsdale, N.J.: Analytic Press, 1977).

7. The essays in Janine Chassguet-Smirgel's anthology *Female Sexuality* (Ann Arbor: University of Michigan Press, 1970), which are non-Lacanian, are particularly problematic for feminists. They share the idea that the early life experiences of girls are much more characterized than those of boys by rage, aggression, and sadism because the girl's mother is not an adequate substitute for the truly adequate sexual object, the father. They also stress how crucial the lack of a penis is for the girl, because she cannot displace onto the penis her fears and her rage—thus they posit not so much envy of the penis (*penisneid*) as some kind of elemental penis need.

8. Of particular importance as markers of the decade of object relations ascendancy are Dorothy Dinnerstein, *The Mermaid and the Minotaur: Sexual Arrangements and Human Malaise* (New York: Harper & Row, 1976), and Jessica Benjamin, *The Bonds of Love* (New York: Pantheon, 1988).

9. Juliet Mitchell, *Women: The Longest Revolution* (New York: Pantheon, 1984), p. 249.

10. Nancy Chodorow is the one of the feminists mentioned who is least given to speculations about prepatriarchal societies. She generally has followed the arguments against matriarchy assembled in the important 1971 volume called

▾ ▾ ▾ ▾ ▾

Woman, Culture, and Society, ed. Michelle Z. Rosaldo and Louise Lamphere (Stanford, Stanford University Press), in which Chodorow published her preliminary study "Family Structure and Feminine Personality." In the 1970s, theorists who supported the idea of early matriarchies generally were Marxist and based themselves on Engels's *Origin of Family, Private Property, and the State,* and those opposed were structuralists. Gayle Rubin, however, is an interesting amalgamator of Marx and Claude Lévi-Strauss.

11. This generalization holds even though the object relations appropriators have very often appropriated Melanie Klein's work, which certainly has a drive theory. Nancy Chodorow relies less on Klein than an Michael Balint, Harry Guntrip, and Ronald Fairbairn, who, she notes, "all argue against the view that the biological requisites of the leading erotogenic zone (oral, anal, phallic, genital) determine the form of the child's object-relations: Rather, with the possible exception of the 'oral' stage, the accession to experienced primacy or preoccupation with other 'erotogenic zones' is a result of particular social interactions concerning the zones . . . Zones, then, do not become eroticized through a maturational unfolding. They become libidinized because they become for the growing child vehicles for attaining personal contact" (*The Reproduction of Mothering* [Berkeley: University of California Press, 1978], pp. 47–48).

12. Simone de Beauvoir, in a 1972 interview reprinted in Marks and Courtivron, eds., *New French Feminisms,* p. 146: "women will not be liberated until they are liberated from children, and children at the same time to some degree liberated from adults."

13. See the exchanges on this topic in Toni Cade, ed., *The Black Woman: An Anthology* (New York: New American Library, 1970). On the history of debates within and at the doors of the women's movement about lesbianism, see Sidney Abbott and Barbara Love, "Is Women's Liberation a Lesbian Plot?" in Vivian Gornick and Barbara K. Moran, eds., *Woman in Sexist Society* (New York: Basic Books, 1971), and, more recently, a retrospective, Katie King, "Producing Sex, Theory, and Culture: Gay/Straight Remappings in Contemporary Feminism," in Marianne Hirsch and Evelyn Fox Keller, eds., *Conflicts in Feminism* (New York: Routledge & Kegan Paul, 1990).

14. In general, it can be said of this feminist appropriation of psychoanalysis that it aimed at a new woman, an androgynous woman—whether this meant a woman on her own terms or a woman no different than a man in terms of status. "Androgyny" was the word of choice (and Virginia Woolf was the patron saint owing to her remarks on androgyny in *A Room of One's Own*) because "bisexuality" was too much connected theoretically with the rejected Freudian drive theory and too much connected practically with earlier visions of sexual liberation from (not in) the family.

15. Elizabeth Abel, in a piece called "Race, Class, and Psychoanalysis" in Hirsch and Keller, *Conflicts in Feminism,* surveys some of the views that emerged during this period, focusing her attention on an essay by Hortense Spillers deal-

ing with African American family life and a memoir by Carolyn Steedman dealing with class consciousness. (Abel herself accuses psychoanalysis of "social irresponsibility" in matters of race and class, and also in the currently very much discussed matters of child abuse and the Freudian "seduction theory"; and her piece is designed as a call to responsibility.) Very interesting use of psychoanalytic work is also made by bell hooks in her several books and in her recent dialogue with Cornel West, in *Breaking Bread: Insurgent Black Intellectual Life* (Boston: South End, 1991).

16. See Angela Davis's *Women, Race, and Class* (New York: Random House, 1981) or the anthology *This Bridge Called My Back* (New York: Kitchen Table Press, 1981).

17. See August Aichhorn's *Wayward Youth;* Anna Freud's *Writings* (vols. 2, 5, and 7); Erik Erikson, *Childhood and Society)* and *Identity, Youth, and Crisis,* which contains the controversial essay "Womanhood and Inner Space"; Peter Blos, *On Adolescence* and *The Young Adolescent;* Edith Jacobson's *The Self and the Object World;* and Samuel Ritvo's essay "Female Adolescence" in Blum, ed., *Female Psychology.* See also Gerald Caplin and Serge Lebovici, eds., *Adolescence: Psychosocial Perspectives* (New York: Basic Books, 1969), and the extensive bibliography of recent work in Moses Laufer and M. Eagle Laufer's very conservative *Adolescence and Developmental Breakdown* (New Haven: Yale University Press, 1984). Among applied analytical studies, Katherine Dalsimer's *Female Adolescence: Psychoanalytic Reflections on Literature* (New Haven: Yale University Press, 1986) is very interesting.

18. See Gardiner and Barrett, "Psychoanalysis and Feminism."

19. Ann Snitow et al., eds., *Powers of Desire* (New York: Monthly Review Press, 1983), and Carole S. Vance, ed., *Pleasure and Danger: Exploring Female Sexuality,* (Boston: Routledge & Kegan Paul, 1984), which contains papers from a Barnard College conference held in 1982.

20. Parveen Adams, "Of Female Bondage," in Brennan, ed., *Between Feminism and Psychoanalysis,* p. 374. We are using Adams's piece as an example, but there have been many other efforts to focus on "transgressive sexuality" in the last several years. See Judith Butler, *Gender Trouble: Feminism and the Subversion of Identity* (New York: Routledge & Kegan Paul, 1990), and Butler's essay "Gender Trouble, Feminist Theory, and Psychoanalytic Discourse" in Linda Nicholson, ed., *Feminist/Post-Modernism* (New York: Routledge and Kegan Paul, 1990).

21. Freud distinguishes two types of nonnormal object choices, inversion or homosexuality and choice of animals and children as objects; only the choice of children incurs his strict moral reproach (see the next note). He also distinguishes two types of perverse practices: those which make something other than the genitals into genitals, like fetishism, and those that make an erotogenic zone other than the genital into the main or the exclusive source of pleasure. As noted, he considered only the exclusive "deviation of aim" to be pathological. (See *Three Essays on the Theory of Sexuality.*)

▼ ▼ ▼ ▼ ▼

22. It is very instructive to observe that Freud, in discussing the deviations of object choices mentioned in note 21, is quite nonjudgmental and free of moral tone until he gets to the third. People who choose sexually immature persons are, he says, cowardly or impotent or without appropriate objects; they "cheapen" their objects or fail to value them—all terms in which clinical judgment and moral judgment mingle (rightly). See *Standard Edition*, 7:148 (and compare Abel's view, mentioned in note 15 above).

23. *Standard Edition*, 23:170.

24. See Rozsika Parker and Griselda Pollock, *Framing Feminism* (London: Pandora, 1987).

25. Laura Mulvey, "Visual Pleasure and Narrative Cinema," in Constance Penley, ed., *Feminism and Film Theory* (London: Routledge & Kegan Paul, 1989). *m/f: a feminist journal* was published annually in London, 1976–1988.

26. Many African American intellectuals in the 1960s—Malcolm X and James Baldwin among them—spoke of what Calvin Hernton called *Sex and Racism in America* (New York: Grove Press, 1988 [1965]). That literature and the topic are reviewed in Charles H. Stember's *Sexual Racism* (New York: Elsevir, 1976). In the 1970s, the discussion, led by African American women, focused not just on sex and racism but also on sexism and racism. See for example, Barbara Smith, ed., *Home Girls: A Black Feminist Anthology* (New York: Kitchen Table Press, 1983).

12. What Happened to "Anorexie Hystérique"?

1. Joan Brumberg, *Fasting Girls: A History of Anorexia Nervosa* (New York: Plume, 1989), p. 120. Brumberg's interesting book has very little to say about psychoanalytic work on anorexia nervosa, and no other writer has produced a thorough review of the literature, although there are many brief reviews, for example Melitta Sperling, "A Reevaluation of Classification, Concepts, and Treatment," in C. Philip Wilson, ed., *Fear of Being Fat* (New York: Jason Aronson, 1983), pp. 77–82. In the most thorough and historically sophisticated recent psychoanalytic study of hysteria, Alan Krohn's *Hysteria: The Elusive Neurosis* (New York: International Universities Press, 1978), there is no mention of anorexia nervosa or, for that matter, of eating disorders in general.

2. Edward Lehman, "Feeding Problems of Psychogenic Origin: A Study of the Literature," *The Psychoanalytic Study of the Child*, 3, no. 4 (1949): 461–488.

3. O. S. English, "Therapeutic Approach to Psychosomatic Problems," in Sandor Lorand, ed., *Psychoanalysis Today* (New York: International Universities Press, 1944), p. 46. See M. R. Kaufman and Marcel Heiman, eds., *Evolution of Psychosomatic Concepts: Anorexia Nervosa—A Paradigm* (New York: International Universities Press, 1964), for reviews of earlier psychoanalytic literature designed to show that anorexia had been misinterpreted as a form of conversion hysteria.

▼ ▼ ▼ ▼

4. Cited in Russell Jacoby, *The Repression of Psychoanalysis: Otto Fenichel and the Political Freudians.* (New York: Basic Books, 1983), p. 102. See Fenichel, "Anorexia," in *The Collected Papers of Otto Fenichel, Second Series,* Norton, 1953–54), pp. 288–295.

5. Hilde Bruch's work had a number of phases, and she adopted a number of different approaches, but we are referring here to her summary work *Eating Disorders: Obesity, Anorexia Nervosa, and the Person Within* (New York: Basic Books, 1973).

6. R. A. Gordon, *Anorexia and Bulimia: Anatomy of a Social Epidemic.* (Oxford: Blackwell, 1990), p. 5.

7. Sigmund Freud, "From the History of an Infantile Neurosis," in *The Standard Edition of the Complete Psychological Works of Sigmund Freud,* trans. James Strachey, 24 vols. (London: Hogarth, 1955), 17:106. Hereafter, quotations from Freud will be noted with *Standard Edition* volume and page numbers.

8. See also 20:139. It was Karl Abraham who took up this focus on the body-as-phallus in the Wolf Man case and first explored its mechanism. In "A Short Study of the Development of the Libido" (in Abraham's *Selected Papers* [New York: Basic Books, 1953–1955], vol. 1, chap. 25), Abraham presented two male patients with this fantasy and noted that they imagined biting off the paternal penis—killing it—and incorporating it as feces—dead matter—so that it became one with them. Sándor Ferenczi followed out the theme while considering female patients in his work on the so-called Gulliver Fantasies.

9. Cecil Mushatt, "Anorexia Nervosa: A Psychoanalytic Commentary," *International Journal of Psychoanalytic Psychotherapy,* 9 (1982–3): 26, describes a male anorectic patient (not, however, one with a full case of anorexia nervosa) who had the following fantasy: "of longing to be in bed with his parents, lying between them with his father's penis in his rectum, and his own penis in his mother's rectum—a blissful state of complete union and sole possession of both parents."

10. See Albert Rothenberg, "Eating Disorders as a Modern Obsessive-Compulsive Syndrome," *Psychiatry,* 49 (February 1986): 45–53.

11. See Otto Fenichel, "The Symbolic Equation: Girl = Phallus," in *Collected Papers, Second Series.*

12. But it may be very important to understand whether an anorexic is exhibiting her thinness primarily in the service of a fantasy of herself as a boy or an erect penis being beaten into shape—in which case she will emphasize her lean strength and (fantasized) muscles—or as a little penis that can be an embryo—in which case the emphasis will be on smallness, shrinking. Helped by the use of intellectualization as a defense, the exhibitionism may also translate into the domain of intellectual achievement, where anorexics are frequently very successful, and there take the form predominantly of triumph over others (possibly including the mother) or winning of parental (especially maternal, but also paternal) praise. Among those who have emphasized body shaping in consid-

▼ ▼ ▼ ▼ ▼

ering anorexia nervosa are Crisp, Kalucy, and Pines (although they do not stress masculinization): "The disorder is primarily one of psychological meaning of body weight with reference to puberty and not of food and its direct relevance and meaning in terms of the mother, as is often the case in childhood feeding disorders." It is not all clear in their work why body weight and food should be construed as an either/or. See M. Crisp et al., "Anorexia Nervosa," *Scientific Bulletin of the British Psychoanalytical Society,* 69 (1973).

13. This line of thought was most fully pursued by Freud's daughter Anna Freud, and the results of her work as it applied to eating disorders was first set out in "The Psychoanalytic Study of Eating Disturbances" in 1946 and then summarized in *Normality and Pathology in Childhood* (1965), in *The Writings of Anna Freud,* 8 vols. (New York: International Universities Press, 1966–1981). She notes that each developmental stage has its peculiar eating disturbances and its peculiar fantasies:

a.) those connected with the oral stage and nursing and weaning, when having and not having food is virtually indistinguishable from having and not having the mother

b.) those connected with eating solid food, when the solid food still represents the mother and her care, which can be fantasized as sweets, for which many children (like the Wolf Man) develop a craving at this time; food can represent felt deprivations of her presence or care as well as means to revolt against being force-fed or over-regulated.

c.) those connected with the anal stage when self-feeding and learning table manners go along with toilet training, and when food fads and reactions of disgust or food selection (vegetarianism as a defense against sadism) become associated with finding substitutes for sucking pleasures and with anal training;

d.) those connected to the phallic and Oedipal phase, when food is less directly associated with the caretaker but strongly associated with sexual theories.

Anna Freud noted that aversions based upon or echoing Oedipal period sexual theories take various forms: fantasies of impregnation through the mouth subtend fears of being poisoned, pregnancy fantasies lie behind fear of getting fat, fantasies of anal birth relate to fear of intake and output, and so forth. Oedipal period conflicts can also give rise to cannibalistic or sadistic fantasies—for example, of eating the parents or biting off a penis—and these must be defended against by, for example, not biting anything, not chewing or eating. In girls, penis envy that expresses itself in fantasies of biting off a penis can result in hysterical vomiting along with food refusal. Similarly, guilt feelings that are aroused in Oedipal competition with the parents or derive from death wishes against them may lead to a masochistic desire not to grow up, not to become a sexual competitor; and this may express itself as food refusal and/or a masochistic turning of the death wish on the self. Each of these fantasies—or combinations of them—can have a role in the various forms of anorexia nervosa, but it seems that anorexia nervosa requires that each—or any combination— come into play with both measures for disidentifying with the mother and measures for obsessional pursuit of thinness (with its masculinizing meaning). (To our knowledge, there is no work in the literature on anorexia nervosa that takes into account the kind of typology of fantasies that Anna Freud's investigations yielded.)

14. To illustrate the controversy in the psychoanalytic literature between interpretations focusing on the interplay of oral and phallic meanings and those focusing only on oral symptomology and its pre-Oedipal object relations meanings, we can note first two case studies from the Chicago group in the 1940s, and then a recent rebuttal of the second case's conclusions. First is Emmy Sylvester's presentation (*Psychoanalytic Study of the Child*, 1 [1945]: 167–186) of an anorexic four-year-old whose mother was constantly preoccupied and sick during largely unwanted pregnancies (five in six years):

> From the very beginning the little girl had seen her mother as a person from whom gratification could not be expected unconditionally... Her disappointment in the mother started with early weaning. It flared up again when, after the birth of her brother, the mother did not satisfy the patient's regressive wishes. The breast which she had denied to the little girl was given to the next sibling, who happened to be a boy. She attempted to gain for herself the gratifying advantages of her rival's position first by the wish to destroy him, and second by the wish to become like him. This took the form of her destructive oral incorporative tendencies toward the brother... [Later] the father entered the picture as a new and more powerful rival for the satisfaction from the mother. The return of the father, whose gratifying relationship with the mother she wished to have, made any relationship to the mother impossible because of its implicit destructiveness as derived from the primal scene [which she had witnessed while she was sharing the parental bed]... Her vomiting then appears as a defense against both aspects [i.e., brother and father] of the destructive incorporative tendencies and in a secondary way serves to restore regressively the dependent relationship to the mother.

The second example (*Psychoanalytic Quarterly*, 10 [1941]: 62–74) is Jules Masserman's analysis of a thirty-five-year-old woman who had begun to suffer from nausea and vomiting when she was fourteen and who had then lost weight precipitously when she was twenty-five. This woman's dreams and associations were interpreted by Masserman as recurrently indicating that assuming "an adult feminine role would necessitate masochistic self-punishment for oral biting aggressions and would also symbolize self-castration" or loss of her masculine strivings. Like Emmy Sylvester's child patient, this woman had shared her parents' bed for a time and was both deeply tied (orally) to her mother and aggressive toward her father, her rival, who had interrupted her bond with her mother.

Finally, to indicate how this "phallic girl" or negative Oedipal dimension of anorexia is rejected by contemporary clinicians focused entirely on the girl in her mother-identified, oral-pregnancy-rejecting feminine mode, here is Johanna Tabin, in *On the Way to Self* (New York: Columbia University Press, 1985), reinterpreting the case of Sylvester's four-year-old: "The patient fused with the mother to achieve intrapsychic balance as a 'little adult' when she was two. The adjustment broke down when her parents' interactions produced a new pregnancy, upon which the child continued her identification with her mother, except on a hostile, self-punishing basis."

15. Freud took a first step in this direction in "The Economic Problem of Masochism" (1924), where he discusses the fusion of the sexual and aggressive instincts, particularly as it is manifest in "moral masochism" where, Freud notes, a person's self-destruction or sadism turned against the self "cannot take place without libidinal satisfaction" (19:170)—which is certainly a way to describe the anorexic's self-starvation.

16. Freud notes that he has not found the fear of being killed by the mother expressed as a fear of being gobbled up—the Wolf Man's fear: "Hitherto, it is only in men that I have found the fear of being eaten up. This fear is referred to the father, but is probably the product of a transformation of oral aggressivity directed to the mother" (21:237). This is an indication of how Freud was continually rethinking the Wolf Man case in light of his revisions in the 1920s.

17. Annie Reich, "The Discussion of 1912 on Masturbation and Our Present-Day Views," in her *Psychoanalytic Contributions* (New York: International Universities Press, 1973), p. 167.

18. See Susie Orbach, *Fat Is a Feminist Issue* (New York: Berkley Books, 1990 [1978]).

19. R. A. Gordon, *Anorexia and Bulimia: Anatomy of a Social Epidemic* (Oxford: Blackwell, 1990), pp. 9–10 and passim.

20. Hannah Decker, *Freud, Dora, and Vienna, 1900.* (New York: Free Press, 1990), pp. 207–208. Decker's remark is indebted to an article by Jules R. Bemporad et al., "Hysteria, Anorexia, and the Culture of Self-Denial," *Psychiatry,* 51 (1988), which, however, argues that both anorexia and hysteria represent an individual's "desperate attempt to escape the conflicts of adult life according to models offered by the prevailing cultural values"—a conclusion that we think weighs against Decker's remark.

The key to the "ethnic disease" approach is to be able to present a typical anorexic family configuration or system and then show the social conditions that make this type widespread or even normal. For a time, this typical family seemed to be discoverable, and it was presented in rather similar terms in Hilde Bruch's work, that of the Italian clinician Maria Selvini Palazzoli, and that of the

▼ ▼ ▼ ▼ ▼

English psychologist A. H. Crisp. The family was given the now often-used title "the enmeshed family" in Salvador Minuchin's 1978 book *Psychosomatic Families*. (The typical family's existence has also been disputed in various recent studies.) Bruch and Palazzoli stressed that, in comparison with others of the well-to-do and well-educated middle class, the anorexic's family is typically rigid and puritanical. This, of course, gave the modern anorexic much in common with her sister the *fin de siècle* hysteric. But, more recent investigators who want to stress the two diseases' *dissimilarities* have been quick to point out the key difference: in the anorexic's family the father is "vain, erratic, and seductive, while the mother is cold, obsessive and self-denying . . . [But] the mother is not demeaned; rather she is the mainstay and strength of the family. The daughter perceives the mother as a model of perfection that is difficult to emulate." The hysteric's mother, on the other hand, was demeaned—she was Dora's mother, at home with "housewife psychosis" while her husband was off with his mistress. In other words, the main difference is that the anorexic's mother is a more "liberated" and formidable player.

This kind of analysis obviously deals with mothers and daughters only on the level of role modeling; and to that limited extent, it may be illuminating. But it does not deal with psychodynamics. It does not ask what the mother—or the vain, seductive father—means to the daughter as an object of love and identification. A child who is overmothered and a child who is inconsistently mothered and a child who is undermothered may each long for the mother (and have to defend against that longing) and feel interfered with by rivals. Similarly, a mother who is cold, obsessive, and demeaned may be just as problematic to her daughter as one who is cold, obsessive, and not demeaned. And so forth.

21. Freud often emphasized that when masturbation is given up it is frequently replaced with an oral symptom, as a displacement upward (such was the case, for example, with Dora's initial asthmatic symptoms and nervous cough). Helene Deutch, in the Freudian mode, says this of an anorexic patient who was aware that her starvation had begun when she made herself stop masturbating: "The main element of her masturbatory procedure was an element of anxiety. The really intense masturbation was in school, and she was always thinking about the danger that her colleagues and teachers might see her masturbating" (Helene Deutsch, "Anorexia Nervosa," *Bulletin of the Menninger Clinic*, 45, no. 6 [1981], 505.) Among contemporary writers, a number in Wilson's *Fear of Being Fat* volume, including Wilson himself, emphasize the importance of masturbation conflicts and their relation to body-phallus fantasies (see pp. 16–17, 339).

13. Feminism, Psychoanalysis, and Anorexia Nervosa

1. Good reviews of the theoretical differences among various types of psychoanalytic feminisms and feminist psychoanlaytic stances exist (see especially

▼ ▼ ▼ ▼

Nancy Chodorow, *Feminism and Psychoanalytic Theory* [New Haven: Yale University Press, 1989], chap. 9), but these are not focused on a clinical topic with salient relations to a social context. I am not going to consider Lacanian theory with reference to anorexia, because I have not found any therapeutic use of it in the American literature addressed here.

2. Luise Eichenbaum and Susie Orbach, *Understanding Women: A Feminist Psychoanalytic Approach* (New York: Basic Books, 1983), p. 34.

3. Jessica Benjamin, *The Bonds of Love: Psychoanalysis, Feminism, and the Problem of Domination* (New York: Pantheon, 1988), p. 20.

4. Sigmund Freud, *Three Essays on the Theory of Sexuality,* in the *Standard Edition of the Complete Psychological Works of Sigmund Freud,* trans. James Strachey, 24 vols. (London: Hogarth, 1953–1974), 7:125–244. Further references to Freud's works are to this edition by volume and page number.

5. Phyllis Chesler, *Women and Madness* (Garden City, N.Y.: Doubleday, 1972).

6. In a recent review essay on feminism and psychoanalysis, "Psychoanalysis and Feminism: A British Sociologist's View," *Signs: Journal of Women in Culture and Society,* 17 (1992): 455–466, the British sociologist Michele Barrett noted correctly that most academic feminists stay away from clinical issues and show an "antipathy to the therapeutic dimension of psychoanalysis" (p. 463) on the assumption that psychoanalytic therapy is conservative and patriarchal.

7. During this five-year period, a vast literature on eating disorders appeared, most of it—including Hilde Bruch's popular *Golden Cage: The Enigma of Anorexia Nervosa* (New York: Vintage, 1978)—not feminist in orientation. Among the feminist works are, in chronological order: Susie Orbach, *Fat Is a Feminist Issue: The Anti-Diet Guide to Permanent Weight Loss* (New York: Paddington, 1978; rev. ed., 1988), and *Hunger Strike: The Anorectic's Struggle as a Metaphor for Our Age* (New York: Norton, 1986); M. Lawrence, "Anorexia Nervosa: The Control Paradox," *Women's Studies International Quarterly,* 2 (1979): 93–101; Marcia Milman, *Such a Pretty Face: Being Fat in America* (New York: Norton, 1980); Kim Chernin, *The Obsession: Reflections on the Tyranny of Slenderness* (New York: Harper & Row, 1981); and Marlene Boskind-White and W. C. White, *Bulimarexia: The Binge/Purge Cycle* (New York: Norton, 1983). See also the related work by Barbara Ehrenreich and Deirdre English, *For Her Own Good: 150 Years of Experts' Advice to Women* (New York: Basic Books, 1978).

8. See Chernin, *The Obsession.*

9. Orbach, *Hunger Strike,* p. 104.

10. Ibid.

11. For example, the *Diagnostic and Statistical Manual of Mental Disorders,* 3rd ed. (Washington, D.C.: American Psychiatric Association, 1980), notes the observed high incidence of urogenital abnormalities and Turner syndrome among anorexics.

12. Orbach, *Hunger Strike,* p. 110.

13. To note another interesting example: Many physicians writing on an-

orexia, and also the third edition of the *Diagnostic and Statistical Manual of Mental Disorders,* note that amenorrhea generally precedes extreme or even noticeable weight loss—a fact that implies that repudiation of sexuality precedes the anorexic's dieting rituals and their effects, and thus that these rituals should perhaps be thought of as ratifying and keeping in place the repudiation of sexuality.

14. Orbach, *Hunger Strike,* p. 165. There is no agreement in the feminist literature concerning this "ambivalence about femininity." For example, Boskind-White and White, *Bulimarexia,* countered one sociocultural explanation for a syndrome they call bulimarexia—that it signifies rejection of traditional female roles—with their own explanation—that it signifies excessive adherence to the very same traditional female roles.

15. Orbach, *Hunger Strike,* p. 154.

16. Harriet Lerman, "From Freud to Feminist Personality Theory: Getting Here from There," *Psychology of Women Quarterly,* 10 (1986): 16.

17. George Devereux, "Female Juvenile Sex Delinquency in a Puritanical Society," in his *Basic Problems of Ethnopsychiatry* (Chicago: University of Chicago Press, 1980), pp. 155–184.

18. Sigmund Freud, *Fragment of an Analysis of a Case of Hysteria,* 7:1–122.

19. Without any indication of her historical sources, and quite out of the blue, Charlotte Prozan simply announced in *Feminist Psychoanalytic Psychotherapy* (New York: Jason Aronson, 1992): "Freud unconsciously protected his father when he protected Fliess and discarded the possibility that girls are the victims of real sexual transgression by their fathers and other trusted men" (p. 326).

14. Gender and Psychoanalysis

1. Jean Laplanche and J.-B. Pontalis, *The Language of Psychoanalysis* (New York: Norton, 1973).

2. This passage is from a 1915 footnote in *Three Essays on the Theory of Sexuality,* in the *Standard Edition of the Complete Psychological Works of Sigmund Freud,* trans. James Strachey, 24 vols. (London: Hogarth, 1953–1974), 7:220 (all references to Freud's works are to this edition by volume and page number); and the passage is echoed in two later statements, one in *Civilization and Its Discontents* (21:105–107) and one in the opening of "Femininity" in *New Introductory Lectures on Psychoanalysis* (22:114–117).

3. See "The Psychogenesis of a Case of Homosexuality in a Woman" (1920), 18:170–172, and "Some Psychical Consequences of the Anatomical Distinction between the Sexes" (1925), 19:243–260.

4. See "Splitting of the Ego in the Process of Defense" (1938), 23:271–278.

5. See Simone de Beauvoir, *The Second Sex* (New York: Vintage Books, 1974), p. 42.

▼ ▼ ▼ ▼ ▼

6. See Kate Millett, *Sexual Politics* (Garden City, N.Y.: Doubleday, 1971).

7. See especially Gayle Rubin's "The Traffic in Women," an often anthologized essay, in R. R. Reiter, ed., *Toward an Anthropology of Women* (New York: Monthly Review Press, 1975). Some feminist social scientists also use the term "sex roles" for behavior stemming from biological sexual differences; for a lexical survey of the territory of these distinctions, see Jean Lipman-Blumen, *Gender Roles and Power* (Engelwood Cliffs, N.J.: Prentice-Hall, 1984), especially the chapter entitled "Sex Roles, Gender Roles, and Power."

8. See Dorothy Dinnerstein, *The Mermaid and the Minotaur* (New York: Harper & Row, 1976), and Nancy Chodorow, *The Reproduction of Mothering* (Berkeley: University of California Press, 1978).

9. For review and criticism, see Ethel Person and Lionel Ovesey, "Psychoanalytic Theories of Gender Identity," *Journal of the American Academy of Psychoanalysis*, 11 (1983): 203–226, and Adria Schwartz, "Some Notes on the Development of Female Gender Role Identity," in Judith Alpert, ed., *Psychoanalysis and Women* (Hillsdale, N.Y.: Analytic Press, 1986), pp. 57–82.

10. John Money, ed., *Sex Research: New Developments* (New York: Holt, Rinehart & Winston, 1965), p. 16.

11. Robert Stoller, *Presentations of Gender* (New Haven: Yale University Press, 1985), p. 16.

12. A preliminary and quite Freudianly phallocentric and normatively heterosexual effort came from Phyllis Tyson, "A Developmental Line of Gender Identity, Gender Role, and Choice of Love Object," *Journal of the American Psychoanalytic Association*, 30 (1982): 61–86.

13. Doris Bernstein, *Female Identity Conflict in Clinical Practice* (Northvale, N.J.: Jason Aronson, 1993), especially "Gender Specific Attribution of Identity."

14. This list is from Susan W. Coates and Sabrina M. Wolfe, "Gender Identity Disorder in Boys: The Interface of Constitution and Early Experience," *Psychoanalytic Inquiry*, 15 (1995): 6–38. Others would, of course, accept a much longer list of verified differences.

15. Ibid., p. 21.

16. Richard Isay, *Being Homosexual: Gay Men and Their Development* (New York: Farrar, Straus, and Giroux, 1989), argues that male homosexuals are innately organized to attract their fathers rather than being merged with and identifying with their mothers, as Stoller claimed.

17. See the *Standard Edition*, 18:170: "The mystery of homosexuality is . . . by no means so simple as it is commonly depicted in popular expositions . . . Tendentious literature has obscured our view . . . by putting into the foreground, for practical reasons, the third feature (the kind of object choice [in contrast to physical sexual characters and mental sexual characters]), which is the only feature that strikes the layman, and in addition by exaggerating the closeness of the association between this and the first feature [physical sexual characters]."

18. Nancy Chodorow, "Heterosexuality as a Compromise Formation," in her

▼ ▼ ▼ ▼ ▼

Feminities, Masculinities, Sexualities (Lexington, Ky.: Free Association Books, 1994).

19. And to show how slippery the terms are, it should be noted that some writers say that the boy is more complex in his gender *role* because of his identifications and disidentifications, while the girl is more complex in terms of gender *identity* because she changes love objects in the Oedipal phase and gives up her phallic strivings. See Tyson, "A Developmental Line of Gender Identity, Gender Role, and Choice of Love Object."

20. See, for example Virginia Goldner, "Toward a Critical Relational Theory of Gender," *Psychoanalytic Dialogues,* 1, no. 3 (1991): "Since Freud collapsed the distinction between biological sex, sexuality and gender, deriving, in sequence, heterosexuality and gender polarity from the anatomical difference, certain kinds of questions could not be asked of the theory because they could not be seen . . . Reasoning backward, we can say that there were three interrelated elements to Freud's thesis: the derogation of femininity, the normative dominance of heterosexuality, and the dichotomous, complementary division of gender. While the first was the focus of heated debates early on, and the second, although inadequately interrogated, was nonetheless always a subject of analytic interest and speculation, the third, the binary division of gender, remained [invisible]" (p. 20).

21. One of the key nonclinical works alluded to in this paragraph is Judith Butler, *Gender Trouble: Feminism and the Subversion of Identity* (New York: Routledge & Kegan Paul, 1990), and see Butler in *Psychoanalytic Dialogues,* 5 (1995).

15. What Theories Women Want

1. It is sometimes claimed that the Freudians who grouped around Anna Freud stand opposed to the turn toward the pre-Oedipal. This seems to me a misunderstanding. Anna Freud criticized any form of *exclusive* focus on the pre-Oedipal in development theory or theory of pathogenesis, stressing instead developmental lines with many key moments. But, of course, hers was a psychoanalysis based on the instinctual drive theory and she did adamantly oppose the various efforts to abandon it.

2. Stephen Mitchell, *Relational Concepts in Psychoanalysis* (Cambridge, Mass.: Harvard University Press, 1988), p. 17.

3. Donald Rinsley, *Developmental Pathogenesis and Treatment of Borderline and Narcissistic Personalities* (Northvale, N.J.: Jason Aronson, 1989), p. 43.

4. Janet Sayers, *Mothering Psychoanalysis* (London: Hamish Hamilton, 1990), p. 3.

5. Nancy Chodorow, *Feminism and Psychoanalytic Theory* (New Haven: Yale University Press, 1989), p. 135.

6. For a recent review of some of these efforts, excluding the Lacanian, see

Jay Greenberg, *Oedipus and Beyond: A Clinical Theory* (Cambridge, Mass.: Harvard University Press, 1991). On Lacan's insistence that focus on the mother-infant dyad obscures how the castration complex operates in females and males, see Juliet Mitchell and Jacqueline Rose, eds., *Female Sexuality: Jacques Lacan and the Ecole Freudienne* (New York: Norton, 1982).

7. See Anna Freud, "The Concept of the Rejecting Mother" (1955), in *The Writings of Anna Freud*, 8 vols. (New York: International Universities Press, 1966–1981), 4:586–602.

8. These debates were informed by Karl Abraham and, particularly, Sándor Ferenczi; and thus it is not coincidental that Ferenczi's work is currently undergoing a revival.

9. Jacques Lacan is one of the few commentators on this period of controversy who has understood that Freud's critics simply substituted their concept of feminine normality—"primal femininity" working out toward heterosexuality—for Freud's concept of universal masculine libido and bisexuality limited in the two normal directions of feminine heterosexuality and masculine heterosexuality. Lacan felt that Freud's work also contained a more fluid, less normalizing theory of sexual identity as *always* indeterminate, and it is this strand that Lacan found in Freud which the Lacanians have taken up with fervor.

10. For a strong argument that Reich was really anti-Freudian, see Bela Grunburger and Janine Chasseguet-Smirgel, *Freud or Reich?* (New Haven: Yale University Press, 1986).

11. Lesbian activists at that time tended to be anti-motherhood, and it is, of course, one measure of the enormous shift in feminism since then that motherhood is now very much a part of lesbian activism.

12. See Nancy Chodorow and Susan Contratto, "The Fantasy of the Perfect Mother," in Chodorow, *Feminism and Psychoanalytic Theory*, pp. 79–96. For a more general approach to theory construction, see Christian David, "A Masculine Mythology of Femininity," in Janine Chasseguet-Smirgel, ed., *Female Sexuality* (Ann Arbor: University of Michigan Press, 1970, [1964]).

13. In *Black Skin, White Masks,* Frantz Fanon argued very persuasively that there were two key problems with the negritude movement: first, the Negro attributes celebrated in the theory had been dictated—as castigations—by the whites, so they were still reflective of the dynamics of racism; and, second, focus on compensatory theorizing draws attention away from the real arena of change, the political. Both criticisms have been leveled against "cultural feminism" by feminist politicos, usually those with a Marxist orientation (who, in the early 1970s, were called "radical feminists"). But such political reflections, crucial as they are, are not really psychotheoretical in the meaning of that term as I am trying to demonstrate it here.

14. Feminine male homosexuals who denigrate men are often, as has been noted clinically, masochistic; they seek a male partner, and that partner's penis, but not for empowerment, as most masculinely identified homosexuals do. They

▾ ▾ ▾ ▾ ▾

denigrate a male who is necessary to them as a punisher, as Jean Genet noted again and again in *Our Lady of the Flowers*. The masculinely identified "sexist" woman is often a woman who has found a safe way to love her father—she has joined his camp, become his son—but is loved by another man.

15. This portrait seems to me to fit, particularly, the interpersonalist theorists of female communitarianism at the Stone Center in Wellesley, Massachusetts, the most idealizing of psychoanalytically influenced feminist theorists.

16. Bela Grunberger, "Outline for a Study of Narcissism in Female Sexuality," in Chasseguet-Smirgel, ed., *Female Sexuality*.

17. It is interesting to note that American psychoanalytically framed academic "queer theory" is generally more influenced by Lacan than by object relations theory, and that it is focused on the Oedipus Complex—called "the Symbolic," where "the Law of the Father" rules—rather than the pre-Oedipal. Like most French theorizing, it does not completely reject instinctual drive theory, although it uses the Lacanian version of this, focused on *joissance* and obsessed with the topic of alienation of desire or failure of pleasure.

18. More precisely, there is only "cognitive narcissism," which refers to the infant's inability to distinguish himself or herself conceptually from the mother while in the primary relational matrix.

19. Heinz Kohut's work on narcissism is focused on what Freud called secondary narcissism, and so are most social theories that take off from Kohut's ideas, like Christopher Lasch's in *The Culture of Narcissism*. The one psychoanalytic social theoretical text that is firmly focused on primary narcissism is *The Future of an Illusion,* and in it Freud stresses that theories—illusions—reflecting primary narcissism (in males only) are nostalgic images of a primal state of merger with the mother, bliss, nirvana.

20. When Freud reiterated these points, which had first been sketched in his early work on hysteria, in his late essays on female sexuality, he was moved to make penis envy even more important than he had made it earlier—penis envy is the main instrument of conversion to heterosexuality (whereas mother identification is a possibility that would have required less male narcissism in his theorizing).

21. Nancy Chodorow, "Oedipal Asymmetries and Heterosexual Knots," in *Feminism and Psychoanalytic Theory*, p. 74.

22. Lawrence Kubie, "The Drive to Become Both Sexes," in his *Symbol and Neurosis* (New York: International Universities Press, 1978). In this 1954 article, revised in 1974, Kubie tends to pathologize this drive (it is "self-destroying") because he views the identities sought as "mutually irreconcilable and consequently unattainable identities." Thus he offers a reading of Virginia Woolf's *Orlando* as a tragedy, not a successful sublimation. Kubie does not inquire whether theories of universal bisexuality, including Freud's and his own, are examples of the drive he studies having been successfully sublimated.

23. It is formulations like this one, of course, that make object relations the-

▼ ▼ ▼ ▼ ▼

orists think that there is no such thing as relationality or mutuality in Freud, for even love here seems to be modified narcissism. Similarly, altruism turns out to be doing unto or for others what you do not allow yourself to do unto yourself. That is, altruism is a reaction formation. But I think that Freud's description of male love reflects a desire to be both sexes—the male's overvaluation of the female is an absorption of her into himself—cast in terms that could be adapted to the "phallocentric" conception in Freud's later work on female psychology.

24. Freudian psychoanalysis cannot be used for refurbishing an ego ideal. After Freud wrote " 'Civilized Morality' and Modern Nervous Illness" (1908), which does offer a social etiology of both neurasthenia and neurosis, he never again offered anything that resembles an image of inborn goodness corrupted, and he constantly criticized Wilhelm Reich and the communist theoreticians of the 1920s for their "illusions" about where "good" and "bad" come from.

25. It is no coincidence that Freud has recently been charged with having abandoned his "seduction theory" out of cowardice or an inability to tolerate the idea of widespread paternal abuse. This is the sequel to the earlier charge that his science as a whole is phallocentric.

▼ ▼ ▼ ▼

Index

▼ ▼ ▼ ▼ ▼

▼ ▼ ▼ ▼ ▼